WHERE HAVE ALL THE COWBOYS GONE?

WHERE HAVE ALL THE COWBOYS GONE?

Madness, Mayhem, and the Making of America

PRIOLEAU ALEXANDER

Where Have All the Cowboys Gone?
Madness, Mayhem, and the Making of America

ISBN 978-1-7329066-7-9

Published by:

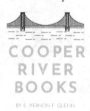

COOPER
RIVER
BOOKS

BY E. VERNON F. GLENN

For my buddy Dabney R "Champ" Yarbrough.
Cheerful in all weathers. Never shirked a task. Splendid behavior.

ACKNOWLEDGEMENTS

My decades long cheerleader and college roomie, Mark Russell. My publisher, E. Vernon F. Glenn and publicist Hannah Larrew. My exceptional history professor, Russ Robinson. Debbie Shaw, of Auburn University. All my friends and family who encouraged me to press on after they read the first draft of this book, 25 years ago. And, of course, my wife Heidi.

Although there is certainly a great deal of artistic licensed in this book, I have attempted to remain true to the facts based on the research and writings of real historians. If an actual historian finds an error, please—you know—keep it between us, and email me at TypingForBeerMoney@gmail.com. There's nothing I can do about it, of course, but I prefer to be typed at in ALL CAPS in private.

EPIGRAPH

History is written by men who've hanged heroes.
RANDALL WALLACE
Braveheart

CONTENTS

MANY PEOPLE FIND HISTORY BORING.

This is a very unfortunate fact, because history is incredibly useful. After all, what other subject offers such a simple formula for success? Observe the actions of those who've gone before you, chuckle at their moronic decisions, and thus discover ways to avoid screwing up *your* life, *your* nation, and *your* children's future.

It goes wa-a-ay back: Ugg make fire. Ugg touch fire. Ugg no more touch fire.

But history rarely gets a fair shake.

This might be because many of the guys who teach it are often relics themselves, cloaked in fraying tweed and tenured since Roosevelt gave away Eastern Europe. Worse yet, history is a required course for college freshmen, so most history-based memories are little more than a collection of piecemeal sound bites from 8:00 a.m. lectures, syphoned through hungover ears and dangling from brain cells weakened by the previous night's battle. Sure, we all recall a few dates here and a few treaties there, but mostly we remember the exams—exams that test little more than one's rote memory skills. Or, in the case of several of my classmates, one's reptilian peripheral vision.

The truth about history is that the memorization games are for naught. One should study history for the *lessons it teaches us,* as these lessons provide the answer to the life-long question, "What the hell do I do now?"

Take for example taxes: A great debate rages as to whether raising taxes is a good thing, or a bad thing. Who's correct?

Fiscal conservatives claim, "Raising taxes is bad. The government takes the money I want to put to work in the economy, and funds pointless social programs. If you seize my money, I can't invest it—and the only way the economy thrives is for me to invest in profitable business ventures, make money and create jobs, then spend the profits on new cars, old whiskey, and women my daughter's age."

Liberals and Federalists, on the other hand, claim, "Oh no, you don't, you rich coupon-clippers. You have more than your fair share of the money, and some deserves to be taken by taxation—all you ever do is roll around naked in it; you never use it to benefit others. With your tax money, we'll build day-care centers, and fund artistic endeavors, and provide everyone with medical care. We need to provide for the people when the people fail to provide for themselves."

So what's the answer? The correct answer?

Well, perhaps we could simply look into the nation's 247-year history of raising and cutting taxes and find the answer. After all, several dozen examples are available from multiple historical records, and even historians have a hard time slanting something as vast and widespread as *how the national economy did when we last raised/cut taxes*—so why don't we just flip to those pages in the history book?

And how about the idea, "Never get involved in a drawn-out guerilla war thousands of miles away from your country—especially when the enemy is trained to fight with guerilla tactics, and believe their cause is worthy of their life." Do we have any experience in this? Hmm… well, since **we the people** utilized this exact formula to defeat the British (twice) and the French, and since the North Koreans/Chinese, Vietnamese, and Afghanis used it to defeat us, I'm thinking—Why, yes! We do know something about this.

So why didn't LBJ at least glance over a freshman World History textbook before sending troops to Vietnam? Or Dubya, before Iraq and Afghanistan? Even if the lessons available failed to dissuade them, confronting reality could have at least inspired a pre-war speech that stated, "My fellow Americans: I'm smarter than history itself, so—Hi-Ho! Hi-Ho! It's off to war we go!"

Wait. Sorry. Correction: "Off to war **your** kids go. Me and mine will be living in our compound protected by Secret Service, so send us a Tik-Tok or something if you need us."

But LBJ and Dubya failed to read the history or give the speech—and here we are, each of us drowning in ponderous awe reading the archives of our elected leaders arguing over who **least** supported the Iraq and Afghanistan Wars after they voted to **support** the war. Just search the Internet for the transcripts:

> **Democrat:** Well, yes, I voted to approve the war, but I protested in the way I pushed the "Yea" button so softly. I felt the war was wrong then, and I feel it is wrong now. Can you feel my pain? I feel yours.
>
> **Republican:** Of course I supported the war—the *first part* of the war, with all that shock and awe! That was fantastic— the military-industrial complex working in harmony, and stuff getting blown up? It was awesome! Of course, no one from the Administration said anything about the media's plan to compare Iraq and Afghanistan to Vietnam. And I'm against Vietnam. Not the troops, of course, the country of Vietnam. I mean, not the Vietnamese people, but the Vietnam-ish way things are happening. Did I mention I'm for the troops? Go troops!
>
> **The Media:** War is bad! People get killed! War is *never* the answer for resolving conflict!
>
> **Me:** Wasn't war involved in stopping the spread of Nazism, Fascism, and Communism?

Here's my question: Where has our country gone? Where are the people who made our country great? We're not a nation forged by lawyers, sommeliers, and yoga instructors. Our forefathers were chiseled out of granite.

Then, we got soft. Next stop, trigger warnings. Now? Military age men in college have and utilize "safe spaces."

What do you think the founders of this nation would say if they saw us now? You know, those madmen who rowed up to Roanoke Island, NC in the heat, humidity, and mosquitoes of August, 1587, got their wool-wearing-asses out of the skiff, looked around, and without seeing a toilet, a shower, a Zippy Mart, or a single regulatory or government aid agency on the entire continent said, "Cool. Let's live here."

What... do... you... think... they'd... say?

It's depressing to even consider: One day we were living as a united group of individuals, each striving in their own way for life, liberty, and the pursuit of a little fun. The next day we're veering off the bridge at Chappaquiddick, slapping each other with sexual harassment lawsuits for accidental contact as we struggle to escape, and demanding the federal government recognize drowning as a disease as the water rushes into our lungs.

So what happened?

It's pretty simple: We failed to learn from our past.

Sure, we held fund-raisers to put up some plaques on historic buildings, and scholars wrote boring books no one reads, but we didn't *learn* anything significant. It seems at times we failed to acquire a single piece of significant information from our forefathers, despite the fact they carefully documented virtually every experience. The thing that makes this so inexcusable is the *extremes* that our forefathers went through to learn these lessons for us. I mean, these people endured some serious country-music-level pain and suffering to acquire the most *basic* knowledge.

So, that's what you and I shall undertake: Spelunk deep into the caverns of the history that shaped this nation, and claw our way back to the sunshine with a basket full of wisdom drawn from the well of blood, sweat and tears shed by our relatives of old.

Before beginning, however, one thing deserves clarification: History can, and does, sometimes lie. Why? Because winners write the history, and the history of our country would read very differently if recorded by, say, an American Indian. I point this out because it's important to remember history *can* be slanted towards the views and opinions of the writer and the "team" the writer feels is righteous. Even today—when we should know better—it is very difficult for a writer to give an historical analysis of a "current event" without offering the "value added" benefit of their slant on how things went down. It's human nature. No writer strives to be a mere factual scribe.

And I'm no different, I suppose.

So what's my point of view? What's my slant? What words best describe my feelings when I study American history and attempt to pass it along to others?

Well, "ponderous" springs to mind pretty quickly.

Allow me to close this section with a commentary about the birth of this nation, because one cannot tell the story without addressing the good, the bad, and the very ugly. During the time periods we will explore, the arriving settlers persecuted and murdered the indigenous people of North America. Call these indigenous people whatever you like, but I'll call them American Indians, primarily because that's what they call themselves. Our treatment of them was barbaric at best, but even that falls short: Barbarians at least *sometimes* acted like humans. Sadly, the blood of our native residents stains our history's hands, and it will forever serve as a point of shame. When combined with the fact that our forefathers owned human beings and forced them to build much of our economy, well... 20/20 hindsight often serves as a very disturbing way to view our past.

One must also remember that life in general was far less precious three hundred years ago. What parent today would even *consider* taking their children on the perilous journeys these settlers risked, simply for a vague chance at "a better life?" The safety-first attitude simply didn't exist with our founders and pioneers—they yearned for adventure, achievement, and the pursuit of happiness—and gambled their families' lives to achieve it. By way of example, let me ask this: How many astronauts would climb into that rocket if they had to have their kids strapped in beside them?

These unfortunate (and at times horrifying) realities must be addressed prior to beginning this book, because to stop and express regret over the atrocities as they arise—well, that's all I'd be writing. Our nation's past is fascinating, educational, brutal, ugly, brilliant, and amazing. What happened, happened, and patronizing, politically-correct gestures isn't going to make it right.

Virtue signaling and a cancel culture won't make it right.

School curricula teaching children they are by nature hateful isn't going to fix it.

Looting, rioting, murder, and arson aren't going to make it right, any more than wearing a white hood and burning crosses will make it right.

The only thing we can do to even try and "make it right" is to understand the issue from 30,000 feet: Every civilization was built on the backs of slaves and serfs. Every single one. And every tribe and nationality arises from a people who were once enslaved.

So let's thank God we aren't those people anymore. There are millions of slaves and sex slaves in Africa, the Middle East, and Eastern Europe—but America put a stop to that cruelty in 1865.

The best we can do now involves committing ourselves to end our nation's "reservation imprisonment" of the American Indians, and end our nation's ongoing low expectations of the African-American community. Very simply put, we need to empower all of our minority groups to achieve success. They can, and they will.

Now strap on your helmet and buckle your seatbelt. We're gonna explore the space and time of America, and I can assure you it's gonna be a bumpy ride.

CHAPTER ONE

GETTING STARTED...

T HE LOGICAL PLACE to start the Great American Story is at the *beginning*. The beginning is usually an easy place to find. Not, however, for Americans.

No, we argue and bicker about the technicalities of who actually sailed here first: Vikings? Irish Missionaries? Some Welsh dude? Spaniards? Tobacco Lobbyists?

Let's not get into it, okay? It's boring and confusing, and like I said, "History is written by the winners." This book is in English because the English eventually came out on top (at least until 1776), so let's just play the game, shall we?

Okay. The English-version of the story unfolds like this: In the late 13th Century, Marco Polo rolled back into Europe from his Chinese road trip with several camel-loads of cool stuff like silk, cotton, jewels, and spices. To a continent whose rich people didn't own these things, and where most meals resembled more of a Fred Flintstone barbeque than a fine-dining experience, the desire to *Keep up with the Polo's* swept the continent faster than a Queen can say, "Momma needs a new pair of spice racks."

Before long, loads of entrepreneurs logged frequent saddle miles between Europe and these far-eastern lands, where everything seemed to feel, smell, and taste good. The demand for these luxuries continued to climb monthly in Europe, where nothing felt, smelled, or tasted good—one's spouse included. After all, we're talking about a continent of people who thought it "unhealthy" to bath, so who *wouldn't* cough up a pretty penny to *stop* smelling like, well, themselves?

In 1453, however, Constantinople fell to the fun-hating Turks, and the supply lines to the good life withered: Very quickly, things reverted back to salted hogs feet and itchy, wool underwear, and a cry arose throughout Europe for a new route to the Far East. What to do, what to do?

Along came Christopher Columbus, who for some odd reason we credit with "discovering America." Captain Chris dreamed a dream of getting to China by sailing in the opposite direction of the land route, and going "around" this thing called a "globe." He pitched the idea to the Kings of Spain, Portugal, France, and England, all of whom responded with a warmth normally reserved for occasions like Ted Nugent keynote speaking to the National PETA Convention.

Determined to achieve fame and fortune, Columbus moved to Spain full-time, where he spent a few years mooching invitations to the beautiful people's cocktail parties, and letting everyone know that he "will explore for food." Eventually, he wormed his way in front of King Ferdinand and Queen Isabella of Spain for a second time, where a conversation something like this takes place:

> **Columbus:** ... and those are the details, your Majesties. When shall I set sail?
> **Ferdinand:** With *our* funding? How about never? How does never fit with your schedule?
> **Columbus:** Uh, wait, Majestic One! Did I mention I'd undertake the venture for only 10% of the loot we discover?
> **Ferdinand:** What am I? Fly paper for freaks?
> **Advisor Luis de Santangel:** A Royal huddle, your Majesties?
> **Ferdinand:** Yes?
> **Luis de Santangel:** This sea dog demands only 10% of the take, and three ships. We have that many ships in your son's royal bathtub. We give him the boats, load him up with some rotten meat and moldy bread, and send him on his way. If

he finds something, we own 90% of it. If not, and he dies, well… he's Italian. It seems like a pretty good gamble for three lousy ships.

Ferdinand: Columbus!

Columbus: Yes, King?

Ferdinand: I've decided I like you. You remind me of myself, when I was young and stupid. You can have your ships.

Columbus: Sweet! Is there an incentive package?

Ferdinand: Sure—uh, as a bonus, you can govern whatever lands you find.

Columbus: It's China and India, my King; they're already governed.

Ferdinand: Oh… and now that's *my* problem?

Columbus: At least give me a fancy title, my King. You know, a little something for my high school reunion.

Ferdinand: Okay, whatever—how about… Admiral of the Ocean Sea?

Columbus: Fitting, Your Highness.

Ferdinand: Great. Now, if I throw a stick, will you leave?

And the deal was sealed.

On August 3, 1492, Columbus commenced to sail the ocean blue. The King and Queen provided him with provisions for the entire 1,000-mile voyage he'd charted, and this was a good thing. Unfortunately, the voyage charted out at 3,900 miles, so it was actually 25% good thing and 75% bad thing. The ships and crew sailed all through August, and all through September, and into October, when—about the time they began chewing off each other's toenails for dinner—Columbus sensed something was up: A mutiny was afoot.

Then, as fate would have it, a siting of land occurred at 2:00 a.m. on October 12th. The sailor spotting it was exceptionally happy, because Columbus promised a hefty reward to the first man to spot land.

Guy in rigging: Laaaand… Hooooooooooooe!

Columbus: What?!! Where?!!

Guy in rigging: There, Captain! There! I can see the moon-light shining off a cliff!
Columbus: Yes! Yes! I see it! I *mean*... uh, so what? I saw that last night. Yeah, *last* night. *That's* when I saw it. So, uh, that means no reward.
Guy in the rigging: But, hey—You suck!
Columbus: Challenging your Captain is punishable by death. Do you wish to repeat that comment?
Guy in the rigging: Sorry, Sir. You're the opposite of suck. You, uh, blow?

Think I'm making this reward story up? This history—*why bother?* It doesn't get any more bizarre than the truth.

The spot where Columbus landed was one of those Banana Republic islands down in Jimmy Buffettville, which most believe to be the island of San Salvador, although some say Watling Island. What do I say? Who cares? The details are completely irrelevant, because they aren't accurate to begin with. Columbus no more discovered the New World than Al Gore invented the Internet. The New World was crawling with explorers before, during, and after 1492. In fact, New Worldmania actually resembled the real estate bubble of 2008, when every King, Queen, Jack, and Ten with a little extra gold in the royal vault offered it by the wheelbarrow-load to every handyman willing to even *claim* they had a general contractor's license.

Sadly, and again like 2008, most of the ventures imploded. Big! Some, however, paid off—Spain, for instance, eventually stumbled onto the riches and gold of South America—no thanks to Columbus—and spent the next couple hundred years doing a their very best *"If AOL Was a Nation"* impersonation.

In the end, Columbus' explorations paid off just like *my* biggest investment, the famous internet site named www.cement-by-mail.com. He died in 1506, still babbling that he'd reached Asia, and whining that his family had a 10% claim to all the riches that were pouring in—from the place he didn't discover, which wasn't the place he even thought he landed.

So why, you are asking, have we even heard of Columbus? Why are the tales of his heroics stuck in our heads, when in fact he proved to be nothing more than a me-too among many?

It's history, I'm tellin' you. Perhaps Columbus' name seemed the easiest to spell for the English writers who wrote our history; perhaps he bought drinks for all the writers at the Annual New World History Writer's Benevolent Ball; maybe he happened onto nude sketches of someone's wife—who knows?

The truth is that Columbus is remembered as *Columbus, Discoverer of the New World*, because the winners of the *Claim America Game*—the English—declared him so. That's what they wrote down, and that's what got passed along.

It's worth noting, however, that we are not the United States of Columbus, which no doubt has the ol' Admiral of the Ocean Sea spinning in his grave. Why are we America? Get this—some dude named Amerigo Vespucci explored sections of the New World in the years between 1497 and 1512, and Amerigo is the guy who apparently coined the phrase *New World*. In 1507, a German mapmaker named Martin Waldseemüller wrote an account of Vespucci's voyages, and included in his book a map of this "New World."

He needed a name (other than *New World*) for these big chunks of land on the map, and since he was writing about *Amerigo* Vespucci's adventures, America seemed a good name. No, it's not a very good reason to be called America, but let's all be happy the Amerigo's name wasn't Dillweedigo.

Now—just consider all the valuable insights we've gained so far, without remembering a single name or date. What insights, you ask?

First, Ferdinand and Isabella demonstrated 1) The rich and powerful always want to be richer and more powerful. 2) If you are willing to risk your life in the service of the rich and powerful, they are more than willing to risk your life in their service. 3) Power corrupts—just ask the poor sailor who actually sighted land on Columbus' ship. 4) We must be cautious with this thing called *history*—often we learn only one account of what happened, and limited facts don't always reveal the truth.

CHAPTER TWO

THERE CAN BE ONLY ONE—

ENGLAND, BACK IN the day, scarcely resembled the England we think of now, with the stiff upper lip and the cute, refined accent. In truth, it was little more than the proverbial trailer park of Europe: You know, located off by itself in a remote area, neighbors fighting all the time, families bashing each other's heads in—everyone's broke, and drunk, and white-trash ignorant. Think in terms of the TV show *Cops*, minus the tattoos, plus shirts.

When Queen Elizabeth was crowned in 1558, she'd had enough of the *"You might be an Englishman if_____"* jokes, and called together her inner circle of advisors:

> **Queen:** Lord Skeeter? Earl of Jim Bob? Ya'll listen up, and listen up good. I 'bout had enough of them damn Continental snobs makin' fun of us, and we're a'gonna do sumpin' 'bout it. I want to *git* me some of that New World stuff everyone's raisin' a fuss about, and I'mma gonna git it **now**. Whatch y'all know about that place?
> **Skeeter:** Gotta git there by boat, I reckon.
> **Queen:** Well, then, *git* a damn boat, and *git* someone to sailin' it. And I ain't kiddin' neither. We gonna git some New World and git some trade rollin' through here, or I's gonna start choppin' some heads.

And so it began.

The mastermind behind the first attempt to "git some of the New World" was Sir Walter Raleigh, who in 1587 inspired the standard *Scream*-theme movie by telling a group of 117 English men, women, and children, "Listen! I think it would be a good idea for us to split up. You go check it out spooky place, uhhh, *I'll* wait here."

Unfortunately for the group, what he wanted them to "check out" was the New World while he "waited" at home in England.

Now before we go one sentence further, let's consider what you just read: *One hundred and seventeen men, women, and children.*

How insane did *that* group have to be? Imagine yourself in those circumstances today:

> **Walter:** Duuuude! I'm gettin' together a group of people to move to Iran to crank up the business world there—make fortunes and stuff. You in, or what?
>
> **You:** Sweeeeet! How will we get there?
>
> **Walter:** I've got a most excellent rusted, old school bus that could explode at any moment.
>
> **You:** What are the business opportunities?
>
> **Walter:** Don't know—never been there.
>
> **You:** Are you going with us?
>
> **Walter:** No way, dude. I'm the guy in charge. I gotta stay here and be in charge—you know, envisioning things.
>
> **You:** Okay, I'm in. I'm sure the wife won't mind me being gone awhile.
>
> **Walter:** Uh, yeah—look, man—you gotta *bring* your wife, *and* your kids. This is a one-way trip. Ready to go for it?"
>
> **You:** (*Please fill in your response here*)

Since 117 of these maniacs offered a **different** response than you, the group set sail for America, and landed on the Outer Banks of North Carolina on Roanoke Island. After snuggling in among the swampy terrain, mosquitoes, humidity, gnats, malaria, and poisonous water moccasins, the group's leader, John White, pulled the old "*Hey, I forgot something*" routine, got in

the ship, and sailed back to England. He told them–get this–he was sailing
back to get supplies. Can't you see Mr. Guy-in-charge explaining it?

> **John White:** Uh, hey, guys, I'm gonna run back to England
> to get some beer, and maybe some ice."
> **Settlers:** Right on! Pa-a-a-a-a-a-a-arty!
> **John White:** Anyone want a pizza?
> **Settlers:** Right on! Pa-a-a-a-a-a-a-arty!
> **John White:** Bye, now!
> **Settlers:** Pick up a DVD of Season 9 of Keeping Up With
> the Queen, too!

With every man, woman, and child counting on him for these
life-sustaining supplies, John White bravely accomplished the five-month
round trip in a blazing *two and a half years*, and was surprised when
he arrived back at Roanoke that... *no one was there.* (Let's put this in a
modern timeframe: You're at a movie and your date strolls off to get some
popcorn, but fails to return for fourteen days. Are *you* gonna be there?)

The only signs of the original settlement were some rusted pieces of
equipment, and the word "CROATOAN" carved into a tree.

Big mystery.

What happened to them? Indians? Starvation? Disease? Historians
have blathered on about it for years. The true answer, of course, sits right
inside the acronym. The settlers formed a committee, discussed the issue,
and decided that John White was not coming back. CROATOAN, it
turns out, actually stands for:

> **C**anned
> **R**oanoke...
> **O**ff
> **A**ttempting
> **T**o
> **O**rganize
> **A**nother
> **N**eighborhood.

With that, the group walked to the Smokey Mountains of the Carolinas, settled, and kept to themselves. The last reported sighting of one of their group occurred during the credits of the movie *Deliverance* as "boy playing banjo."

Okay, nothing groundbreaking here—everyone remembers the Lost Colony of Roanoke. But *why* is it worth remembering? Because we learned two more very cool and useful lessons: 1) The guy in charge always looks out for himself. 2) Committees always produce *something*, but usually that something is group stupidity.

DON'T STOP THE CARNIVAL

With the Lost Colony of Roanoke now, uh, lost, the English decided to "give it another go, eh? Hip! Hip!" This decision arose largely due to the fact that all of England's starving peasants were complaining about, well, starving, and the merchant class found themselves short on buyers for their miniature figurines of the Tower of London and kegs of warm, flat beer. The nation's budding Artisan class fared about the same, although they *were* able to proudly describe themselves as "starving artists" without a hint of irony.

On December 20, 1606, another group of madmen gathered their families and set sail from England, including some rich men to sit around and give orders, and some poor men to actually do all the work. The poor men, interestingly, paid for their passage by agreeing to be indentured serfs for seven years, but—good news—most avoided the burdensome commitment because—bad news—they died. But I'm getting ahead of myself. Sorry.

Anyway, thirty-nine of the one hundred forty-four passengers died during the treacherous ocean crossing, resulting in an unthinkable zero lawsuits filed against the ship's captain, doctor, owner, or board of directors. The group collided with the coast of Virginia, and instead of sailing up and down the coast looking for a survivable "location, location, location," decided the malarial swamp in front of them looked just peachy. (A decision possibly hastened by the olfactory trauma of having thirty-nine corpses as bunkmates.)

They disembarked, named the place Jamestown, and the rich men began their jobs of posturing, while the poor men began working. This division of tasks didn't last long, as within a few months the policy became an "all-hands pitch-in" situation, instigated by the fact that an additional fifty-one of the settlers were no longer "pitching in" at all, and were instead being pitched into a six-foot-deep hole.

In the winter of 1609-10 the remaining settlers discovered the true meaning of "there's no place like home." The men were so busy burying everyone that they'd forgotten to do little extras—like gather food. With the cupboard completely bare, they endured this period known as "The Starving Time" by eating the settlers who'd been courteous enough to drop dead. This new source of food gave them energy... not enough energy to improve their situation, but enough energy to dig up the people they'd buried a few months previous, and eat them, too. The whole affair redefined the idea of being chewed out by a neighbor.

Finally, the guy you learned about in school—Captain John Smith—stepped to the front, took charge, and began giving orders (hopefully the first of which was for everyone to floss their family and friends from between their teeth.) Much of what the modern world thinks about Captain John Smith is based on Smith's writings about himself; in addition to being a mercenary, he worked also as The New World's first a spin doctor. In reality, his primary accomplishments were:

a) Befriending the Indians
b) Convincing the Indians to share their food and knowledge
c) Killing the Indians.

Although many may consider this barbaric, an even larger number would consider it "leadership," given the uncanny resemblance between Smith's behavior and the behavior of most U. S. Presidents.

The Indians, of course, weren't particularly fond of Smith's system of diplomacy, and resorted to old-fashioned creative thinking to retaliate.

Brave #1: Yo, Homebrave, these Settlers are harshing my mellow.

Brave #2: They're not all bad. Some are dead.

Brave #1: Hey! I got an idea. Remember how last winter we told them we eat corpses in the winter? So then they ate theirs?

Brave #2: Yeah?

Brave #1: Let's tell them we light tobacco leaves on fire and suck the smoke into our lungs.

Brave #2: Dude, tobacco leaves will kill you. Even an idiot knows that.

Brave #1: We're talking about people who ate their dead.

Brave #2: Good point.

And so it happened.

The settlers bought into the idea, got hooked on nicotine, introduced tobacco to London, and the population of London (because there was no Surgeon General's warning) became addicted. Thus, tobacco became the "cash crop" that saved Jamestown.

Unfortunately, the word "cash" popped little Jamestown up as a blip on the greed-adar screen back in England. Of course, as we know in hindsight, the Jamestown settlers remained in daily hand-to-hand combat with the Grim Reaper himself, but the fact that they weren't eating their dead anymore offered proof positive to the government bureaucrats that all the really hard work was done, and it was *time* for *payday*.

The lust for said payday led to bickering between private enterprise (The Virginia Company who funded Jamestown) and the public sector (The King and his bureaucrats), which then led to the formation of Committees, Sub-committees, Oversight Committees, Ways & Means Committees, and a Task Force on Forming New Committees. All these committees eventually agreed that "greed is good," and declared the New World open for 'bidness. (They failed, however, to notice that the only people thriving were undertakers and members of Gravedigger's Local 001). Before long, droves of fortune seekers began to bum rides across the Atlantic to Jamestown, where they found primarily that:

a) All the chicks here were taken (and many eaten as part of a low-carb diet).

b) This settling stuff is a lot like hard work.

These predicaments were addressed in 1619, but at a fairly steep price: They solved the lack-of-ladies dilemma issue with the importation of English brides-to-be. Price? 120 pounds of tobacco. The "hard work" situation was solved with the importation of the first African slaves. Price? A lot of money, and what would certainly be a very, very, very uncomfortable conversation with St. Peter outside the Pearly Gates.

By 1624, over 6,000 settlers departed the comfort of Great Britain for the fourth circle of Hell in Virginia. Despite the booming immigration numbers, a census held in Jamestown in late 1624 indicated that only 1,277 of those 6,000 were still above ground. The rest, of course, were killed, starved, died, lost, eaten, or carried off by Indians.

Vexed by the obvious, one of the Royal Committees queried, "What has become of the five thousand missing subjects of His Majesty?"

So, let's take a look at the next nuggets of wisdom we've unearthed:

1) From the settlers at Jamestown, we found that if one is *truly* hungry, anyone "will work for food."

2) From John Smith, we learned autobiographies can be fudged by the autobiographer, which tends to shatter the facts into a million little pieces.

3) From the Indians' kindness, we learned a twist on the wise-old saying that goes, "Don't feed the hand that bites you."

4) From those first Americans who bought into the idea of sucking the smoke of a burning weed into their lungs, we learned that there is no limit to the gullibility of the public.

5) And from the King's committees we learned, once again, that committees lead to mass stupidity.

THE PURITANS, AKA PILGRIMS...

First, a little background: In 1536, King Henry VIII told the Pope he didn't like his policies regarding divorce (and beheadings), and formed his own church, The Church of England. The partying began, and continues to this day in Anglican and Episcopalian congregations around the world.

As usual, one group of party-poopers didn't want to join in the fun, and they moaned and whined and told all the "Whiskey-palians" that they were headed to Hell lest they knock it off. All the whining of these self-proclaimed "Separatists" hampered the Anglican's buzz, so they got the Chief Holy Henchman (the King of England) to rally some bullies to bully these Separatists into leaving for Holland.

After a few years, the Separatists became grumpy at their Dutch neighbors—the whole place was just too windmilly and tulipy—and they decided to move somewhere they could better squelch the level of fun going on around them. They heard through the grapevine that the settlers in Jamestown were no longer eating each other, so, hey—how hard could it be?

So in 1620, after years of meetings, and discussions, and arguments, they proclaimed it was time to set sail for America on the Mayflower.

There is, however, an interesting side note here, having to do with the passenger manifest: Of the thousands of these "Separatists" *claiming* they wanted to go to America, almost all of them bowed out, saying (one supposes) that they had a really important Pot Luck church dinner to attend, and... uh... 1620 was just a bad time to sail off into almost certain death.

In fact, only fifty Separatists arrived at the docks when it came time to weigh anchor, so they invited some adventurers along to help pay the freight. In the tradition of acceptance and brotherly love taught by Jesus Christ, they dubbed this not-like-us-group as "Strangers," and themselves "Pilgrims."

You can almost hear the after-dinner conversation up on the bow:

Stranger: So, Pilgrim, what are your plans when we get to the New World?
Pilgrim: We planneth to construceth a colony and government where only we have religious freedom. And ye-self?
Stranger: Aww, you know—try and scare up a little coin, pound some beers, chase squaws—the usual stuff.
Pilgrim: Hmmmm... bound for Hell, methinks.
Stranger: Really? I thought we were headed to the New World. Oh well, whatever. I just wanted to get out of Liverpool.

After 65 days of listening to the Pilgrims froth at the mouth about persecution in England, and how they couldn't wait to get to America so they could launch their own monopoly on persecuting, the Strangers began to feel a bit like Siegfried's tiger. They noticed, however, that Massachusetts in late December isn't the world's most welcoming environment, and decided to work together through a document called the "Mayflower Compact." It said, in essence:

"We admit it: We'd like to kill each other. But we were stupid to come here, stupid*er* to land someplace up North, and stupid*est* to do so in the winter. As a result, we will work together and not nag each other. If we survive, the Strangers can begin their business of stealing land from the Indians, and the Pilgrims can persecute any additional, follow-on settlers stupid enough to follow on."

Unable to use their newly signed Mayflower Compact for food, the Pilgrims and Strangers decided they better put some irons in the fire. Of course, surviving a New England winter with no planning is impossible, so they considered the advice of Shawshank Prison's very own Andy Dufresne: *Get busy living, or get busy dying.* Since this was the Mayflower group, and they couldn't agree on which half of the advice to heed, they split the difference. Half chose living, and half chose dying. By spring, everyone had accomplished their individual goal.

The reason the *entire* group didn't put on their running suits and Nikes and hitch a ride on Haley's Comet came about because a nearby Indian tribe, Wampanoags, helped them survive by teaching them a few tricks of the trade. Why, you ask? The Pilgrims discovered the source of their kindness during one of the feasts that led us to celebrate Thanksgiving Day as a national holiday:

> **Head Pilgrim:** Wow! I'm as stuffed as Roy Roger's horse. How 'bout you, Chief?
>
> **Chief:** Ugh, me happy, too. Maybe one more slice of pie.
>
> **Head Pilgrim:** Say, by the way, why didn't you just leave us to die when we got here? Is it because you are—by nature and cultural upbringing—friendly, loving, family-oriented, happy, peaceful, and committed to environmental sustainability like those Indians in *Dances With Wolves*?
>
> **Chief:** Ha! Good one. No, actually, we gottem major beef with them Massachusetts Injuns. We hoping that tomorrow you use those sticks-that-go-boom to give them some hot lead injections.
>
> **Head Pilgrim:** Tomorrow??!! Chief, do you have any idea how much *shopping* I have to get done tomorrow? It's Black Friday!
>
> **Chief:** Hey, Buckle Head—you wantum me and my posse to keep droppin' off food, then you best start putting some lead down range.
>
> **Head Pilgrim:** Huh… Well, one Massachusetts Indians massacre, comin' up!

Word filtered back to England that the Pilgrims somehow actually survived their first year, *and* that they were enjoying an unlimited supply of Indians to lecture, persecute, and bore.

As a result, Puritan Separatists back in England hopped onto the bandwagon. Between 1629 and 1642, close to 20,000 Puritan-come-lately's bolted England for the New World, settling places in and around New England. (Their settling was made decidedly easier by the fact the Old School Plymouth Pilgrims had already killed off most of the pesky

Massachusetts Indians). Ironically, the grumpy Old Schoolers resented their arrival, so instead of helping they spent these years yelling at the new arrivals to get off their lawn.

So, what did we learn from this discussion? 1) From the Puritans we learned that immigration is inevitable, and the smartest thing you can do is plan for it as part of your master plan. 2) From the Strangers and Puritans we discovered that people are different, and don't always get along. 3) And from the Indians, we re-learned that lesson we all tell our kids: Don't talk to strangers, no matter how interesting, charming, or sincere they seem.

SALE OF THE CENTURY... NEW YORK.

The study of American history reveals one shocking fact after another. Take for instance this mind-blowing revelation: At one time, the Dutch actually mattered.

I know, I know—it *seems* impossible, because they're so, well, cute, with all those canals and dikes and wooden shoes—but it's true. In fact, during this brief period of significance a Dutch leader, Peter Minuit, "purchased" Manhattan for $24 in trinkets and named it New Amsterdam.

In reality, of course, the deal transpired as a two-way rip-off, because Manhattan Island's teeming forests were zoned as hunting grounds, and Indians no more believed in "ownership" of hunting grounds than in "ownership" of the clouds that drifted above them. A stenographer recorded the deal like this:

> **Minuit:** Here, Chief... here's some real shiny junk. Can I have Manhattan?
> **Chief:** Sure, Manhattan... Bronx... Queens... Whatever. Got any firewater?
> **Minuit:** You bet! ("Sucker... ")
> **Chief:** Thanks! ("Idiot... ")

As the head honcho for the Dutch interests, Peter Minuit focused on one goal: the pelts of cute/dead animals. The Indians found this arrangement to be a-okay, for the same reason people don't mind when the carnival sets up down the road—provided the carneys don't actually remove the wheels from their mobile homes and settle in. The Dutchmen's lack of plows and oxen gave them an air of temporariness, which suited the Indians just about fine.

After a while, the cute animal population became the vanishing animal population, and the Dutch found no other choice but to start busting sod. From the Indian perspective, this looked a whole lot like the carneys not only moved in next-door, but they'd parked their Funnel Cake truck on the front lawn. Relations further soured with the arrival of a Governor named William Keift who, being *centuries* ahead of his time, implemented an extortion racket—extorting protection money out of the local Indian tribes in exchange for his "protecting them" from the Mohawk Indians. Like all good racketeers, of course, he actually put the Mohawks on the payroll—and anyone who refused to cough up the wampum enjoyed a sudden visit from the boys with the really cool haircuts. The scheme worked like a Swiss watch.

Even a little power corrupts greatly, and Keift lost track of how much was too much. In 1643 he dispatched the Mohawks to muscle a tribe that lived upriver, which inspired the tribe to flee to the area that's now Jersey City. When the terrified tribe sent a team to Keift to ask for some help, Keift dropped a dime to the Mohawks that their mark was over in Jersey City.

After the Mohawks got through doing their thing, Keift sent in his troops to finish the job, which entailed the cowardly massacre of men, women, and children. His troops returned with more than 80 heads, which the settlers and soldiers commenced to use as soccer balls. Aristocrats.

As one can imagine, this particular public relations maneuver drummed up a feeling among the locals normally reserved for sea otters attending an Exxon shareholders meeting, and resulted in all of the area's Indian tribes ripping the *I (heart) New Amsterdam* bumper stickers off their horses. Now bound together in an all-things-Dutch jihad, the Indians went about making life as miserable (and short) as possible for all the Palefaces in the colony.

The Dutch colonists quickly forgot that it was *they* who'd been playing hacky-sack with the Indian heads, and threatened to revolt against Keift for *his* failure to control the Indians. Eventually, the Dutch West India Company (who invested all the coin in play) fired Keift, and replaced him with a peg leg minister named Peter Stuyvesant.

Stuyvesant's job proved impossible, because New York *then* was like New York *today*—an insane asylum/trading post best described as a controlled riot, where chaos ran the show, and good men died like dogs. He brought a few laws and a little order, and some public works to the colony, but made the fatal mistake of restricting the sale of alcohol. A *drunken* mob is manageable because *eventually* everyone wanders home to grab some shuteye, and the next day everyone feels like hell and sleeps in. A mob denied of its booze, however—well, all they have is all day to sit around hating you.

When you add the fact that the Dutch farmers worked as *share-croppers* and did not enjoy land ownership, you've got the perfect recipe for an anger martini, seasoned with bitters and a splash of apathy. In short, pretty much no one (hearted) New Amsterdam, and the winds of change blew through the five boroughs like the Witch of November.

In 1664, the Duke of York sent four English frigates and 1,000 soldiers into New Amsterdam Harbor, and announced the arrival of a new sheriff in town. The people of New Amsterdam took one look, and said, "Four frigates? Frig it." When word spread that the Duke of York liked to belly up to a good Happy Hour, they pitched the old boss out and the new boss in faster than you can say, "Gimmie a Long Island Iced Tea." The insane pace of life in the newly-named New York continued without missing a beat.

RELIGION BEGATS RHODE ISLAND...

Okay, in talking through New York we leapt a little ahead of ourselves, so let's rewind to the 1630s, when a Puritan named Roger Williams emigrated from England to Boston. Perhaps all the fresh air boggled his mind or maybe he drank too many Sam Adams' lagers, but the unselfish, loving things that came out of his mouth *enraged* his fellow Puritans. Before long, he began espousing such concepts as a civil government *not* creating or enforcing religious laws. Next, he blathered that government should be representative, and founded on the principle of religious *freedom*. Finally, the guy even had the big brass ones to insinuate the white man *buy* land from the Indians instead of stealing it.

To the veteran Puritans, this stunk of pure blaspheme, and they ordered Williams to purify his mind of such thoughts. When he refused, they kicked him pure out of the colony.

Shortly after receiving the boot, Williams led a small band of followers to what is today Rhode Island, and purchased it from the Indians. Now removed from the day-to-day insanity that engulfed the other colonies, the Rhode Islanders realized they had a good thing going, and decided to lay low and keep quiet—for the next 350 years. Think I'm kidding? Have *you* heard from Rhode Island lately? Me neither.

... AND MARYLAND, TOO.

When the orthodox Puritans heard that Williams successfully relocated a group of Christians to Rhode Island, smoke began billowing out of their stovepipe hats: Who in the *hell* did those jerks think they were, worshipping God as *they* pleased? What would be next? Demi Moore portraying them in the worst movies ever made? Nope—even worse. At almost the same time the pagans in Rhode Island were praying without supervision, the Papal Heathens known as *Catholics* moved into Maryland, *with* permission from the King, no less! The question began to circulate: What's the point of freedom if everyone else gets it, too?

To *really* make the Puritans mad, the newly-arrived Catholics passed "The Act Concerning Religion," America's first law explicitly providing for freedom to worship as you please. (Provided, of course, you were at least Christian.) This was almost more than a hateful, bigoted, mean-spirited Puritan full of God's love could stand! Something had to give.

THE PEQUOT WAR...

In 1634, an English pirate named Stone got whacked on board his ship while anchored in the Connecticut River. As a shining example of Early American white trash, resplendent with an extensive rap sheet, Captain Stone's demise failed to generate a great deal of boo-hoo-hooing, but it did open up an opportunity to blow off some steam.

Here's why: The murder was pinned on a tribe called the Niantic—but since the Niantic usually answered to a tribe called the Pequot, and the Pequot lived right there in the neighborhood, the cry for revenge trumpeted out against the far-more-conveniently-located Pequot.

The Pequot tribe attempted to calm things down by coughing up some protection wampum, and asking for forgiveness, and generally telegraphing the message that they didn't want trouble. The peace held for a little while, but the Pequot lived on desirable land, and undesirables living on desirable land never works out well for the undesirables. This is what happened next:

> **English Soldier:** My Lord, the Indians have killed another man.
> **English Bigwig:** Who?
> **English Solider:** Captain John Oldham, off Block Island.
> **English Bigwig:** Who did it?
> **English Solider:** I told you... the bloody Indians!
> **English Bigwig:** Do we have at least a tiny-tiny grain of proof the Indians did it?
> **English Solider:** Ha, ha, ha! What a kidder! Of course not!
> **English Bigwig:** Good point... slaughter the Pequot!
> **English Solider:** Women and children and old people, too?
> **English Bigwig:** Ha, ha, ha! What a kidder! Of course!

The cry for revenge went out, and the English dispatched Captain John Endecott to the Pequot village with orders to steal everything, kill all the men, and capture the women and children so they could be sold into slavery. The Pequot anticipated the English would do something ruthless, so they'd vacated the premises. Endecott didn't want to depart without leaving an appropriate calling card, so he torched their villages.

The Pequot did not think this particular maneuver was too cool at all, so they responded by putting the match to English settlements all over the Connecticut Valley. (Pulling for the Indians now, aren't you?) Unfortunately, this dispute ended like all disputes with the Indians: The settlers finally got it together, recruited some Indian rivals of the Pequot, and mounted an effective counter-offensive.

As a coup de grace, a guy named John Mason won that year's *One-Way Ticket to Hell* Award by attacking a tribe of Pequot in Connecticut and slaughtering over 600 women, children, and old people. The Pequot attempted to respond in kind, but were unsuccessful due to the fact that they were all now dead. (It's kind of hard to cue the patriotic music in the wake of this war, no?)

THE CAROLINAS...

While most settlers flocked into the northeast, freezing their family jewels off in the winter and brawling with some understandably angry locals, a couple of small southern colonies were getting underway. Strangely, these folks found the lung-crushing humidity, black skies of mosquitoes and gnats, and limitless supply of poisonous snakes more appealing than the cold weather up north.

The Carolinas came into being in a way this historian finds suspicious. For some undocumented, unexplained, unbelievable reason, King Charles II *gave* South Carolina and North Carolina to eight dudes called the Eight Lords Proprietors in 1663. Although there is no information to support my opinion, I have a difficult time believing a "gift" of this size didn't involve some pretty damning dirt on the guy with the crown.

Then, in a move almost as stunning as Charles' gift itself, the first people to settle the area *didn't* pick the absolute worst spot: No malarial swamps, no deadly temperature swings, and no jealous, Colonial neighbors. They just sailed into Charleston Harbor in 1670, found a peninsula that offered natural defenses with access to the open sea, and announced the bar would open at five.

Without the usual trials and tribulations and 75% death rates, these "Charlestonians" had time available for little things like business and profits, and soon made fortunes in the business of exporting: First furs, then timber products, then rice, and then indigo (whatever that is). All this wealth created an atmosphere of arts, and culture, and livin' la vida loca. The religious leadership came from the French Huguenots and the Anglicans, so everyone felt it was okay to live life like one big party, as long as God was invited to attend. It is worth noting that one of the early leaders of Charleston, a Huguenot minister named Samuel Prioleau, began a family line that would one day result in one of America's least-respected historians... me.

While life boogied on in Charleston, things were, uh—a little more nuanced in North Carolina. Settlers struggled to get things underway, and the early years saw fights with Indians, squabbles with Virginians, corrupt government, and the birth of Jesse Helms.

In 1712, the owners split the colony of Carolina into North Carolina and South Carolina. In 1729, George II *bought* the Carolinas back from the Lords Proprietors, most likely to slip his hands into the Charleston cookie jar, or at least around the shoulders of some of the city's debutantes. With an absentee King in charge, the economy of the Carolinas boomed, because any fool knows that when you decrease regulation and reduce taxes, the inevitable result for the economy is—oops, sorry. Trying to avoid economic politics here.

PENNSYLVANIA...

A little background on Pennsylvania: During the 1600's, an English dude named George Fox founded a group called The Society of Friends, which quickly earned the nickname "The Quakers." This dangerous, radical group's founding beliefs included such ideas as:

a) The relationship between man and God is personal, thus churches, and preachers, and collection boxes aren't necessary for worship.

b)   People should be nice to each other.

The concept of *no sermons* and *no collection boxes* seemed so repugnant to the status quo that England imprisoned these Quakers, and all the colonies except Rhode Island passed laws against them. (And how in the world were the poor Quakers *ever* gonna find Rhode Island?)

Fortunately for them, a young aristocrat named William Penn thought minding your own business and being nice to people sounded like a good idea, and certainly not a hanging offense (as the Massachusetts Puritans believed). From his home in England, Penn proclaimed the rest of the world could kiss his... the backside of his leather breeches: He called in a marker from the Duke of York in the form of Pennsylvania (*I don't know about you, but I think that's a serious, whopper-sized marker*) and invited the Quakers to make themselves at home there.

Penn also included a few forward-thinking concepts in his new colony, one of which included the elimination of debtors' prison. (*Debtors' prison was a truly brilliant invention: You owe money, so they put you in prison, where you can't earn money, so you can't pay anyone back, so you stay in prison.*). He also created a sort of Bill of McRights, establishing that your life, liberty, or property could not be taken away without a jury trial. We're talking a radical big deal here, because in taking these steps Penn surrendered potential *personal* power for the common good.

How many politicians *these* days are willing to do that? Or stated another way, what sectors of government have *shrunk* in the last 50 years? As you can see, early America brought forth some fairly amazing men right from the start.

GEORGIA...

By 1682, English settlers swarmed to America like movie stars flying private jets to global warming events. At this point there were—in order of founding—Virginia, Massachusetts, New York, Maryland, Rhode Island, Connecticut, Delaware, New Hampshire, North Carolina, South Carolina, New Jersey, and Pennsylvania.

Georgia, the last original colony to come aboard, was founded in 1733 by James Oglethorpe, a military general turned humanitarian. A number of theories remain as to why Oglethorpe took so long to found his particular colony, but some say he spent too much time on his side-business, which was thinking up "Arms Are for Hugging" slogans and stitching them onto t-shirts.

Just consider his masterplan: Oglethorpe proclaimed Georgia would be a Utopia, where criminals and debtors would enjoy a new start. To help the new Utopia along, he and the other 19 wealthy do-gooders behind the plan agreed to take no profits for 21 years. He set up all sorts of "Envision World Peace" rules, banned the sale of rum, and staked the first 100 settlers on 55-acre tracts of land that they couldn't sell or transfer. (You know, a chunk of land big enough to be cute and profitable, but not so big that anyone would get—*shudder*—greedy or boastful.)

The plan for Georgia worked flawlessly about the same of time it takes a team of Apple attorneys to figure out how to avoid paying corporate taxes: Let's be optimistic and say 20-minutes. This was because before he could even round up the next wave of desirable undesirables to move there, the first 100 settle-repreneurs figured out ways around the rules and set themselves up plantation style. Disgusted, Oglethorpe threw up his hands and walked away—something capitalists have been trying to convince socialists to do ever since.

CHAPTER THREE

TO THE PAIN...

DESPITE THE FACT that all of America's 13 Original Colonies (except Georgia) were *geographically* created by the year 1682, the word *"settled"* is a lousy way to describe them. Here is a brief list of the luxuries they lacked:

1) Everything.

This hostile New World served as home to a group of pioneers who, at best, existed as an unruly mob of crazy people, plagued by disease, a shortage of survival skills, a shortage of supplies, and a shortage of chicks. The only thing in ample supply was death and extremely bad moods.

Think Thurston Howell on Gilligan's Island—The New World held no regard for whether you were rich or middle class or poor, or what religion you were, or what colony you lived in: Life sucked, and "aid" of any sort did not exist: No stores, no medicine, no building contractors, no roads, no heavy machinery, no bars, no mail service, no grocery stores, no building supply or lumber stores, no *nothing*. It wasn't a nation—it was Hell, with clean air.

Out of this craziness, however, emerged something amazing— something more powerful than all of the world's monarchies, and all the world's armies, and all the world's political ideologies before or since—something called The American Spirit.

The swamps and the mud and the death and the shared suffering gave birth to an ideal proclaiming **Don't tread on me:** *I* left the comforts of home, and *I* took on this untamed world, and *I'll* be damned if *you* are gonna tell *me* what to do. And with this American Spirit came the most obvious historical reality in modern times: Down to our very DNA, Americans are tough, adventurous, independent, and resourceful. And every single year, from then until now, our national gene pool is freshened and mixed with the DNA of adventurous, hard-working immigrants who bring with them the dreams of a better life. The American people are mutts, and simply different than other citizens of the world.

So, America overflowed with tough, resourceful men and women, all of whom nursed a very bad mood. But during this era of bad moods, the American Indians also felt a little grumpy. At least the settlers *chose* to slither into the belly of this insane beast—but the Indians made no such choice. They were sitting around minding their own business, growing corn and hunting deer and smoking the peace pipe on weekends, and in stomps Whitey to upset the entire apple cart.

Bad moods, bad business all around.

KING PHILIP'S WAR

On June 11, 1675, in Plymouth, Massachusetts, a farmer shot a Wampanoag Indian he claimed was rustling his cattle. That Indian's Chief was a guy named Metacom—nicknamed "King Philip" because he dressed like Whitey—and ol' King Philip demanded some retribution. At this time America boasted zero TV lawyers around to "fight" on his behalf (for 40% of the wampum, plus expenses), so King Philip traipsed on over to see the local "Man." The Man summarily dismissed the Wampanoag Chief without so much as a cost-to-defend token payoff.

King Philip found this response entirely unsatisfactory, and decided to dispense his payback via a mafia-baker's half-dozen: He killed the farmer, plus six other folks.

The settlers in the area were overcome with glee. *Finally,* a reason to do something other than wallow in the misery of pioneer existence. Everyone signed up for a *Kill Someone/Anyone* team, but they ended up signing for a variety teams with no head coach to organize their efforts. As a result, King Philip's War began slowly as nothing more than a series of attacks, counter attacks, counter-counter attacks, and counter-counter-counter... you get the picture. It was really just a series of drunk-frat-boy punches, with no one getting any *really* serious damage done.

By the end of the year the Colonists got it together, and in December threw a really vicious blow during an attack in Rhode Island—a blow that included the gutless murder of women and children. They were surprised, however, when they found the Indians also understood the concept of a well-regulated militia, and began acting as an organized unit. They were even *more* surprised when the Indians showed the nerve to win a number of the clashes. And then they were really, really surprised when they crunched the numbers and figured out the Indians wiped out a total of twelve of New England's towns.

Unfortunately for the King Philip and his Indian Braves, the area now hosted more settlers than they had arrows; to make matters worse, the settlers also managed to recruit a number of anti-Wampanoag Indian allies (who still didn't understand that these Colonists treated every cooperative tribe like the sorority girl with the bad reputation, and no engagement rock was ever gonna be produced).

The result? King Philip's head rested on a stick, and his wife and son were sold into slavery. In a twist of fate only Satan himself could dream up, King Philip's soon-to-be-enslaved son was the grandson of none other than Chief Massasoit... the same Chief Massasoit who saved the Pilgrims from starving to death.

An even sadder epitaph goes to the Indian tribes who converted to Christianity due to the teaching of the English clergy. These poor souls were ruthlessly attacked and murdered by King Philip's warriors as traitors, and left to die undefended by the English because, well, they're just *Indians*, right? It's *good* that they converted, but it doesn't *really* count, does it? Jesus couldn't possibly love Indians, right? What would he have in common with a savage Indian? It's not like Jesus was a *persecuted minority*, and the Indians were a persecuted minor—uh, hmmmm. Maybe we could get back to that later.

I'LL GET YOU, MY LITTLE PRETTY...

With the successful conclusion (from the Colonists' perspective, at least) of King Philip's War, everyone reluctantly returned to the agony of their day-to-day life. An Indian War wasn't available at the moment to occupy their time (having committed virtual genocide on the troublesome tribes) so, two things topped every Colonists "To Do List": a) *hate life* and b) *try to hunt food versus being hunted as food.*

Up in Salem Village, however, they discovered a creative solution to the mind-numbing boredom of life. This is what happened: Two little girls began acting "strangely," which, given the fact that they were living in a Puritan village probably meant they were acting like normal little girls. A village doctor, board-certified in eye-of-newt remedies, logically pronounced them as under the spell of a witch, and pointed his wizened finger at the girls' nanny as the chief suspect. One thing led to another, and soon everyone was accusing everyone else of witchiness:

> **Woman #1:** You're a witch!
> **Woman #2:** No, you're a witch!
> **Woman #1:** No, you're a witch!
> **Woman #2:** No, you're a witch times infinity!
> **Woman #1:** I accused you first, and there's no takes back!
> **Woman #2:** Well, I'm rubber and you're glue, and...
> **Mayor:** Women of *rubber*? Of *glue*? Hang them both.
> **Husbands:** Excellent idea, sir.

Some real milestones of legal brilliance emerged from Salem Village's witch-hunt trials, including these "rules" of proceedings:

1) If you fail to confess, you're guilty.
2) If you criticize the proceedings, you're guilty.

3) If you plead innocent, you're guilty.
4) If you refused to implicate others in the crimes you haven't confessed to, you're guilty.

Is this beautiful, or what? Sure, it's not unlike our current "justice" system, but think about how far ahead these guys were! Engage your best Monty Python accent, and think about the exchange between the minister and the accused:

> **Minister:** Do you, Suzy, confess to your crime of witchcraft?
> **Suzy:** No.
> **Minister:** Oh… so, you're guilty.
> **Suzy:** Huh? I'm innocent.
> **Minister:** Now you're double-guilty.
> **Suzy:** This sucks.
> **Minister:** Now you're triple-guilty.
> **Suzy:** Oh, so you're gonna hang me? How about my six-year-old daughter? Gonna hang her, too?
> **Minister:** Ah, you're cooperating now... you must be innocent.
> **Suzy:** Huh?
> **Minister:** Release her... go get her daughter.

By the time some semblance of sanity emerged, nineteen "witches" were hanged—and it's fair to say, in retrospect, that they were *probably* innocent of their crimes. It's also possible that this sort of nut case behavior is a reason the Puritan movement eventually died out, and had no lasting effect on the future history of the nation.

Oh, and we learned a fairly valuable lesson: Governance by religion doesn't work so great.

THE FIRST RULE OF FIGHT CLUB IS...

America in the early years was not nice. Most residents would qualify as racist, cruel, greedy, and merciless. The national pastime evolved into nonstop fighting, and half the time it was European disputes being fought on North American soil. The nation engaged in King William's War, Queen Anne's War, King George's War, and the French and Indian War.

I'm going to gloss over some of these for a couple of reasons. First, I find military history boring, and that's an opinion coming from a former Marine. It's all a snoozefest of acronyms, where *this* guy flanked *that* guy, and *that* guy got re-supplied with fresh troops, and *this* guy ran low on supplies, and *that* guy repositioned his artillery—I mean, who cares, unless you're a military officer commanding a battalion?

The other reason for my glossing is that most of these wars offer few history lessons. They took place simply because the spoiled, inbred brats that comprised European royalty couldn't stand the idea that *another* Monarch owned as much stuff as they did. What follows is a conversation that *actually* occurred IN MY MIND:

> **Prince Buttmunch:** Boo-hoo-hoo.
> **Duke of Suckup:** What's wrong, your Highness?
> **Buttmunch:** It's dreadful! My Uncle, the Second Duke of Mustard, died yesterday, and he didn't pick me to replace him as the Earl of Whiners.
> **Suckup:** So what, my Lord? You're knee-deep in gold, you own all the land for three days ride in any direction, and you have your choice of any Sheila you want, any night of the week.
> **Buttmunch:** Yeah, but, but, but—if the King *dies*, the Earl of Whiners is fourth in line for the throne. And if I was *that* Earl, I'd only need to murder *three* relatives to become King. As it stands now, I have to murder nine! Boo-hoo-hoo.
> **Suckup:** I have an idea, my Lord! Let's get the Queen of Soul and the Duke of Earl to support your claim to the Whininess. We can draw the King of Pop into the fray by pointing out *he* divorced the Princess of Rock n' Roll, while remaining illegally aligned with both Queen Latifa and the Prince formerly known as Prince. From there, we'll instruct

Sir Mix-a-lot to muster his colonial forces, and attack Forts
Rhythm and Blues.
Buttmunch: Will that make me the Earl of Whiners?
Suckup: No, but it might grab us a few acres in the Colonies.
Buttmunch: Oh, Suckup… I feel so much better. Fetch me
a serf to throttle.

A FAAAAILURE… TO COMMUNICATE.

One of these early wars mattered, however, in a really big way: The
French and Indian War. I'm not sure why we've slipped this particular
war down the national memory hole, but it just doesn't get a lot of play.
If forced to guess, I'd say it's because it's one of those wars with multiple
fronts, and lots of names to remember, and pit us against the French.

Ever since WWI we Americans haven't had too high of an opinion
of the French military, so we may be looking back in retrospect and
saying, "We beat the French. Big deal. I used to beat up my little sister,
but no one gave me a ribbon from that, either."

Anyway, the French and Indian War mattered a great deal. It started
because no one could produce a proper deed to the Ohio Valley, and
both the French and the English wanted it. The French claimed it; the
English claimed it; the French moved in; the English moved in; the
French built forts; the English built forts… blah, blah, blah. We all
know where this is headed.

In 1753, the English sent a young Captain named George Washington
to outer Pennsylvania to advise the French loitering there that they were
trespassing and needed to vamoose. The French chuckled a bit, gave a
George a wedgie, and sent him packing. George subsequently returned
with a group of 150 militiamen, and managed to fire off a few potshots
before the French killed most of his men and sent George home.

After this, the English got really mad, and launched a fairly significant force under a guy named Major General Edward Braddock,
a career military officer who graduated Magna Cum Lousy from the
Forest Gump School of Intellectual Prowess.

With *Lt. Colonel* George Washington in tow, Braddock planned to attack the French Fort at the site where Pittsburgh now stands. As a value-added part of the plan, Braddock dispatched forces to attack Nova Scotia (Nova Scotia? WTF?), where a bunch of French-speaking fishermen were minding their own business and trying to reel in enough fish to make enough money to buy enough whiskey to forget they were stuck in Nova Scotia reeling in fish for a living.

The attack against the French fort transpired as one would expect (if Forest Gump served as the master strategist), and the French—supported by lots of Indians who preferred French trappers to English farmers—put the smack-down on some serious English fanny.

General Braddock took the Big One for the team, and once again George Washington headed home. (Am I the only one getting a funny feeling about George here?) This victory emboldened the Indians, who ravaged the countryside with a joy not unlike ANTIFA when the Main Street Footlocker gets a new shipment of Jordan's. The British responded by running around building forts and doing their best Chicken Little impersonation, and generally acting like their world was falling apart, because, well, it was.

[Interestingly, the French and Indian War sparked a spillover effect in Europe, a phenomenon not unlike what occurs within the audience during a particularly exciting World Wrestling Entertainment match. Here's the deal: At a really good wrestling match—a chair-swinging, microphone grabbin', blood spurtin' cage match—the voyeuristic audience gets caught up in the moment, and forgets they are watching the show and aren't **in** *the show. As a result, when Captain Madman smashes HellCat with a chair, HellCat's posse takes offense at the Madman fans demanding he follow up with his signature Windpipe Removal move. This bloodlust among the fans builds and builds, until finally someone puts down their beer, and starts throwing fists. And so it was with Europe: England, France, The Holy Roman Empire, Bohemia, Prussia, Spain, Russian—everyone got caught up in the thrill of the fight, joined the brawl, and the whole mess became known as "The Seven Years War." The only positive thing one could say about these spin-off European wars was, well, it resulted in less Europeans.]*

Anyway, over in the Colonies, The French and Indian War started out very badly for the British, and they reacted by putting William Pitt in charge of Colonial affairs. Pitt possessed a couple of very radical theories concerning warfare, centering mostly around the creative concept that the point of war is winning. This point often evaded the British because of their strict and unwavering code of manners. As a result, difficult conversations were, uh, difficult to have among military men, thus hard decisions and leadership was difficult. Here is a conversation uncovered in my research:

British General: I say, Colonel, what brings you back to the fort?

British Colonel: Well, Sir, the situation *required* my return.

General: Ah, yes... the situation. Might I inquire about the situation?

Colonel: Right... yes... well, seems my regiment was wiped out. Quite a loss, really. But I had a very exciting view of the action from atop a nearby mountain.

General: The *entire* regiment?

Colonel: Afraid so, Sir. Every man-jack of them.

General: My son was in your regiment.

Colonel: Was he? Oh, bother... I'm sure he died well.

General: Hmmm, yes... and you did everything you could?

Colonel: Everything I could?

General: Yes, you know, to lead the men from the slaughter that—

Colonel: *General!* Might I remind you that my ex-step-brother-in-law-once-removed is married to the second cousin of the Duchess of Grovelingham? And that my father was the assistant to the under-secretary of the Royal Sanitation Engineers?

General: Quite so... my apologies, Colonel. Why don't you go take over the 5th Regiment? It's commanded by one of those horrid Colonials... he won't mind.

Colonel: Very well, then. And your wig looks wonderful today, General. The powder is holding quite nicely.

William Pitt, a leader who clearly failed his etiquette training, maintained the barbaric notion that to win one must choose the best officers for the job and spend the money needed for beans, bullets, and band-aids. With good officers and decent supplies and the shared understanding that the point of all this was to break things and kill people, the English managed to turn the war around (I'm glossing over the boring stuff), and by 1760 the unpleasantness petered off. France gave up the proverbial ghost as a power in North America, and the British strutted the streets like a Hunter Biden on his way to deposit his Ukrainian oil check.

So why does the French and Indian War matter so much to history? *Because England ran up a fairly significant war debt, and decided that imposing debt-relief taxes on the Colonies was a terrific idea.* The Colonies, however, took the victory to mean something a little different… namely that *"their* victory" on behalf of England proved their worth, and they deserved enough respect from the mother country to determine their own tax burden.

Thus, the French and Indian War ended, and everyone (except the Indians) got what they deserved: Territories were divvied up, the Europeans returned to sipping tea, and the settlers returned to the life of settling, which still really, really sucked.

A problem surfaced, however, when no one explained to the Indians that the war ended, and (also) that no one really cared what they thought about it. In response, Chief Pontiac of the Ottawa Tribe gathered as many pissed off Indians as possible and pointed out the obvious: They got nothing but screwed for their efforts. The participating tribes cut loose like a horde of vegans at the annual meeting of the Texas Cattlemen's Ball, and initiated a very successful campaign to kill and torture settlers in the western areas. (Not that there's anything wrong with that).

The English, tapped out from the previous war, took steps that the modern mind finds almost unthinkable: They called a pow-wow, and as gifts gave the Indians blankets infected with the smallpox virus. As the Indians had no natural defense immunities to smallpox, the disease caused an epidemic. Before long, Pontiac's Rebellion ended, but the rebellion planted in the settlers' minds that Indians were murderous demons.

Now, let's end this chapter by discussing a couple of things we learned:

1) Americans are, and always have been, tough, independent thinkers. It just comes as part of the gene pool. 2) From those folks in Salem, we learned that theocracies don't work that well. 3) From our on-going, inhuman treatment of the American Indians, we learned that sometimes the good guys aren't. 4) From Chief Pontiac, we learned that defeating people who feel *they have nothing left* to lose is much harder than defeating people who have plans for after the war.

LET THE HISTORY LESSONS BEGIN

As discussed earlier, the entire point of studying history is to **learn** from the past. We, as a nation, fail miserably in this seemingly simple concept—even in these modern times of digital data. We have access to virtually unlimited amounts of accurate historical research *and* analysis, and yet... yet... we keep sticking our hand back into the fire to see if it's hot.

So, let's reverse that trend! Let's recap *The Lessons We Should Have Learned.*

I will offer the lesson learned, and your challenge is to come up with examples of when we clearly failed to act on those lessons learned.

I could fill in the answers to these screw-ups with numerous examples, but then I'd be removing the opportunity for you to challenge yourself—and thus I am hereby challenging you—gentle reader—to come up with your own examples of historical lunacy. Maybe buy 10 copies and form a book club to discuss the ideas. Or 10,000 copies, and send them to the "professors" at the Ivy League schools to use in their freshman history classes.

Keep in mind that most failures come from our elected leaders, bureaucrats, political appointees, courts, and the private sector, but here is an extremely important fact: Often times the failure to learn from the past rests on the shoulders of *we the people*.

By way of example, consider this:

> **Lesson:** The guy in charge will always look out for himself.
> **Who gets the F?** We the people, for re-electing career pol-
> iticians based on the insane belief they are in Washington,
> D.C. focused on taking care of our needs.

Makes Sense?

Here's the game:
—You read the lesson learned.
—You decide on the leaders, institutions, companies, groups,
or individuals who clearly failed to learn the lesson, while
analyzing how their failure to learn the lesson has impacted
recent history.

Lesson: If you're willing to risk it all for the rich and pow-
erful, the rich and powerful are more than happy to let you.
Lesson: A little power can turn anyone into a com-
plete dictator.
Lesson: As history is written by men who've hanged heroes,
we must jealously guard the truth in order to learn from it.
Lesson: Jumping to conclusions can lead to mistakes.
Lesson: If truly hungry, anyone "will work for food."
Lesson: History can be manipulated by the historian.
Lesson: Don't feed the hand that bites you.
Lesson: The gullibility of the public can never be overstated.
Lesson: Committees lead to group stupidity.
Lesson: Immigration is inevitable, so you should plan for
it in your masterplan.
Lesson: People are different by design.
Lesson: You shouldn't talk to strangers, no matter how
interesting, handsome, or powerful they are.
Lesson: People like to hang around people like themselves.

Lesson: Americans are opportunistic, so don't send a fox to guard the henhouse.

Lesson: Americans are tough, independent thinkers.

Lesson: Theocracies don't work so well.

Lesson: Sometimes the "good guys" have very bad apples in the mix.

Lesson: An enemy who has nothing to lose is a fearsome opponent.

CHAPTER FOUR

DON'T TREAD ON ME...

AS STATED EARLIER, most of the bloodshed during the first 65 years of the 1700s resulted from European conflicts fought on North American soil. A real problem arose, however, when the King George's accountants balanced the Royal Checkbook and discovered a mysterious reality: Wars are expensive. Solution? Make the Colonists pay their "fair" share of the cost. This logic, of course, is not unlike the U. S. Department of Defense sending Iraq a bill for the damage their buildings did to our bombs.

As a tax-raising "strike one" the King implemented the Sugar Act of 1764, placing a tariff on sugar, coffee, wine, and every other imported pleasure-providing item that might momentarily take your mind off the fact that half of your friends, neighbors, and family died fighting on behalf of the guy taxing you. (*George, let's think that through: Is it wise PR to have your Subjects muttering "Death to the King" every time they sit down to relax? Isn't that a bit like putting a picture of the Capitol Building on every Starbucks lid and on every wine label?*)

Next, he created the Stamp Act of 1765, which required a Royal "taxes have been paid" stamp on every **paper** document—from newspapers, to legal documents, to playing cards. (*All right, Your Georgeness—now that you infuriate them every time they relax, pass a tax that will infuriate them every time they do something requiring thought—and not a wimpy* *trade tax that gets hidden within the price, but a direct tax, so they can see right there how much you're screwing them. They'll love it!)*

The Colonists, of course, began seething—and since Colonists technically retained a right to representation in Parliament, some spin doctor spun up with the phrase *"no taxation without representation!"*

In truth, the educated Colonial leaders knew representation in the English Parliament was as useless as a warning sticker on a hip hop CD, but—hey, *it was a cool slogan.* And *people like cool slogans.* Plus, it planted a feeling of "unfairness" among the Colonists, even among the uneducated farmers who wouldn't understand "representation" if it bit them on the shin. *(What do you think, Clem? I want me some representin', that's what I think.)*

Add to this overall atmosphere the coming riots, and the coining of the phrase *"Sons of Liberty,"* and you're brewing a tempest in a beer stein. *(I'm with you, Billy John... I even joined them Sons of Libations. I want me some dang liberty, and I'm fixin' to git it.)*

Seeking a nomination for **The Cluey**, an award presented each year in Liechtenstein to the world's most clueless monarch, King George soon passed the Townshend Acts, which taxed imported glass, lead, paper, paint, and tea—and also provided his military with the right to use "blanket search warrants" and hold juryless trials.

Can you hear the Colonists grumbling?

The King reacted to their grumbling and boycotts by sending 4,000 soldiers to Boston, a city of only 16,000 people. He then cinched the Cluey by passing the Quartering Act of 1765, which proclaimed, "Not only will you put up with my Redcoats, but you will house them, wine them, and dine them... at no charge."

The folks in Boston got downright uppity, among them Samuel Adams, a man probably losing a fortune in beer to all the thirsty Redcoats. One thing led to another, and the Bostonians took to the streets protesting, and no doubt wearing angry-slogan t-shirts and chanting things like "Hey, you, Redcoats, we don't want you here! But if you're gonna stay, at least pay for beer!"

On March 5, tragedy struck. A group of drunken longshoremen-types confronted some Redcoats, and pelted them with snowballs. One of the longshoremen violated the *most* sacred of all snowball fight rules by putting a rock in his snowball, then bonking it off a soldier's head. Well-versed in the rules of snowball fighting, the Redcoats felt they had no choice but to retaliate—and responded not with cold snowballs, but with hot lead.

Five Colonists were dead, the "Boston Massacre" became a rallying cry, and King George got a standing ovation when he collected his *Cluey.*

As you can see, my friends, the lessons learned are pouring in. 1) People really, really, really dislike taxes. 2) From King George, we've learned that you can learn a lot by watching a bad example in progress. 3) We learned a fairly subtle lesson from those British troops: No matter what the reason, firing into an unarmed crowd makes for bad press and lousy poll numbers.

A MOMENT FOR COMMENTARY...

As a former U. S. Marine, I know better than most about the concept of "shared suffering" and its impact on a man's psyche.

I know what it feels like to stand in a downpour, and feel the rain soak its way through 'til it runs down your private parts, and know that you're going to *eat* in that rain, *sleep* in that rain, and *live* in that rain for the next five days. I know what it feels like to move across a mountain at night on cross-country skis, then dig a snow cave for shelter—not as an adventure, but to keep from freezing to death. I know what it is like to risk your life on a routine basis—not silly-fun-risk-your-life stuff like rock climbing and skydiving, but this-has-got-to-get-done-risk-your-life stuff like training with live ammunition and conducting an amphibious assault in rough seas on a moonless night. I have *not*, in deference to those who have, experienced the most intense shared suffering experience of all, combat.

But what I know of shared suffering is this: It bonds you. It bonds you with utter strangers, and makes you one with them. It bonds you tighter than blood, and creates an almost unhealthy intolerance of those who have not shared your suffering. It endows you with a feeling of strength, and superiority, and empowers you to do things together the uninitiated view as madness: Things like storming the beaches of Okinawa, Tarawa, or Normandy, or fighting house to house in the streets of Baghdad. It breeds relationships that defy all else, except for the relationship between God and a man in a foxhole.

It is my theory that in Colonial America, around the early 1770's, an entire nation of people held doctorate-level degrees in the field of suffering. Some born and raised in it and some immigrated into it, but they shared a bond between them as tight, and unique, as the world had ever seen. This is not to say that plenty of people before these American settlers didn't possess graduate-level work in suffering—clearly the serfs caught up in the feudal system knew the meaning of "this sucks".

The difference, however, is the uniqueness of Colonial America. You see, since time began, whenever a king or nobleman sought to oppress people, he did so geographically and physically—that is, he ordered a Knight to gallop up to your geographic location, and as you stood there defenseless, said Knight physically smashed you in the head with his mace.

Everything was different in Colonial America—but here's the big thing: The people possessed arms. In fact, they owned the same weapons as their potential oppressors, which offered them the ability defend themselves from the King's henchmen.

Another uniqueness of Colonial America revolved around the people's feelings of independence, brought on largely because new colonies lacked the European class system. The Duke of Butthead didn't come to America, because it was uncomfortable. He already had his castle, his stables, his lords a' leaping and maids a' milking in Limeyshire, so why bother? He sent over some mercenary-types to make money and send it back, but why go himself? Besides, Lord Beavis had a really cute niece, and they arranged for a picnic next week. Without the "nobility" around to make everyone feel inferior, the Colonists began to feel *equal*... then *better*... then *superior* to the Duke of Butthead and Lord Beavis.

And that's it, friend.

There's the recipe, simple as it may be: The recipe that led to the greatest nation, the greatest government, and the greatest melting pot of immigrants the world would ever see. Cooking this mighty pot of potential took only a time and a place where human beings could:

a) Benefit personally and directly from all their labors.
b) Feel mutual respect for their neighbors.
c) Possess the arms to defend themselves.

The rest, they say, is history.

TEA, ANYONE?

Following the Boston Massacre, the King lost out on his chances for induction into the **Cluey** Hall of Fame by suspending most of the Townshend Act taxes—except the one on tea. This repeal of taxes spurned the economy, and history got its first look at what the average American does when the economy takes a turn for the good, which is primarily lie down in front of the fire and wag his tail.

Unfortunately for the King, the idea of true freedom began to play ping-pong in the minds of men like Samuel Adams, Patrick Henry, and Thomas Jefferson, and they spent much of their time trying to speed up the pace of the game. They poked around at a few technical issues, and sought to fire up the locals, but—like I said—the economy roared like a lion, and Americans aren't very energetic when there's enough dough coming in to keep Momma happy and in the fashionable clothes and shoes from *Really, Really, Really* Old Navy. To ensure proper communications existed when these leaders *did* find a significant issue, the Virginia House of Burgesses formed a Committee of Correspondence, which is a fancy way of saying they put together a newsletter committee to keep all the colonies "in the loop" about upcoming potluck revolutions.

Eventually, of course, guys this smart *did* find a rallying point for the Colonists, which turned out to be tea. They pointed out that it was *not* the *taxes* on the tea, but the fact that all the tea sales funneled through a handful of loyalists, which made it almost impossible for even a hardworking tea smuggler to make a living.

They spun up a story that this "Good 'ol King" Network was nothing short of price fixing, and this idea inspired the Colonists curled up in front of the fireplace to sit up and take notice. After all, if the King shut the tea smugglers out of *their* livelihood, who would be next—you? Me? Sure, it hadn't actually happened, but it might, and everyone knows the best way to prevent trouble is to stop it *in advance*, right?

The tea issue so excited the Colonists that they didn't bother to growl or bark, but lunged straight to the bite: On December 16, 1773, 150 men dressed as Mohawk Indians boarded three ships in Boston Harbor, and dumped 342 chests of tea overboard.

Why they dressed as Mohawk Indians has remained largely a mystery, because it's not like they were fooling anyone. A mystery until now, that is. As I am wont to do, I dug deeper than other historians, and discovered the truth.

Here is the real story: Sam Adams was rolling out a new beer called Indian Summer Ale, and invited over a group of regulars. After a dozen pints, he announced, "Men, I've got the artist on the way who's gonna paint the scene for the Indian Summer Ale poster, and—don't know if y'all remember, but we've pretty much killed anyone that can sit for the painting. Any volunteers?"

Five pints later, he had them all in buckskins. Right about pint 20, the gang was laughing, staggering about, shaving their heads, and rubbing war paint on their faces.

A man with a keen ability to manipulate others, Sam then proclaimed: "Men! The artist has been kidnapped! Unless we ransom him, there'll be no painting.!"

One man spoke up, and spoke for all: "Sam! If you think my ass is goin' home to wife lookin' like this and stinkin' of alcohol, with no damn fame to show for it, you been drinkin' more than just beer! Whatta we gotta do???"

Sam explained tea smugglers kidnapped the artist, and now had him in a row boat in the harbor. All they needed to do was board the ship tied up at the pier, throw the tea into the harbor where the smugglers could get it, they'd release the artist, he'd paint the painting, and his painting would bring forth the fame!

When steps 1 and 2 came about, but 3, 4, and 5 failed to, Sam never did get to release his Indian Summer Ale... these dudes looking like retired Mohawks stopped by every day at 5:30, and after about a month drank the kegs dry.

So, what is the historical significance of the Boston Tea Party? It's actually easier to understand if we eavesdrop on a conversation between rich fathers and sons this very day... Dad is England, his son is America:

> **Father:** Your behavior is totally unacceptable! As long as you live under my roof, you'll live by my rules!
> **Son:** Your rules are stupid!
> **Father:** My house, my rules!
> **Son:** In case you haven't noticed, I don't live under your roof anymore! I live in Aspen, and you live in Boston!
> **Father:** Yeah? Well, I own the condo you're living in, and I say you will stop sitting around drinking beer, and get a job!
> **Son:** I pay the rent!
> **Father:** With the allowance I give you!
> **Son:** Oh yeah? Well, listen to this! (*Smash*) You hear that? That was your framed picture of you and Frank Sinatra! Want to hear some more stuff break, Pops??!
> **Father:** You sit right there, young man—*I'm on the way.* We'll *see* who's the head of this family!

Indeed. And so it occurred with the Boston Tea Party—and like many father and son spats, things moved quickly from harsh words and symbolic acts of defiance to real, no-fooling action. Steam poured from British ears, because the value of the dumped tea came in at about 9,000 British Pounds, and seeing how that represented the annual income of 90 average Colonists... well, it wasn't brushed under the rug like "The King is fat" graffiti. It added up to lot of dough, and the Crown wanted someone's allowance to pay for it.

Now, before moving on, let's take a look at the lessons learned. 1) From the repealing of the Townshend Acts, we know Americans get lazy and complacent when the economy is good. 2) And from the reaction of the Colonists to the tea situation, we learned that "if a dog is asleep and you kick him, he'll wake up and bite you."

I SEE DUMB PEOPLE...

Following the Boston Tea Party, King George huddled with his Prime Minister, Lord North, and formulated a plan. Most historians agree that while King George loved to read governmental documents and policies, he wasn't exactly a foreign policy rocket surgeon, resulting in Lord North calling most of the shots. This historian surmises that the planning session unfolded something like this:

> **King:** Wow. The Colonists have gone totally colonial. Even with troops occupying Boston, the little brats pulled off that Tea Party thingee.
>
> **Lord North:** Your Highness—Let's institute the *Boston Port Act*, which will close the port until they pay for the tea they dumped in the harbor.
>
> **King:** How can we enforce that? We can't even keep them from dumping our tea into the harbor.
>
> **Lord North:** We'll institute the *Massachusetts Government Act* which more or less nullifies their charter and puts us in control.
>
> **King:** What if they complain?
>
> **Lord North:** We'll pass the *Government Act* and make town meetings illegal.
>
> **King:** What if they lash out?
>
> **Lord North:** We'll pass the *Impartial Administration of Justice Act*, so that after our soldiers kill them for lashing out, we bring the soldiers back here for, uh, *trial*."
>
> (Wink, wink)
>
> **King:** It's almost unbelievable—Your understanding of compassionate conservative ideals is unsurpassed—High five!

Not surprisingly, the Colonists considered these acts intolerable, and in a stroke of creativity lumped them together and dubbed them "The Intolerable Acts."

In order to decide what to do, they formed a "Continental Congress," which met in Philadelphia from September 5 to October 26, 1774, during which they decided that a meeting that lasts almost two months is damn near as intolerable as the Intolerable Acts. They accomplished very little, except for their decision to boycott imported British stuff, and a bold declaration that if things didn't get better they'd... they'd... they'd... they'd meet some more.

THE COLONISTS DID WHAT??!!

Shortly after enacting the Massachusetts Government Act, the King fired the elected governor of Massachusetts, and appointed British General Thomas Gage in his place; he figured that Gage was already unpopular enough—serving as the Commanding General of all the troops in Boston—so who cared about one more job description?

The Colonists responded by acting all revolutionary, and across the river in Lexington, militiamen drilled with muskets, declaring they'd be ready to fight the British on a moment's notice, and earning the nickname "Minutemen." *(Oddly, they did **not** earn the additional nicknames "extremists," "gun-nuts," "rednecks" or "Boogaloo Boys.").* In Boston, a silversmith named Paul Revere sat stakeout on the British, and told his fellow Patriots he'd created a church steeple signal with an employee of a Boston Church to advise him if General Gage headed to Lexington. (The old "one if by land, two if by sea" trick).

Sure enough, General Gage eventually tired of sitting around Boston, and when he heard that John Hancock, Samuel Adams, and a bunch of guns and ammo were cached just across the river waiting to be captured, he busted his move. Paul Revere got the signal, then took off on his horse towards Lexington and to give warning to everyone along the way.

Note: Before continuing with the exciting parts, there's something you need to know: Paul Revere wasn't alone—in fact, two other cats played just as big of a role in the ride: Sam Prescott and Billy Dawes. The historical truth be known, a British patrol detained Revere, and only Prescott made it to Concord to warn the folks there. After his release by the British, Revere rode back to Lexington, where he found Hancock and Adams sitting in the same place, still running their pie holes about the coming British, and what they should do.

"*What should you do?*" Revere said. "Hey, I've got an idea—Why don't you get the *$#&!!* outta here before the British show up and cut off your *#%&!!s!*" Hancock and Adams heeded his advice, and headed for Philadelphia immediately.

The other factual buzz-kill concerning Paul Revere entails the fact that he didn't actually roar past the homes at a full gallop shouting, "The British are coming! The British are coming!" He *actually* knocked on people's doors to wake them up, then told them, "The Regulars are out!" (*History*, man—when can we start trusting it?)

So, you ask, why is Paul Revere the famous one? Because Henry Wadsworth Longfellow wrote a poem entitled *The Midnight Ride of Paul Revere*, and unfortunately for Dawes and Prescott, *Revere* rhymes with all the easy stuff: Hear, fear, rear, gear, mere, steer, dear, jeer, beer… I mean, imagine you're Longfellow. Who are you going to choose? (*Listen my children, stop smoking pot, this is the story, of Sam Prescott?*).

Anyway, after crossing the river, General Gage marched his troops to Lexington, where he encountered a small group of very brave Minute Men, all of whom needed a minute to get organized. Sadly, it took the British soldiers only about a minute to shoot them, then continue their march to Concord.

What happened next seems pretty amazing. But allow me to explain: In Europe, the *real* advantage of rifles and cannons remained undiscovered. As a sensible person, *you* understand intuitively that the entire point of a rifle is that *it enables you to shoot the other guy before he sees you, often from a spot that provides you with cover.* If you **aren't** using the rifles in this way, then why bother using them, right? Why not fight with swords, or axes, or those brightly colored swimming pool noodles?

Who knows, but the intricacies of the concept appear to be more than the English could handle. As a result, the approved style of battle in Europe was:

- Good guys march out
- Bad guys march out
- Good guys get aligned and looking good
- Bad guys get aligned and looking good.
- Load, Aim, Fire!
- Reload
- Repeat until dead.

The training methods used by the British taught a twelve-step movement for the reloading of their "Brown Bess" muskets, which a decent soldier could accomplish between two and five times every minute. It must be noted, however, that should a soldier become *distracted*—perhaps by the guy next to him getting his head blown off by, say, a cannon ball—well, the number of reloads per minute may prove significantly less.

Given that the enemies' weapons were just as complex to load, the victory usually tilted to the army that could reload the fastest. Yes, literally a reloading contest.

And since that's the case, why shoot each other? Why not have three-legged sack races, and dizzy-izzy relays, and apple bobbing contests? The overall winner is the, uh, overall winner?

Doesn't that sound more sensible? More sensible than the insanity of having a reloading contest where the only available prizes are life and death? Yes?

Well, to the Europeans, this idea of battle seemed *honorable*... and the idea of seeking cover or concealment was viewed as *cowardly*. (All cowards, please raise your hands.) (My hand went up first.)

So, as the British troops neared Concord (marching in their usual formation through open fields), an unexpected reality developed:

> **British Colonel:** I say there, Lef-tenant... have you noticed that our chaps keep falling about? It's almost as if they're *dead*.

British Lieutenant: Well, Sir, now that you point it out, it *does* seem that we have a few motionless bodies strewn about here and there.

British Colonel: I don't *see* the enemy. Who could be shooting them?

British Lieutenant: Well, sir, I *do* see some blokes shooting at us from behind those rocks.

British Colonel: *Behind* the bloody rocks? That hardly seems cricket.

British Lieutenant: Colonists... worse than the French.

British Colonel: Ha! Jolly good point, Lef-tenant! Oh well, have the Sergeant fire a few proper volleys, then let's collect up the dead—back to Boston we go, eh?

It's safe to say the British and the Colonists maintained different views of what transpired at Lexington and Concord. The British General Gage reported to his boss of "an event that happened here on the 19th." The Colonists, however, launched a "fair and balanced" version of the events via their newsletter express, and within a couple weeks the stories spread throughout the Colonies.

The Facts? The British suffered 73 dead, and 174 wounded; the Colonists suffered 49 dead and 41 wounded. One can only imagine the story once it reached an illiterate farmer in South Carolina, filtered through six tellers of the tale, and several jugs of whiskey on a dozen front porches:

> *And then! Then! Then them English Lobsterbacks scalped the children, and ate 'em! I ain't lying—heard it personal from a fella who saw 'em doin' the eatin! Covered 'em with hot sauce and such! But our boys—well, some of 'em can fly, and they swooped down like an eagle with a musket in its talons and a knife in its beak!*

Within a month, a 2nd Continental Congress of almost 350 delegates gathered for more meetings. The first order of business entailed forming an army, that being a fairly important part of any war, especially given they didn't have one. Now, if it was me there, *I'd say, "Hey, let's just do the same thing we did at Concord, and let's do it every day until the British leave."* To me, several thousand hard-as-oak backwoodsmen and farmers launching a hit-and-run campaign against the Brits would be an absolutely unbeatable force.

However, the Continental Congress felt it vital to have a traditional, national standing army in order to fight the British in the traditional, standing European manner. (As usual, it wouldn't be the deciders doing all that "standing." If that were the case, my three-legged race concept might have received serious consideration.)

As the commander in chief they chose George Washington. Today, we Americans accept this fact as just another point of history, but the Father of our Country actually deserves much, much deeper consideration: When George accepted that job, he stood alone as the very first person to accept *guaranteed* death if the Revolution failed. For him, and him alone, the decision offered victory or death.

Yes, of course, dozens of the Founding Fathers risked everything, and understood their actions *could* result in their hanging, but these were very civil times, and one could easily see some of them getting acquitted because "ye glove did not fitteth." But General Washington? He agreed very publicly to bear arms against the Crown and the world's greatest military, and the punishment for that would be a very stretched neck.

The fact that George Washington accepted this appointment is, in reality, shocking. Raised as a stereotypical Virginia preppie, he inherited a money, married even more, and lived a life of semi-leisure at Mount Vernon. Like most trust-fund frat boys, work wasn't really necessary, so he worked as a surveyor because he liked surveying. By all accounts opting out of the whole affair was the wiser choice. *(I'll be out on the veranda with a mint julep. Inform me when you've dispatched those dreadful Brits.)*

Isn't that what virtually everyone with his bloodline and privilege would do today? Do you see a lot of Obamas, Bushs, Trumps, or Clintons in the infantry?

Not George. He and his fellow Founding Fathers believed Britain was violating natural law, and stomping all over the rights granted to the

Colonists by the Lord above. In order to right that wrong, he stepped into the breach, and in my book that fact alone is reason enough for all the historical praise he receives.

However, there is another and lesser-known theory (The Alexander Theory) as to why Washington agreed to take the reins of the Continental Army. The Alexander Theory is based on the true fact that his Mom was such an unbelievable pain in the ass that George stepped to the front.

Yes, that's right—the Father of our Country had a nagging, complaining, whining mom. In fact, in 1781, when General Washington's work made him perhaps the busiest, most-preoccupied human being on the planet—he carved time out of his schedule to deal with the members of the Virginia House of Delegates, who received a letter from George's mom claiming she was living in poverty and needed help.

Needless to say, she lived in the sort of poverty borne by such women as Bill Gates' Mom, but the fact that *one* servant fanned her while George's wife Martha enjoyed *two servants*—well, the humiliation and pain must've simply been too much.

Interestingly, this Continental Congress appointed the committee that "created" the motto "E Pluribus Unum," which means "From many, one." If you're like me, you probably envision this very cool, very appropriate motto being handed down from on high, complete with rays of light, rainbows and doves with olive branches. Sorry, not the deal. After discovering the true source of the motto, it becomes much easier for me to envision the way its development likely occurred:

> **Man #1:** Dude—it's 9 am. Are you already fixing a
> Bloody Mary?
> **Man #2:** I've got to—this convention is killing me. I've been
> out for 14 nights straight.
> **Man #3:** Where'd y'all go last night?
> **Man #2:** Ladies of Liberty Review… did you go out?
> **Man #3:** Dude, I crashed. We better declare independence
> soon, or my liver is gonna transform from one organ, to many.
> **Man #1:** Guys, we gotta get serious about this stupid motto.
> Anyone got any ideas?

Man #2: I don't even know what day of the week it is.

Man #1: Well, Old man Franklin is gonna insist we use one of his stupid wise sayings if we don't come up with something.

Man #3: I got nothin'.

Man #1: Hey, what are you reading?

Man #3: *Gentleman's Magazine*—it's some sort of English rag. I found it under the sofa.

Man #1: What's that phrase on the cover? Looks like Latin, or Greek.

Man #3: It says, *E Pluribus Unum.*

Man #1: Sweet! What does that mean?

Man #3: I don't know. I don't speak Latin.

Man #1: Exactly! And neither does anyone else! We'll just use that, and everyone will be too embarrassed to admit they don't know what it means.

Man #3: What if it means, *Spank me, King, spank me.*

Man #1: Dude, it's just a stupid slogan on the front of a magazine. At the most it'll be put on a lapel pin for the old codgers at the convention.

Man #2: True 'dat! Someone hoist the "Mission Accomplished" banner, and make me a Bloody!

"What??!!!" you're now saying. "Did I read that right? Was the national slogan *E Pluribus Unum* swiped from the cover of some lame British men's magazine?!!" And my answer is "Yup." It's like I told you at the beginning of this book, this is history—you can't make this stuff up.

Anyway, the big decision rendered at the Continental Congress entailed the raising of a formal Army, and the word went out. Before the end of 1775, the Continental Army boasted over 25,000 soldiers, with men at arms representing all 13 Colonies.

I LOVE THE SMELL OF GUNPOWDER IN THE MORNING...

Shortly after the Continental Congress met for the second time, relationships between the Colonies and the British took a turn for the worse. It
shook out like this: British General Gage had done a brilliant job thus far
of infuriating the Colonists, but his ability to quell the rebellion ranked
up there with Al Gore's ability to reduce his personal carbon footprint.

The Crown caught on to this, and sent to his aid three underling
Generals: William Howe, John Burgoyne, and Henry Clinton. No
sooner did this 'A Team' arrive than the current Commander (General
Gage) called Major General Howe in for a meeting:

> **Gage:** General Howe, we've got to crush these rebels.
> **Howe:** I'm ready, Sir. How can I assist?
> **Gage:** *Howe* can you assist?
> **Howe:** Yes, Sir. Absolutely I can. That's what I just said.
> **Gage:** Good! But Howe?
> **Howe:** Yes, Sir?
> **Gage:** I'm saying, *Howe* can you assist?
> **Howe:** I'm sure I can, Sir.
> **Gage:** No, fool... I want to know *Howe!*
> **Howe:** Oh, you'll get to know me, Sir... by the way I fight!
> **Gage:** Ughh... Howe can we end this conversation before
> I go insane?
> **Howe:** Certainly, Sir. Enough talk. Why don't I go
> attack someone?
> **Gage:** Howe about you do that...

Howe designed his first move as a biggie. His plan centered on the
taking of Bunker Hill, a piece of high ground outside Boston, then
establishing it as a key area for crushing the Colonial rebellion. The
Colonists, however, got word of the plan, and marched to the area first,
where they dug in on nearby Breed's Hill. (History claims the decision to
occupy Breed's Hill was a tactical one, but I served as a compass-carrying
Marine Corps Lieutenant, and I tend to think they were just lost.)

The British commenced to bombard the area with naval gunfire, but the Patriots hunkered down in their foxholes, so the casualties were minimal. The British troops then began the slowest amphibious assault in history—so slow, in fact, that some witnesses claim a couple of dolphins actually evolved into humans and joined the ranks.

Through a semi-miracle of luck and courage (combined with the usual boring lingo about flanking, and fresh troops, and re-supply) the Americans stood their ground for most of the battle, and killed an impressive number of Redcoats—thanks in part to the wisdom of Patriot Officer Israel Putnam, who ordered "Don't fire until you see the whites of their eyes!"

(Note: For any future military men out there, "Don't shoot until you see the whites of their eyes" is literally the worst tactic available, times infinity. If you ever give that order to your subordinates, they'll probably shoot you in the whites of your eyes).

When all was said and done, the Redcoats pushed the Patriots into punt formation, but the Pats inflicted the greater number of casualties. For the Patriots, the cost tallied to 450 casualties, 140 of which died. On the British side, things were much worse: Over 1,000 casualties, with 226 of those beaming up to party with Henry VIII.

No, it failed to qualify as a great and horrific battle by any stretch of the imagination, but two things occurred as a result: First, it clued the Patriots into the fact that the British Army wasn't invincible. And second, it let the British know that running up the score against the Patriots may prove very difficult.

GOOD NEWS, BAD NEWS...

Although the mathematical victory at Breed's Hill offered good news, some bad news tagged along: The loss depressed the Brits, who walked down the hill to mope in Boston. This proved to be a significant problem, given that Boston served as more or less the seat of the revolution, and having four British enlisted men sleeping in your living room puts a hamper on your potential revolutionary activities.

As a result, over half of Boston's residents wandered off to less revolutionary climes. The Brits, of course, viewed this as a good thing, because now they could move out of the living room and into the empty bed, plus they could drink all your liquor and look through your drawers to see if you had any Playcolonist magazines or cool games to play.

Now, as you may recall, George Washington accepted command of the Continental Army on June 15th, 1775. Well aware that the British lay awake at night envisioning his neck in a noose, Washington advanced post-haste to a place where he could keep an eye on the British (and their coils of rope). From his siege position overlooking Boston, Washington watched the British, and fretted. Fortunately, this was also the British strategy under General Gage—so there was fretting and counter-fretting for several months. The conversations that occupied the two generals' days told a great deal, especially if one reads a little between the lines:

> **Washington:** Okay… what's on tap today?
> **Aide de Camp:** Well, Sir, there's a Major Paine waiting—he'd like a position under your command.
> **Washington:** Excellent. I need good men willing to serve in the Infantry.
> **Aide de Camp:** Actually, Sir, he asked that I explain he's unavailable for service in the infantry.
> **Washington:** Hmmm… what then? Artillery? Tanks?
> **Aide de Camp:** He was quite specific, Sir. Even wrote it down. Let's see… yes, here it is. He wants a position *close enough to the combat to win ribbons and medals, but not so close as to get hurt or hear men screaming. A position with lots of face time with you, but no contact with the enlisted men. A position where he nods along with tactical decisions, but doesn't have to develop the decisions or actually authorize them. Oh, and he asked that I mention his record concerning TPS Reports and cover sheets.*
> **Washington:** Does such a job even exist?
> **Aide de Camp:** Yes, Sir. Mine.
> **Washington:** I see. Anyone else waiting?

Aide de Camp: Actually, there are 255 other officers, waiting to ask you for, uh, the exact same job.

Washington: Great. Anyone else?

Aide de Camp: Yes, Sir. Some enlisted men are standing in line behind the officers. Their enlistment is up, and they are waiting for you to sign their discharge papers so they can go home.

Washington: How many enlisted men?

Aide de Camp: Let's see, Sir. There are... well, look at that. It's **all** of them.

For General Gage down in Boston, the daily routine wasn't a great deal more productive.

General Graves: So, what's on tap today?

Aide de Camp: Well, Sir, yesterday you asked me to clear the schedule so you could spend the day discussing how much you hate the Royal Navy.

Gage: Ah, yes. Excellent. Have they done anything productive this morning? Popped in with some men, or ammo, or food, or—

Aide de Camp: No, Sir.

Gage: You *see*, Lad? You *see* how my gut instincts serve me well? Gather all the Generals and Colonels, and advise them we'll be telling Navy jokes here in my tent straight through dinner.

This stalemate may have gone on until, well, yesterday afternoon, but one man stepped forward with an idea that General Washington couldn't refuse.

Colonel Knox: General Washington... I have an idea. I think it would be smart for me to go to Fort Ticonderoga, gather together about a zillion pounds of artillery cannon and ammo, put together a team of men and animals, and drag the whole mess through the wilderness here to Boston, and we can use it to bombard the British.

Washington: It sounds impossible, man! Think of the backbreaking labor! Think of the poor roads! Think of the nightmarish 300-mile journey! I have but one question...

Colonel Knox: Sir?

Washington: Do I have to get involved?

Colonel Knox: No, Sir.

Washington: Permission granted.

Incredibly, Knox accomplished his mission, and upon his return Washington positioned the new artillery on high ground overlooking Boston. After eight months of fretting about each other, Washington now had something for Gage to fret about. Gage ceased the fretting, and found a reason to like the Navy: It was they who evacuated the Army to Nova Scotia. By early spring, 1776, Boston was a Redcoat free environment.

THE MIGHTY PEN...

In January of 1776, a fairly new immigrant to the Colonies named Thomas Paine wrote a pamphlet called *Common Sense*, which argued effectively that:

1) The colonies should be independent.
2) The idea of a hereditary succession to the crown makes as much sense as using an axe and chopping block to divorce your wife.
3) We'd all make more dough if we didn't answer to the King.
4) England sucks.

The pamphlet was printed and sold, and eventually achieved sales of a half million copies; proportionately, that means that, per capita, *Common Sense* buried the record sales of Michael Jackson, Elvis, and U2. Needless to say, Paine's ideas proved popular, and provided the Colonists with a boost both logically and emotionally.

Okay, let's wrap up this chunk, and briefly look at what we've learned: 1) From the commitment of George Washington and our nation's minutemen, we learned it can be very unhealthy to underestimate a group who's willing to die for their cause. 2) From Colonel Knox and his 300-mile artillery parade we learned that doing something impossible is possible if you have the right men and motivation to do it. 3) And from Thomas Paine, we learned that a well-communicated message *can* change the world.

CHAPTER FIVE

LET'S GET READY TO RUM-BLLLLLLE!

MOST AMERICANS REMEMBER very little about the details of the Revolution from their history classes. If water-boarded by a crack troop like Lindy England, most people could produce these basic facts:

1) Some dudes signed *The Declaration of Independence*.
2) For some reason, George Washington crossed the Delaware, standing in the bow of a boat.
3) Valley Forge is cold.
4) The British surrendered.

The reason so little is recalled is because, as I said, military history is boring.

War *movies*? Awesome. War *history*? Please—unless you've been in the military, it all makes less sense than the lyrics to a Yoko Ono solo project. Here is the abridged, *Alexander's Notes* version of the Revolution, and hopefully it will be easy for you to remember:

> The world's military superpower nation finds itself disagreeing with a small nation of nobodies, located halfway around the globe in a place none of its supercitizens really care about.

This superpower nation is *mad*, but not *"kill 'em all and let God sort 'em out" mad*—just mad enough to send troops to wreak some havoc. Sadly, droves of their supertroops are killed right away because:

1) The nation of nobodies is very serious.
2) They sometimes fight in a tricky, guerrilla-style fashion, and the superpower generals don't understand it.

Things get worse, and the super-troops continue to die, and the super-citizens complain. To make matters worse, the superpower's super-rival supplies the guerrilla army with beans, bullets, and bandages. The superpower responds by refusing to adjust its tactics, and instead simply sends more super-troops. At this point, Presidents LBJ, Nixon, Dubya—oops, sorry, wrong wars.

Korea, Vietnam, Lebanon, Somalia, Iraq, and Afghanistan comparisons aside, however, I feel I would be cheating you if I didn't at least give you a brief overview of the Revolution. Failure to do so would prove an insult to the incredible accomplishments of these American Warriors.

WILD-EYED SOUTHERN BOYS

As we all know, the British are snobs of the highest order, and after receiving the boot out of Boston they yearned for a place of equal snob-appeal to relax and sip their tea. Things in the New England area felt downright hostile, and Nova Scotia seemed so *common*, so in June of 1776 they decided to try and grab Charleston, SC, where hopefully the locals still retained their manners and at least some semblance of a proper English accent.

Upon sailing into Charleston Harbor, the Royal Navy found themselves under attack by a ragtag group of Patriots on Sullivan's Island under the command of Colonel William Moultrie. The British fleet returned fire, expecting to make short work of the small fortress—but for some reason the fort just absorbed their cannonballs. They didn't realize that the Charlestonians built the fort out of sand and Palmetto logs, which are Mother Nature's squishy-stuff quicker-absorber-upper.

After a while, the Brits realized the tiny fort wasn't going collapse and their ships were de-masted, so their desire for the city's famed Mimosas would have to wait. With hurt feelings and several badly damaged ships, the Brits sailed north.

Word spread quickly through the Colonies that the undefeatable British Navy had been, well, defeated.

THE DECLARATION OF INDEPENDENCE

On June 7, 1776, Richard Henry Lee presented a three-part resolution to the Continental Congress stating that the Colonies should be free states. Everyone liked the idea, but the writing lacked gravitas, so they sent it to a committee—and everyone knows what happens there.

The chances are good that the document would *still* be in committee today, and we'd actually care about Meghan and her milquetoast husband Harry, but someone in the committee had the foresight to turn the rewrite over to Thomas Jefferson. Jefferson wisely edited the original document with a match, and began over.

According to historian Alan Axelrod, Jefferson admired the work of English philosopher John Locke, and Locke (years earlier) listed three "inalienable rights" in his writings. Jefferson agreed with Locke's first two, and listed them accordingly: Life... and Liberty. *However,* Jefferson *clearly* did not believe the third of Locke's "inalienable rights" to be an ultra-important "inalienable right."

You see, Locke claimed the three to be "Life, liberty, and ***property.***"

Jefferson believed them to be "Life, liberty, and ***the pursuit of happiness.***"

Get out your mental highlighter, because this is important.

We *know* that Jefferson got the idea of "inalienable rights" from Locke. We *know* he considered them at length. And we *know* he decided that, in ***America***, listing ***property*** is an "inalienable right" was **not** necessary.

Why? Here's **my** take on Jefferson's thinking: Locke was an Englishman, and in England your personal property was not safe from the "Above the Law" King. If you owned the nicest horse in the kingdom, and the King decided he wanted it, he could send someone over to just **take** the horse. Why? Because he's the King and the King is above the law... even if it's *your* property. In Locke's *English* mind, this was a violation of "natural law," and the English people deserved to feel safe in *their ownership* of property.

Jefferson, already formulating in his own mind the essence of "the United States," *knew* that there'd be no thieving, untouchable King ruling, and that people might be **truly** free. Because of this, I believe Jefferson *specifically* deleted "property," and replaced it with "the pursuit of happiness." If *owning* stuff makes you happy, you were free to "pursue property." If owning nothing and living a Grizzly Adams existence was what you desired, grizzle away.

According to Jefferson, your *pursuit* of the good life deserved protection. Note, however, that he specifically wrote the "pursuit of happiness" and not just "happiness." Why? Because *failure* and *unhappiness* are both potential outcomes of any pursuit, especially if one chooses to lie in bed all day and pursue nothing.

The Declaration of Independence effectively explained to the British and to the world community at large why the Colonies demanded freedom, and the Continental Congress adopted it on July 4th, 1776. (Yes, the Revolution had already started, but as you know the government moves a little slower than everyone else).

At the signing, John Hancock said, "There must be no pulling different ways; we must hang together."

"Yes," replied Ben Franklin, "we must indeed all hang together, or most assuredly we shall all hang separately."

Regarding the "revolutionaries," there's an interesting parallel these days: We the people tend to think that the EarthFirst yo-yos who throw themselves in front of a bulldozer represent environmental *revolutionaries*. I'm curious, though: How members of EarthFirst would show up for their protests if their "revolutionary" antics resulted *not* in media coverage, but with the guarantee they'd be ground into a meat waffle by the bulldozer?

NEW JACK CITY...

After the boot out of Boston, and the rebuff from Charleston, the British decided their next move should center around taking New York City. New York offered a very central location for conducting follow-on operations, and since it proclaimed to be *The City That Never Sleeps*, the enlisted men would always be able to find something to do regardless of what time they came off guard duty.

As an added benefit, New York was virtually indefensible by a Colonial Army that had no Navy. Seeing how it was "No Navy" versus "The World's Most Powerful Navy," the British had good reason for invading New York.

Before we skim over the New York campaign, it's important to understand great changes in warfare that occurred over the centuries: It would be *centuries* before the concept of maneuver warfare came about. Maneuver warfare, what we practice today, says, "Hey, let's avoid smashing heads with the enemy. Let's maneuver around until we find him in a weak position, *then* attack. If he's in a strong position, we'll leave him alone."

I point this out because it may seem fairly odd to you that George Washington arrived in New York in April of 1776, and committed most of his army to defending this indefensible position. These days? You'd give up on New York, and fall back to a place where you have a chance to win. But in those days... well, let's just say that creative thinking has never been the military's strong suit.

Anyway, General Washington sprinkled his men around New York and Long Island the best he could, and waited for the Brits to arrive. When they came, they came to the tune of over 30,000 troops.

The initial battle took place in late August on Long Island, where the British simply overwhelmed the Patriots—at the very moment the Patriots faced the peril of annihilation, the residents of Long Island rushed out and demanded the Brits repair all the picket fences they'd broken, then dragged them into the curio and health food shoppes and forced them to browse.

Washington used the time to rally the troops, and organized an orderly retreat to Brooklyn. After setting up a defense in Brooklyn, Washington decided it was an all-around bad spot, so he retreated to Manhattan. After a couple of fights on Manhattan, Washington decided that this wasn't such a wonderful place either, and retreated to White Plains, NY. The Brits attacked there, and Washington retreated to North Castle. Finally in early December (and one wonders now if retreating became sheer force of habit) Washington retreated across the Delaware River into Pennsylvania.

Despite General Washington's Retreat-a-thon, something positive occurred—not necessarily *on-purpose-occurred*, but occurred, nonetheless. What? The British grew tired of all this hit-and-run stuff. It just wasn't cricket. Armies should stand, fight, and die... and when *enough* men die, the officers get together over a few whiskeys and discuss the terms of peace. This whole "marching about the countryside looking for the enemy" sucked, and the folks back home didn't much like it either.

The Patriot Army failed to clue into the enemy's general unhappiness, and as a result felt pretty droopy-dog themselves. The cure? A doggie biscuit arrived in the form of another essay by Thomas Paine, who was actually assigned to Washington's Army in Pennsylvania.

It was during the frozen month of December that some of his most famous prose circulated, which stated that "sunshine patriots and summer soldiers may fold, but the real studs would not." His words bolstered the morale of the troops currently freezing their liberty bells off... and wanting to be counted amongst the studs of the world they quit whining and remembered, "Hey, this is Colonial America. We may be short on everything else, but we got **plenty** of firewood."

SOMETHING YOU'LL ACTUALLY REMEMBER...

A few things occurred to General Washington as he shivered around the campfire in Pennsylvania: First, the fact that his Army hadn't moved in a *forward* direction since they'd become an army. (Maybe sideways a couple times, but never actually forward).

He also thought long and hard about the British Army and their German mercenaries, all snuggled up with barrels of hot buttered rum over in New Jersey, singing show tunes and making limey-kraut-eyes at the barmaids. And finally he considered his men, pumped full of Paine-fully injected testosterone, but unable to put it to any good use.

The solution? Give his men a heartwarming Christmas present—the chance to kill some of the enemy.

On Christmas Night, he and his men loaded up in boats and… and… anyone? Anyone? Yes, you in the back? Correct! ***Crossed the Delaware***, and executed a bayonet attack on Trenton, where his men killed more than 100 enemies and took more than 900 prisoners.

About a week later, Washington struck again when he attacked and took Princeton. With two winter victories under his belt, General Washington decided to retire for the season, and withdrew to New Jersey high ground to wait for warmer weather. This was more than all right with the British, who much preferred dying in nice weather anyway.

BLAH, BLAH, BLAH…

Come spring, the Brits stood ready to start fighting again, and brought onto the team General John Burgoyne, a British dandy who played the role of tough guy with all the effectiveness that kid from Harry Potter might've brought to the role of John Wick.

General "Gentleman Johnny" Burgoyne formulated a plan to gather a bunch of Britain's "fresh troops" in Canada and attack Fort Ticonderoga in northeast New York, enabling Britain to… *blah, blah, blah…* win the war. King George (actually Lord North, of course) approved Burgoyne's plan, and tapped him to carry out the plan personally. Unfortunately, this resulted in hurt feelings among the other generals, who moped about, grumbling over who out-ranked whom.

Despite the *general* unhappiness (get it?), Burgoyne launched the plan, and his troops did an amazing, hump-busting job of slogging their way through hill, dale, and hell to move from Canada to New York.

In the cool and collected manner made famous by his boss George Washington, the commander of Fort Ticonderoga took one look at the Brits sweating just to get themselves into the *position* to fight and said, "You know what? Those dudes want this fort a **lot** more than me."

Yet again the Americans retreated—and the sweaty British troops got so angry they actually managed an effective pursuit. The Americans suffered some casualties, and thus ended the day bruised, bloodied, and minus one fairly important fort. History reports that King George felt so giddy about the taking of Fort Ticonderoga, he squealed to his wife, "*I have beaten all the Americans.*" (Note to King: All you did was lounge around like a limey poofter reading three-month-old reports about what the actual men were doing.)

Like most wars, the Revolutionary War continued on—yielding a long, boring yarn. The Indians continued to support one side (or the other), the Hessian mercenaries continued to fight and die for fairly low wages (considering the risks associated with the job), the British continued to attack (and mostly win), and the Patriots continued to somehow stay alive as an army. In late September of 1777, tragedy struck:

> **General Washington:** Bad news, old friend. The British have taken Philadelphia.
> **Ben Franklin:** Philly?
> **George:** Philly.
> **Ben:** Huh. You know, I gotta say, I never much liked Philly.
> **George:** Me neither, now that you mention it.
> **Ben:** And if the Limeys have it, maybe we can move the capitol someplace else.
> **George:** Hmmm… someplace with a better water view? Maybe *closer to my house?*
> **Ben:** Dude, your crib is a most excellent spot to party! You think Martha will mind?
> **George:** No problem, Dude—she parties!! We just can't put the Capitol on, like, the actual property. Maybe somewhere across the river, but easy to get to on the weekend?
> **Ben:** DC! DC! DC!

General Washington's excitement about the post-war parties inspired him to try and end the war right then by attacking the British stronghold at Germantown, just outside Philly. Like every other battle he commanded, this one was a disaster, but somehow the war didn't end. Why? Because the fighting patriots across the Colonies were becoming "Americans," and the feeling that they were fighting for the right cause began to take deeper root.

PAY NO ATTENTION TO THAT MAN BEHIND THE CURTAIN—

Remember General Burgoyne? The Harry-Potter-looking guy who took Fort Ticonderoga? Well, he was still milling around, smoking cigarettes and wondering what to do. As you might recall, The King himself authorized the launch of Burgoyne's plan, but his approval still hurt the other Generals' feelings:

> **General Howe:** Seriously—I'm not exaggerating! The Duke of Sandwich just *sat* there, staring, while I boldly sipped my tea without extending my pinkie!
> **Aide de Camp:** Sir, you're such a rebel!
> **Colonel:** Sorry to interrupt, General, but the brigade is mounted and ready to go.
> **General Howe:** Go where?
> **Colonel:** To participate in General Burgoyne's attack plan.
> **General:** Ahhhh…; Yes. I've opted out.
> **Colonel:** Opted out, Sir?
> **General:** I researched the issue last night, and it turns out that Burgoyne is 894th in line for the throne, and I am 735th. As you know, this means he's not the boss of me.
> **Colonel:** Couldn't agree more, Sir. There may be the issue of, er, losing the war, and a few thousand dead soldiers.
> **General:** Colonel, if you start giving in on important issues like this, where does it end?

Burgoyne couldn't know for sure if all of Britain's Generals were paralyzed by their poisoned panties, so he decided to do what military folks are trained to do: In the absence of orders, you follow your last orders. Burgoyne's last orders came from, well, himself, so he ordered himself to do what he'd ordered himself to do—march to Albany.

Eventually Burgoyne's army arrived at a place called Saratoga, where a ferocious battle ensued with the Patriots. Much flanking and maneuvering and counter-attacking transpired, seasoned with some heroics by Patriot officer Benedict Arnold, and some skilled fighting on the part of the Patriot troops—and, at the moment of truth, the truth was discovered: The hurt feelings were too much for the other British Generals to overcome, and thus no one came to help poor "Gentleman" Johnny Burgoyne.

On October 17th, badly outnumbered (and badly in need of a hug), General Burgoyne surrendered his Army to Patriot General Horatio Gates. Following the surrender, General Burgoyne and his troops were sent to England with no supper, and told not to return until the adults were through fighting.

AN OVERDUE CONVERSATION?

By mid-1777, some disturbing conversations circulated amongst the power brokers of the revolutionary nation. Although some folks schemed and plotted more aggressively than others, the general chat went something like this:

> **Patriot Officer:** Uh, hey—umm, you know what I just noticed?
> **Colonial Congressman:** What?
> **Officer:** Well, uhhh—uh, never mind.
> **Congressman:** What?
> **Officer:** It's just that… uh, you know General Washington?
> **Congressman:** Yes?
> **Officer:** Have you noticed—maybe it's just me—but have you noticed that his primary strategic plan involves a great deal of losing, and retreating?
> **Congressman:** What are you saying?

Officer: I'm just wondering if he actually knows what he's doing.

Congressman: Hmmm. Well, he is, after all, George Washington.

Officer: Yeah, you're right. He is George Washington.

Congressman: Word on the Hill is that he cannot tell a lie.

Officer: Plus, he's George Washington.

Congressman: Besides—we don't know his next plan! Winter is coming, and he may have some excellent plan in store for taking care of our fine volunteer army.

Officer: You're right! I think I'll go re-join his army right now. It's gonna be a great winter to serve under George!

VALLEY FORGE

For some reason, everyone remembers the Continental Army's winter of 1778 at Valley Forge. Most likely this is because people have no concept of what it's like to have their jaw blown off by a cannon ball, but everyone knows what it's like to be really, really cold. We all agree, of course, that being really cold really sucks, as does being hungry. Being really hungry *and* really cold is apparently really memorable.

However, it's worth noting that things weren't *all* bad at Valley Forge—on the rare occasions when the men *did* get food it was usually fried dough, which they referred to as "fire cakes." Of course, nowadays we call fried dough "Elephant Ears" and "Funnel Cakes," and everyone loves to go to the County Fair to eat those! Yum! I'll bet they even had corn dogs, and just aren't telling us.

But, aside from the tasty food, life at Valley Forge registered as a zero on the Continental fun meter. In response, General Washington did do something right.

You see, if given the opportunity, enlisted men love nothing more than to bitch. And if conditions are bitch-worthy, as they certainly were in Valley Forge, they do it with a gusto normally found only in Yankees fans after a shut out by the Sox. In fact, I'd bet that, left unsupervised, the entire Continental Army's enlisted ranks would have been happy to cram into one 11x17 tent, and forsake food and water in exchange for the opportunity to complain for three straight months.

However, troops that are *training* are too busy to bitch, and if you train them hard enough, then they have to *sleep* at night versus sittin' 'round the campfire, jaw jacking about how the Officers are doing them wrong.

Fortunately, this great truth finally dawned on General Washington, so he used the winter to train his men **hard.** As an added benefit, hard training really pisses off the troops, which instills in them a real desire to kill *someone.* Once a commanding officer achieves this anger trifecta, he need only point his herd of furious, rabid dogs toward the enemy and say, "Dinner time."

1778...

The year 1778 started on an upbeat note: The French agreed to help the Patriots, the charismatic French officer Lafayette—actually, Marie-Joseph Paul Yves Roch Gilbert du Motier, Marquis de La Fayette—arrived, and the overall mood in camp was lifted by Lafayette's impersonation of the French insult lines from *Monty Python and the Holy Grail.* Oh, and the Continental Army looked lean and hungry after a winter of hard training.

The British, so proud about capturing Philadelphia, came to the conclusion that no one cared they'd captured Philly. As a result, in early summer, they abandoned the city and moved troops to New Jersey, where they *hoped* someone might care.

General Washington *did* care, and ordered his second in command, General Charles Lee, to attack. General Lee quickly demonstrated his finely-honed levels of incompetence, and blew the operation. Fortunately, since losing seemed to be the Patriots primary tactical strategy since day one, the British felt no great sense of triumph.

Shortly after Lee's defeat the Patriots mounted an attack so manly it pains me to even acknowledge without claiming U. S. Marines conducted it. The attack? A "bayonets only" assault on a British fort in New York.

WHERE HAVE ALL THE COWBOYS GONE?

This clearly-insane gang of over 1,300 Patriots simply fixed bayonets on their unloaded rifles, mounted a nighttime attack on a fortified position, and overran it.

Although I've uncovered no evidence to support this theory, I cannot help but think the Patriots were afforded *some* degree of protection from the wheelbarrows they used to carry their incredibly large cojones. It's worth noting that one of the heroes of this battle was "Light Horse" Harry Lee, whose grandson became a fairly well-known military man himself—General Robert E. Lee.

LOOK AWAY, DIXIE LAND...

Although the Patriots weren't really winning that much in the northeast, the Brits were unable to run up the score at will. This caused significant concern by the Brits, who enjoyed seeing Colonial backs and butts after a few minutes of fighting. This new development encouraged the Brits to once again look down South, in hopes that the outright defeat of any one particular area would cause the overall revolution to collapse like a Congressman without free booze.

They targeted first Savannah, Georgia, a key port city for the Colonial south. Landing in late November of 1778, they arrived in the midst of the debutante season, and everyone was way too busy going to brunches, lunches, dinners, cocktail parties, and fancy-dress balls to worry about participating in a revolution. The city's hostesses saw the red uniforms, assumed they were the caterers, and invited them in—where they remained until well after the war ended.

The following spring, fresh off their taking of Savannah, the Brits made a move on their next target—Charleston, South Carolina, the city that so skillfully repulsed their first invasion attempt in 1776. This go-round, however, the Brits had the good sense to arrive after 6:30pm, by which time everyone was drunk. The next morning yielded both a hangover, and an occupying army.

I hate to say it, but the Revolutionary War down south didn't look much different than the one up north, with the British pretty much smashing the Patriots time after time. Occasional good news reared its elusive head—like when Francis "The Swamp Fox" Marion launched some sneaky Rambo raids and harassment operations—but for the most part the average Patriot looked at his intolerable quality of life and thought the Intolerable Acts might have been more *inconvenient* than intolerable.

Then! Then! Yes, that's right—Something good actually happened. The Patriots scored important victories at Kings Mountain, NC and Cowpens, SC.

Now before you get too excited, we're not talking massive, end-of-the-war victories like, say, the U. S. nuking Japan—but, hey, half a loaf is better than none. These battles yielded more dead Brits and Loyalists than Patriots, and the good guys were pretty much looking for any reason to tap a celebratory keg in late 1780. The mere fact that the Patriots felt good about *anything* gave the British commanding officer Cornwallis a bad case of gas, and he decided all the happiness need to be stomped out.

Stripping his army down to their jock straps and rifles, Cornwallis set out to chase the Patriot army, which was now moving north. The chase culminated in a battle at Guilford Courthouse, NC, where the two sides slugged it out in March of 1781. The battle proved to be a tactical victory for Cornwallis, but cost him about 25% of his army.

LOONEY TUNES IN VIRGINIA...

In 1781, the state of Virginia hosted a cast of commanders and armies that seemed more *Looney Tunes* than history-altering. Playing the role of the long-suffering Wylie Coyote? Patriot-turned-Traitor Benedict Arnold. Starring as the narcissistic windbag Foghorn Leghorn? General Cornwallis. The smooth and effective Pepe LePew? Marquis de Lafayette. The bold and buff Tasmanian Devil? Patriot General "Mad Anthony" Wayne. The loud and inept Yosemite Sam? The French Navy. And as the cool and collected Bugs Bunny, none other than George Washington.

Now, as everyone knows, Pepe, Taz, and Bugs would beat Wylie Coyote and Foghorn Leghorn any day—the issue would be Yosemite Sam. Could he, and *would* he, accomplish his mission, or act with his usual complete incompetence: Sure, shootin' irons are a good thing in a gunfight, but only with the discipline to show up, then firing the guns in the right direction. (Not a strong point of the French Navy).

But, my doubting friend, every 'toon has his time, and in the early fall of 1781, the French Navy actually did—for the very first time in the entire war—what they were supposed to do. The Colonists surrounded Cornwallis at Yorktown, the French Navy lay siege from the sea, and Cornwallis admitted "Th-Th… That's all folks" on October 19, 1781. The Patriot Band struck up a Merry Melody.

And that was that.

Okay, let's take a look at some of the lessons we learned during the Revolution.

First, from King George, we learned that "might makes right" only when you possess the might to make yourself right.

From Thomas Paine and Thomas Jefferson we learned that powerful words can stir a powerful reaction, so it's not a bad idea to contemplate exactly what the words are saying.

And from the American Revolution in general we learned perhaps the most obvious lesson in all of history… *and yet it seems to be the one we simply cannot commit to memory.*

But, in case you become President one day, here's lesson to learn, so that you don't become lumped in amongst Harry Truman, Jack Kennedy, Lyndon Johnson, Richard Nixon, George W. Bush, and Barack Obama.

You ready? Get out that Big Chief pencil and write this down.

If you're a really slow learner, maybe copy it ten times. Here it comes: *Don't get involved in a land war fighting a guerrilla army on their turf, halfway around the globe, unless you're willing to kill 'em all and let God sort 'em out!*

OVER??! WAS IT OVER WHEN THE GERMANS BOMBED PEARL HARBOR?

Most Americans think the Revolution ended when… well, when it ended. You think this because we *won,* and usually *winning* means the bad guys go home and the winners pour Gatorade on the coach, drink champagne, and go to Disney World.

Not so when you defeat Britain.

First, there was the King, and he didn't take the news too well:

> **Lord North:** Well, your Highness—there's good news, and bad news.
>
> **King George III:** Yes?
>
> **Lord North:** The bad news is that we lost the war with the Colonists, but the good news is I just saved a bunch of money on my carriage insurance by switching to GeorgeCo!
>
> **King:** Oh, I get it... like humor... but different. Now listen to me, North: I'm the King, and the war cannot *end* without my okay.
>
> **Lord North:** Right—well, see, there's the little problem of having actually *lost* the war, and the Parliament voted to *end* the war, and your secretary of state for the colonies said he'd quit if you tried to *continue* the war, and all your subjects are actually *glad* the war is over.
>
> **King:** Well, I didn't expect things to be easy when I ran for King, did I?.

Now, in all fairness, it should be noted that King George III was not the sharpest tool in the shed. In fact, historian J.H. Plumb states bluntly, "Had he been born in different circumstances, it is unlikely that he could have earned a living except as an unskilled laborer." In addition, he ascended to the throne at a mere twenty-two years old because his dad croaked when a tennis ball nailed him in his windpipe, and killed him coffin dead. (Note to self: *Get more elected officials interested in tennis*)

Right about the time the revolution ended, King George was (in the words of my beloved grandmother) "about ready for the nervous hospital." You see, in addition to inheriting a throne and no brains, he inherited a disease called *porphyria,* one of the less desirable side effects of which was going insane. And in the delicately crafted words of the royal website www.royal.gov.uk, *"George became permanently deranged in 1810."*

At this point, old George was out like a fat kid in dodgeball and sent all the way to his private apartments, where he spent much of his time in a straight jacket, behind bars. (Yes, yes, I know what you're thinking. And no matter how logical this solution it sounds, we are not going to do the same with our Presidents. This *is* America, after all.)

In addition to King George's objections, there remained the issue that a handful of the British soldiers in the U. S. weren't about to give up their disco-inferno lifestyle, especially amongst the beautiful people of Savannah, GA and Charleston, SC.

With or without Cornwallis, these guys dug in their heels and insisted they weren't going anywhere. Fortunately, it turned out to be nothing more than a misunderstanding. Within Charleston and Savannah, the British Soldiers seemed to be little more than over-extended guests, and no one wanted to be rude by asking them to leave. Eventually, the ladies quit putting out the cucumber sandwiches and the men locked up the scotch, and it finally dawned on the Brits it was, indeed, last call. Savannah was evacuated in July of 1782, and Charleston in December— more than a year after Cornwallis had thrown in the towel.

The British impersonation of "the thing that wouldn't leave" was, however, nothing compared to the lunacy Ben Franklin, John Jay, and John Adams encountered in Europe as they worked to negotiate the terms of peace and the recognition of the United States. Simple job, right?

America – 1
England – 0

Give us the trophy and our parting gifts and we'll be out of your hair.

Nope. Couldn't be that simple. Spain cahooted with France, and France cahooted with Britain, and the treaty plans proposed the French get this land, the Brits get that land, and the Spanish get back this land—the burning question of the day seemed to be one whether the people who won the war got anything.

After months of re-explaining the concept of victory and defeat, the reality finally stuck. On September 3rd, 1783, the Treaty of Paris was signed and notarized and stamped and put in place: The British and their European counter parts admitted the obvious: They lost. We won.

ROUND UP THE USUAL SUSPECTS—

One of the great things about an entry-level knowledge of history is the fact that it empowers you with cocktail party knowledge. After all, what could be more fun than having an acquaintance spew forth a lame opinion cloaked in "historical fact," after which you interject, "That would be *fascinating*, if it contained a shred of truth."

Having done it a few times myself, I can assure you it rivals the joy of having a copy of the Constitution in your pocket when some doofus starts spouting off about their Constitutional Rights.

So, while it's true you won't gain any great *lessons learned* from this upcoming section, it's worth inclusion. It's fun to have some back-story, and these are the men who shaped the life in America we now enjoy.

George Washington: George is one of the few men discussed at any length in this book, primarily because he stood up and out during the entire revolutionary process. While it's true he was no strategic or tactical genius, he was *there,* and several million bullets were launched in his direction by men intending to do him harm. As we all know, there weren't any camcorders in camp with General Washington, so we'll never know the real magic behind his mojo, but the fact is that he held together an army under the worst of circumstances, then never bragged about it—in fact, it was his officer corps that told the stories that made him such a national idol. (Trust me, junior officers don't tell good stories about bad leaders.) Following the Revolution, the military men felt they'd been treated so badly they began bantering about the idea of marching on Congress, throwing the bums out, and crowning Washington as King.

George himself called his Officers together, and talked them (and thus their troops) down off the cliff. In addition, he walked away from the opportunity to serve a third term as president, a move in sharp contrast to the politicians of today, who fight like Hollywood starlets for just one more day in the spotlight of pathetic relevance. When it comes down to the *important* issues, Washington served as an example for all citizen-patriots After all, we're talking about a man who married a rich chick, spent most of his career in the business of breaking things and hurting people, and gave his retirement speech at a bar.

Thomas Paine: Writers are rarely heroic figures, except in their own minds. Thomas Paine, however, was different. He was a writer of talent, ideals, and action, the likes of which we haven't seen since... since... uh, we haven't seen again. For reasons that defy my simple brain, Paine returned to England after the Revolution where he was tried for treason for writing *The Rights of Man*. This, of course, really shouldn't have surprised Mr. Paine, since the Revolution was pretty-much fought because *"the rights of man"* in England sucked. Anyway, he fled England to France, where the French Revolution was brewing, and everyone *really* liked into his thinking. Apparently, the French were *so* into his thinking that eventually they decided to chop off his head, and have a look inside. Fortunately for Paine, the French changed their minds, and he returned to the United States. Once back here, Paine turned to criticizing the new government's power brokers, all of whom loved his critiques of the King, but now... not so much. Paine faded from favor with a George Dubya-esque efficiency, and died in a leaky van, down by the river.

Nathan Hale: Nathan Hale was the fellow the British caught spying for General Washington on Long Island, and subsequently hanged without so much as a trial. His official last words are not really known, but they're claimed by history to be *"I regret that I have but one life to give for my country."* Given the discrepancies in some of the history we've discussed thus far, it's possible he said, "I regret that I'm giving up my one life for this country!" But, let's assume it's the former—for the children.

Samuel Adams: With a tasty brew on the market in our 21ˢᵗ Century, Sam Adams is enjoying a fairly epic *Extreme Makeover, Historic Guy Version*, and is emerging as a cool, beer-brewing Patriot (and what could be cooler than that?). This makeover is fortunate for ol' Sam, because his legacy needed the help. The truth is that he managed to blow through his inheritance, ruin his father's beer brewing business, and fail at every other job he attempted. (Not that there's anything wrong with that). So, like many of our 21ˢᵗ Century hard-core unemployables, he turned to professional protesting. Fortunately for Sam, the issue of his day involved changing the world, not protecting the rights of a down-on-its-luck *snail darter*, so he actually earned some national respect and fame for his work. With the shooting done, however, Sam didn't have the cash flow needed to continue to party with the big boys, and more or less faded from view.

John Hancock: Best known for his really, really big signature, John Hancock should be known for his really, really big wallet. Mr. Hancock, in fact, covered many of the costs associated with hosting a Revolution. He wasn't that different than today's political fat cats, because he wanted something in return for donations—namely, command of the Continental Army. (*Yes, yes, I know I don't have any experience as a soldier, but **I paid** for all that cool military stuff, and I should get to **play** with it.*) Fortunately, the politicians back then didn't act *exactly* like the politicians of today, thus didn't cave to the fat cat's desires. Hancock spent most of the actual war fulfilling the pastime that seems to be emanating from his own last name.

Thomas Jefferson: Arguably the most brilliant man in the Revolutionary mix, Thomas Jefferson didn't play a particularly significant role in the revolution itself. He made up for it, however, after the war, when his insistence on preserving the rights of the individual created much of the freedom we enjoy today. Without Jefferson, it's possible that the Federal Government could have evolved into an ultra-powerful totalitarian institution. Wait a minute. I guess I should say "could have evolved into an ultra-powerful totalitarian *faster than it did*."

Benjamin Franklin: Few men have managed to cloak their earned reputations as successfully as Mr. Ben Franklin. A man of many, many talents, Franklin was most notably an inventor, publisher, diplomat, a tireless womanizer, and one of the Top 10 worst fathers of all time. It's true. Kindly old Ben 'sicced' the authorities on his son William, a Loyalist and the Royal Governor of New Jersey, which led to his arrest and imprisonment following the adoption of the Declaration of Independence. While William rotted in prison, Ben took custody of William's son (his grandson), and forbade any contact between the two. The conditions of William's confinement proved so horrid that he emerged three years later bald, toothless, and unmarried—because his wife died while he was in prison. Many years later, Ben and his son William met in Europe for a final time, during which William hoped for reconciliation. Ben wanted to reconcile things, too, but from a different playbook—the playbook where the son signs over to Dad all his property in the United States in order to reconcile their debts. What debts? The usual—for the clothes William wore as a child, and the mad money William had given him to buy lollypops and such. As an eternal reminder of what he thought of his son, Ben removed all references of him from his autobiography (and you remember what we learned about autobiographies, right?). One can't help but think that maybe Ben himself was "Richard" in his famous publication *Poor Richard's Almanac.* Who else could it be, given what a "Dick" old Ben was?

Benedict Arnold: Benedict Arnold spent the first part of The Revolutionary War playing the role of Colonial SuperStar: Not only did he co-command the capture of Fort Ticonderoga along with fellow stud Ethan Allen, he led, heroically, at the Battle of Saratoga, which played a big role in turning the tide for the Colonists. When Arnold failed to receive the proper ribbons and rump smooching he felt he deserved, he became embittered, and to soothe his wounded ego got himself reassigned to a command position in Philadelphia, where he did his very best Keith Richard's lifestyle impersonation. As part of the rock star life, he married Peggy Shippen, an eighteen-year-old celebu-tante twenty years younger than he. Like most young trophy wives (to use the parlance of our times), this one felt a constant need to keep up with the Kardashians, which put Arnold in constant feed-the-monkey mode. After attempting a few underhanded deals to earn some extra fun tickets, Arnold found himself being court-martialed by the Continental Congress, which led him to sell his services to the British. From there, things went downhill for the famous traitor, and he died bitter, broke, and exiled in England, whining to the very end.

Alexander Hamilton: The more I read about Alexander Hamilton, the less I like him, but I admit my dislike is largely personal. My problem? He turned his back on his kind, a trait I won't abide in a man. You see, Hamilton came into the world as a poor and illegitimate baby, born in the West Indies and destined to live the life of an island scrapper. Hamilton got lucky, though—the Good Lord blessed him with brains, then right-place-right-timed him into a scholarship at Columbia College. From there, he earned a commission as an Officer in the military, got noticed by General Washington, married a society gal, and skyrocketed to the top, where he developed into a staunch Federalist—meaning he felt the power of the government should be only in the hands of intel-lectuals like him. (*This from a guy who was one scratch-off lotto ticket away from sweeping floors in a West Indies tavern for a living.*) It is, of course, understandable that many people admire Alexander Hamilton, because of the brilliant things he accomplished as President Washington's Secretary of the Treasury but, sadly (boo-hoo-hoo), we'll never know what else he might have accomplished—because Aaron Burr reminded him from hence he *ultimately* came—that being *dust*—to which Burr helped him return.

Marquis de Lafayette: An idealist who sailed from France to help win America's freedom, Lafayette is included in this list primarily as lesson in self-discipline on my part. Yes, he became an important player under General Washington, and yes, he loved America and what the nation stood for. However, you'll never know how difficult it is for me to com-pliment a Frenchman in the wake of their decisions following September 11th, 2001. I've done it, and please let's move on, quickly.

John Paul Jones: As America's only naval hero, John Paul Jones was literally without peer. But, that's not saying a great deal, since it's hard *not* to be without peer when you have no peers because the nation possessed pretty much no Navy. However, he did raid British ships and managed to avoid getting hit in the coconut by any cannonballs, so he emerged as our premier Naval Officer. Jones is the guy who proclaimed, "I have not yet begun to fight" during a naval battle with the British ship *Serapis*, which remained America's most over-used expression until a very stoned skateboarder came up with *"Go for it!"*

CHAPTER SIX

DUDE, WHERE'S MY GOVERNMENT?

O KAY—SO THIS IS it. Time to "invent" a government: A government of the people, for the people, by the people. As you undertake this challenge, here is a list of things you will **not** have at your disposal:

- A reference model
- A power-point business plan to steal from
- A smart kid at the next desk to cheat off of
- Advice-dispensing lobbyists from organizations with names like *Concerned People For the Development of Stupid Ideas*
- A single website for research, much less a website entitled www.create-your-own-government.com with a downloadable departments' matrix, complete with fill-in-the-blanks articles of organization and pop-ups offering free checks and balances
- Built-in royalty and/or hereditary titles
- De facto laws

The tools you may use are:

- A quill pen
- Parchment
- Prayer

Before we begin this chapter, let's imagine that a spaceship full of 21st Century lobbyists, lawyers, and politicians travel back in time, and sneak into the Constitutional Convention. Wouldn't it be great? The ability to provide the framers of the Constitution with 225 years of valuable perspective and experience? Here, listen to their additions, and see if the Founding Fathers might have clarified their writings as a result:

- I think that if my cousin, Jim "No Arms" McIntyre, wants to be a miner, anyone who owns a mine should be required to hire him. And if he doesn't get hired, the owner should have to pay my cousin and his lawyer huge sums of money.
- I think that, if I'm poaching on someone else's land, and a mountain lion bites me, the land owner should pay me and my lawyer for my pain and suffering.
- I think that we should pay farmers not to grow crops.
- I think if another settler beats me up, he should go to jail. But, if we find out that he beat me up *not* because he loves me but because he *hates* me, he should go to jail even longer.
- I think we should exempt the arts from the inconvenience of free enterprise, and take money from people and give it to artists so they'll have time to be creative.
- I think we should establish a political system so that people can literally purchase laws they want made by bribing their Representative with campaign contributions, free booze and coke, and lots of parties where "friends" show up and contribute more money.
- I think we should regulate every facet of our citizens' lives— how they run their businesses; what they do to (or put in) their bodies; what medicines to take; how safe their transportation methods must be; how they use their privately-owned land; what safety issues must be implemented before doing anything; and how many gallons of water they're allowed to use to flush their waste in the outhouse.
- Hey, I think we should do **all** that stuff, plus take their money through taxes and spend it to buy off our constituents, which will lead to re-election, so we can start the whole process over again!

Unfortunately, time travel is a fairy tale, and the Founding Fathers had no way to anticipate the depths of our future, collective stupidity. Without any insights into the 21st Century "intellect," there was no way for them to create a document to prevent such stupidity from becoming law. As a result, what happened transpired pretty much like this:

The war ended, the treaty got signed, and eventually everyone sobered up. Sobriety, always overrated, revealed a few ugly, morning-after realities:

- A crushing debt from the war hung around the Colonies' neck
- No government existed to accept responsibility for the debt
- The means for raising the money needed to deal with the debt didn't exist
- There was no national currency to pay the debt

Well, with all that depressing news, everyone simply assumed a little more personal debt at the local tavern and knocked back four score and Seven and Sevens. Unfortunately, they sobered up again—and because people in this era weren't allowed to operate under the *Fiscal Rules of Fantasyland* like we do today, they realized something must be done.

The overall situation was exacerbated by the fact that the army had all gone home, the Indians on the Western frontier were playing musical tomahawks on settlers' skulls, and the post-war economy was as flat as Kiera Knightley.

On May 25, 1787, a bunch of unbelievably smart dudes gathered in Philadelphia to try and figure out "What now?" Oddly, the meeting was *not* a case of a bunch of victorious revolutionaries smoking cigars, bumping chests, and yelling "You da mahn!" "*No*, You da mahn!" A more accurate description might be a bunch of retirees descending on a garage sale, each in a full-blown anxiety attack to ensure they nab a fair share of the good stuff. Every state sent delegates except Rhode Island, but as discussed earlier, Rhode Islanders are big into the low-profile thing. It doesn't take a lot of imagination to hear the discussions being bantered around the room:

Northern Merchant: I cannot support slavery in any way! It is against my moral convictions! To support it would mean turning my back on *everything I believe in!*"

Southern Plantation Owner: Okay, give us the slavery issue, and we'll agree to that thing where you get *more* representation if you have *more* people in your state.

Merchant: Everything I believe in likes the sound of that—*if* you'll agree to the slave trade being taxed.

Plantation Owner: With the equal representation Senate?

Merchant: With checks on the President's power?

Plantation Owner: Assuming there are checks on the Legislative branch?

Merchant: Assuming you'll agree to term limits for Senators and Representatives?

Plantation Owner: Term limits? What are those?

Merchant: You know... where we set down rules that an elected official can only serve for so many years.

Plantation Owner: Dude, are you *high*? What kind of complete moron would **want** to serve in the Senate or House more than one or two terms? I don't know about *you*, but Washington, DC will *never* see my happy ass unless I get *forced* to serve by the people in my state. I've got a job. I've got money to make. Running around begging for campaign contributions and kissing people's asses ain't my idea of making a living.

Merchant: Okay, you're right. Forget term limits. Where were we?

Over the next four months, a stone-cold-God-was-involved, a miracle took place. Through compromise, negotiation, and rational debate, the delegation created a document that addressed everyone's concerns for fairness and equality (Everyone that is, except the slaves and Indians... who, had they been able to read, would have thought *The Constitution* sucked).

It's staggering to think a convention hall full of successful men could agree on a lunch menu, much less a new form of government. Think of how easily this convention could have resulted in a civil war, or a splintering of the new McNation into a mere confederation of nation states.

But it didn't happen! And among the really, really, really smart things the group at the Constitutional Convention accomplished included the creation of:

- An equal representation Senate
- A population-based representation House of Representatives
- A Congressional Branch, an Executive Branch, and a Judicial Branch, each of which had "checks and balances" on each other. (Which means, as P.J. O'Rourke brilliantly points out, that on a perfect day they all *undo* whatever the other just did, thus ultimately leaving us alone.)
- A declaration that *something* needed to be done about slavery, but not 'til sometime later (when all the Founders hoped they'd be dead).

On September 17, 1787, the delegation quit delegating, and took a vote. The consensus was that *The Constitution* was good enough for government work, and thus it was sent out to the states for ratification. The debate over the *Constitution* wasn't done, however, and boiled down to one essential issue, and the philosophies of two strong-willed men:

1) Alexander Hamilton—a big government federalist, who said that bigwigs like himself should be given "*a distinct permanent share of the government.*"
2) Thomas Jefferson—a, uh, Jeffersonian, who said, "*Do these ideas just **spew** out of your cake hole, or do they actually spend time in your brain?*"

The debate between these two heated up fast and furious, because Hamilton believed that the *Constitution* allowed for a certain degree of interpretation, and he interpreted it to be a document that called for a large, powerful, central government—a government that taxed, and regulated, and thought things like ObamaCare would be good.

Jefferson, however, felt the document provided for self-government and freedom of the individual—a government that picked up the garbage, protected the borders, and allowed Socialized Medicine Fans to blather on about whatever they liked, just not in front of Senate subcommittees.

Here is how Jefferson reacted to his rival, and a possible theory on why he did it: To Jefferson, a guy like Hamilton seemed to be simply a guy who slipped into the gene pool when the lifeguard wasn't looking. And Jefferson believed that *since* the *Constitution* allowed for true self-governance, within one generation "the people" of the nation would saddle the horse and take the reins, and elitists like Hamilton would fall prey to social Darwinism. In order to buy time for individuals to assume this role of self-governance, and to keep men like Hamilton from oppressing them before this happened, Jefferson and other Anti-Federalists insisted on a *Bill of Rights* as amendments to the *Constitution*.

With Jefferson serving overseas as America's Minister to France, the orchestration of the *Bill of Rights* fell largely to James Madison—and he did a terrific job writing them so they are not difficult to understand. Here's a brief run down:

First Amendment–

A) **There is to be freedom of religion, and no official national religion will be established.** *Please note:* This section ensures that Christians, Jews, Muslims, Hindus, Buddhists, and Rocks-Have-Soulsians alike can worship whomever they choose. There is, however, *nothing* to even remotely indicate that school prayer is verboten.

B) **People are free to worship as they please.** *Please note:* There is no mention here along the lines of "unless they live in Waco, and have lots of guns, and seem really weird."

C) **There will be freedom of speech and press.** Sadly, there was no provision put in place for criminally stupid speech.

D) **People are free to assemble and petition for changes.**

Second Amendment–
A well regulated militia, being necessary to the security of a free state, the right of the people to keep and bear arms shall not be infringed. *Please note:* The Second Amendment is today an issue of great controversy, because many people claim the Founding Fathers didn't intend for it to give *individuals* the right to bear arms. Critics say this amendment empowers the government to arm and regulate militias as they are needed. Who's right? Instead of my giving you fifty pages of my opinions, let's ask the Founding Fathers ourselves, by reading what they wrote: Alexander Hamilton, in *The Federalist Papers: "The best we can hope for concerning the people at large is that they be properly armed."* Thomas Jefferson, in *The Thomas Jefferson Papers: "The strongest reason for people to retain the right to keep and bear arms is, as a last resort, to protect themselves against tyranny in government."* James Madison, in *The Federalist Papers: "Americans have the right and the advantage of being armed—unlike the citizens of other countries whose governments are afraid to trust the people with arms."* Ambiguous? You be the judge. Note to the "guns only for hunting" crowd. The 2nd Amendment was not put in place because the Founders thought deer would attack.

Third Amendment–
U. S. citizens enjoy the right to not have soldiers quartered in their homes if they don't want them there. *Please note*: As in the Second Amendment, the Founding Fathers recalled the birth of the nation, and took steps to protect the nation's citizens from the natural tyranny of government.

Fourth Amendment–
This amendment protects the public from "unreasonable search and seizure," and states that search warrants must be specific in nature. *Please note*: There is no provision in this Amendment that indicates "but if they're really scary, you can do warrantless searches." There is also no indication in this amendment that a misspelling in the search warrant invalidates it.

Fifth Amendment–
The Fifth Amendment says… that I don't have to tell you what it says, should doing so incriminate me.

Sixth/Seventh/Eighth–
These amendments ensure that, if you are going to commit a crime, your rights will be a lot better than that dude in the movie *Midnight Express*.

Ninth Amendment–
This amendment states that rights spelled out in the Constitution do not eliminate the rights that reside with the people. What rights? Please see below:

Tenth Amendment–
Any powers not *specifically given* to the federal government, or *denied* to the states in the *Constitution* belong to the states or the people. *Please note:* There is no mention along the lines of *"unless the Federal Government really, really, really thinks we need it,"* which comprises 80% of the things the Federal government now oversees.

Fortunately, in 1791, America's evolution had not yet begat a nation of room-temperature-IQ whiners or media-seeking lawyers. The *Bill of Rights* made sense, people liked them, and their addition to the *Constitution* enabled people all across the land to pretty much agree that we had come up with one righteous framework for a government.

And so… what are we taking away from the Constitutional Convention? What lesson did we learn? I have an idea: The American people who ratified the original Constitution, wanted "the people" to run the government—not vice versa.

HOW LUCKY CAN YOU GET?

Again, consider how easily and how quickly the young Republic could have all fallen apart. Throughout human history, virtually every revolution resulted in replacing one tyrant with another. *The Who* nailed it in nine simple words: Meet the new boss, same as the old boss.

The infant nation of America, however, hit the leadership Lotto with one George Washington. In April of 1789, Washington—not a member of any specific "political party"—became the only US President elected unanimously by the nation's electoral college, which inaugurated him in New York City on April 30. Instead of surrounding himself with an entourage of dimwitted yes-men, then rushing out to Camp David for some martinis and a round of golf, Washington went to work.

First up, the creation of key executive posts, which he filled *not* with political cronies and successful fund-raisers, but with the men most qualified for the job. It became quickly evident that Washington was serious about receiving good counsel when he appointed Thomas Jefferson his Secretary of State, and Alexander Hamilton his Secretary of the Treasury.

Everyone knew that Jefferson would view *Hamilton's* appointment as a clear case of depriving a village somewhere of their idiot—and Hamilton considered *Jefferson* to be someone who should go far (and the sooner he got going, the better)—but Washington didn't care. He knew they'd both accept the appointments, then fight like Michael Moore and Rosie O'Donnell for first-in-line at a Shoney's food bar—enabling him to hear *both* sides of every argument, and thus make better all-around decisions.

The truth be known, President Washington's views skewed a little more Hamilton than Jefferson. Hey, let's be honest—his pedigree was rich, preppy Virginian, and the idea of giving away all the power to the people probably ran counter to his selectively wrapped DNA. As a result, his administration appeared largely "Federalist," which is to say he believed that he and his "educated, rich inner circle" made better decisions than the average taxpayer.

Now, if you're like most folks, you probably always assumed that Washington and Jefferson thought alike, and the fact that Washington had Federalist leanings may surprise you. Remember, however, that Washington spent a lot of time around the "average American" while in command of the Continental Army, and probably retained a pretty good feel for their abilities regarding rationale governance. (Knife fights, for instance, are probably not the very best way to settle civil disputes).

Thomas Jefferson, as much as I personally admire him, probably never ate a meal with an "average American," much less spent an entire winter at Valley Forge smelling their feet and wondering if they even owned a toothbrush.

Washington was, by any possible measure, a great President, most likely because he didn't arise every day feeling the call to do something "significant." What he did, instead, entailed gently steering the ship of state, without trying to show everyone onboard how to tie their particular knots.

He listened to both Jefferson and Hamilton, based his decisions on the overall good of the Republic, and generally avoided foreign conflicts so the young nation could grow strong. This is not to say President Washington wasn't an *effective* President—one could argue he was our greatest President ever, because he provided *leadership*, not stupid new laws and regulations. He was one of the principal men involved in the design and siting of Washington, DC and the White House; he selected West Point as the site of, uh, West Point; he wrote to a Jewish community in Rhode Island that he envisioned America as a country "which gives bigotry no sanction," and a place where the Jews would live as equals; and he entertained more VIP's and foreign diplomats than Jeffery Epstein ever dreamed about.

Then, in 1794, George Washington sealed once and for all who the coolest President in the nation's history would be. In fact, they retired the category because it would be pointless to ever reconsider the issue. Imagine a college running back rushing for twenty-thousand yards. Or an MLB slugger hitting 750 homeruns in a year. Or an NBA team going undefeated, with a spread of eighty points per game. Do you feel me, here? The nominations for coolest President ever were closed, forever.

What happened? Well, a few years earlier, Alexander Hamilton urged congress to institute a 25% tax on scotch whiskey. This went over with the Scotch and Irish farmers of western Pennsylvania like a fart in a bagpipe: The Scots because they distilled the whiskey, and the Irish because they bought it. Hey, they had a tight little economic circle going, so who were these "Feds" to extort a share of the profits? The situation became so unruly, in fact, these rebels tarred and feathered one of the tax collectors, and torched another one's house. (Not that there's anything really that wrong with that.). Soon, this Whiskey Rebellion was getting some traction.

So what did El Presidente of the United States do? He put on his frickin' Commander-in-Chief uniform, and personally led an army of 13,000 to put down the rebels. (Please—imagine former President Nixon astride a horse, waving a saber and leading men into battle). Then, after putting down this Whiskey Rebellion, President Washington said, "Hey, if you're going to *rebel*, whiskey taxes are a pretty good reason to do so—so I hereby pardon the survivors."

You want to cure global warming? Get Chuck Norris to hold a séance, and bring George back. Two guys that cool in the same room, demanding action? World-wide temperature will drop ten degrees, easy.

Before leaving the timeframe associated with President Washington's administration, we should segue to one hilariously tragic event that transpired during his watch in 1796. Here are the facts: As General "Mad Anthony" Wayne returned from fighting some Indians in Michigan, an illness overwhelmed him and he died in Erie, Pennsylvania.

In accordance with his wishes, the locals buried him there. Thirteen years later, his son pulled into town looking for his father's body, expressing his desire to return the old man to the family plot in Radnor, Pennsylvania. What followed is almost unbelievable:

> **Son:** I'm here to collect up my daddy's remains.
> **Erie Chamber of Commerce President:** Not going to happen, Son.
> **Son:** Why not? He's my daddy, and I'm taking him home.
> **Chamber Prez:** Sorry. He's ours. We, uh, honor him here. It hasn't got a thing to do with the tourist money we make on visitors.

Son: Well, how are we going resolve this?

Chamber Prez: I have an idea. Let's each drink five bottles of moonshine. I'm sure a good, logical, Christian idea will come to us.

(Ten bottles of moonshine later)

Son: I's tryin' to think, but izz just not workin'.

Chamber Prez: I got it! I got it! I! Got! It! Izz the perfect s'lllution!

Son: Can't read your brain, Man. Speak Ing'ish.

Chamber Prez: We'll git ol' Doc Walters down here, and he can boil yer deddy up good, and get all the guts and skin and bones separated, and we'll keep the flesh and the clothes, and you can go home with the bones!

Son: Man, that's perfect! *Perfect!* Just perfect! I'm sure that's what daddy would want. I love you, man. Another round?

And so it happened: The son got the bones, the town got the flesh and clothes, and everyone went their separate way. Aristocrats.

NEXT!

After his second term, Washington was a shoo-in for a third, but the unthinkable happened: *George Washington thought of his country before himself.* I defy you to name a President in the past fifty years (except LBJ and Reagan) who wouldn't be willing to cheat at the Special Olympics to win the title of President-for-life. Washington had that very thing within his grasp, and walked away from it.

Why? His concern about the young nation looking to him like a king. He knew the Republic needed to grow through new, fresh ideas, so he stepped down to return to life at Mount Vernon. The mere thought of it gives me the chills—and then chills again at the thought of how far our elected leaders have plummeted down the slippery slope of narcissism. But as we leave George behind us, let's keep in mind one simple lesson—a great President can simply be a great leader, without feeling the need to be an activist on behalf of everyone who gave fifty bucks to his campaign.

President Washington's reason for leaving—to allow for the injection of new, fresh ideas—fell short, literally and figuratively, with the election of the next President, John Adams. President Adams is not well known by amateur historians because, well, the things he did aren't the sorts of things that impact history. In addition, the poor fellow stood only 5'7", so he had the whole Sean Penn attitude going on; add to that, the fact he looked a bit like a hobbit, and top it off with a Harvard diploma and a law degree, and you've got a guy who's *going* to succeed, just not in the area of making friends. So, what were Mr. Adams claims to fame? Let's see:

First, he emerged as a world-class whiner, and everyone's love for George Washington topped his *List of Things to Mope About*. It tore him apart that he wasn't getting proper credit for the important role he and others played in the birth of the nation. Of course, John Boy remained home snuggled up under a goose down blankie while General Washington froze the winter away at Valley Forge, but—hey, somebody's got to keep the milk and cookies economy going, right?

Am I exaggerating? You be the judge. John Adams actually took the time (and used the ink and energy) to compose a letter to a friend listing the Top Ten Reasons that Washington was popular, and then went on to complain that none of them required brains. Among these, Washington was handsome... he was tall and elegant... people told great stories about his bravery... he was born in Virginia... and no one tattled on him when he did something wrong.

Is it possible to dislike John Adams any more than you do right now? Sure! Why? Because he also managed to rival Ben Franklin as the world's worst father. How bad? When his sons failed to excel at Harvard, he informed them not to come home until their class rankings improved. "I feel nothing but sorrow and shame in your presence," he told them. At the end of his presidential term, Adams informed one of his sons he would be returning home to oversee the son's life, so the son promptly threw himself into Long Island Sound and drowned.

Adams did, however, do one thing that should have resulted in a lesson learned, as demonstrated by the following conversation:

Yes-Man: Well, Sir... last day on the job. How do you feel?

Adams: You know, looking back on my Presidency, I'd have to conclude I've been a pretty insignificant dude.

Yes-Man: I feel your pain, Sir. It was President Washington's fault... he did all those great things, and was such a great leader, and his greatness was so great that-

Adams: Good grief, shut up, man. I'm depressed enough as it is. Plus, that jerk Jefferson is going to come into office, and he's going to give the common trash all sorts of rights and personal power—those people don't need rights! They need someone smart like me to govern them! They need a big, powerful government—and we need to keep it that way!

Yes-Man: You know, Sir, it's a shame we couldn't create a few dozen new federal judgeships, then pack the federal courts with Judges who agree with us—I mean, *you.*

Adams: Come again?

Yes-Man: You know, choose a bunch of lapdogs who think like us, and make them Federal Judges. Even if they aren't qualified, they'd have their position for life, and your political beliefs would live on through them.

Adams: Ah, yes... my ideas living on. Excellent.

Yes-Man: Just think, Sir. It's a golden opportunity for you to be a tumor on the Republic—your beliefs will spread wider and wider like an invasive cancer, and even when you're gone the host body will be unable to—

Adams: I have an idea!

Yes-Man: Sir?

Adams: I'll create a bunch of new judgeships, then pack the courts with minions who think like me!

Yes-Man: Brilliant, Sir! One great idea after another! How *do* you *do* it!??

And so it happened.

Adams signed appointments for judges based on their political views until well past midnight on his last day in office, and "midnight appointments" became a presidential "privilege." So let's use a privilege associated with hindsight, and learn a lesson: Many federal appointments are nothing more than an ideological abuse of power.

ON THE SHOULDERS OF A GIANT...

Our third President, Thomas Jefferson—by any standards a brilliant man—played a key role in ensuring the United States ended up as a government "of the people, by the people, for the people." (Okay, at least for a while). In order to help folks pull themselves up by their boot straps, Jefferson even advocated free, public education—a radical idea at the time, because education traditionally ensured the elite were able to distinguish themselves from the rabble, and if *everyone* was offered an education—well, it could lead to… lead to… uh, the smartest, freest, most successful nation in history?

Even during his days in Congress Jefferson advanced these "liberal" positions, serving as the chairman of the committee that made it possible for western territories to be self-governing, and ultimately to become equal members of the government by becoming states. This might seem to be common sense to you, but we're talking about really radical thinking back then. This was the time when "royal" families weren't a joke, and did a lot more than just attract tourists and provide whiney interviews to Oprah. Thomas Jefferson possessed the foresight to know America needed to get *away* from the tyranny that comes with "royal," "centralized" power—even though it meant he personally wielded less power as a governmental leader.

As Jefferson came into office as our third president, a very important event transpired. To make understanding the event possible, I have hacked through the legalese. Here's the deal:

A) One of Adam's biggest (and most blatant) "midnight appointments" entailed the appointing of John Marshall (his Secretary of State) as the Chief Justice of the Supreme Court.

B) In his rush to dump his business suit, don his judgeship robes, and act aloofishly superior to everyone, Marshall failed to complete his Secretary of State chores, one of which was to sign off on all of other the "midnight appointments."

C) Jefferson settled into office, found the unsigned appointments, and filed them under "W" for "When monkeys fly out of my butt."

D) One of the unsigned "midnight appointees" was for William Marbury. Needless to say, Mr. Marbury was bad bitter, because that appointment was his ticket to an address on Easy Street, so he sued *Jefferson's* Secretary of State, James Madison. The case ended up in front of the Supreme Court. (Marbury v. Madison)

E) Marbury (the appointee) figured he was in high cotton, because the Chief Justice hearing the case was (Yahoo!) the exact guy who'd accidentally failed to sign his appointment to begin with— fellow Adams-appointee John Marshall.

F) Chief Justice John Marshall, however, totally screwed Mr. Marbury by ruling—on a technicality—that the Judiciary Act of 1789 was unconstitutional, *and thus overturned an act of congress.* This left Marbury with no job, no hope of appeal, and no one to turn to who'd listen to his bitching. On the other hand, of course, it made Chief Justice John Marshall more famous and powerful than ever before. Why? See below:

G) No one objected, so the "checks and balances" that established the Supreme Court as "the court of no appeals" survived its first test.

President Jefferson threw himself into the job, doing the work of the people, and undoing a number of laws passed by Adams that he felt were anti-immigrant, anti-free speech, and anti-common sense. He established himself quickly as a popular president, reducing taxes and standing up for the rights of the individual. He was, quite frankly, what most politicians claim to be in their campaign ads: A man who thought about the rights of the common man when pursuing his agenda.

One of Jefferson's early maneuvers entailed a political risk, but certainly no more so than, say, having sex with an intern then mounting your defense on what the definition of "*is*" is. Jefferson's maneuver came

about because, due to some complex and boring reasons, Spain closed
the Mississippi to trade. Jefferson foresaw this as a problem, and sent
his bagman to France to talk to Napoleon's man about buying New
Orleans, and Florida. This reportedly how it went down:

> **Jefferson's Man:** Hey, Froggie. I want to buy New Orleans
> and Florida.
> **Napoleon's Man:** Impossible! Eet would cost you a gazillion
> francs! Do you have thees?
> **Jefferson's Man:** Nope. Hey, let's go cruise for some babes
> with hair under their arms!

Moments later, Napoleon's Man was handed a letter from Napoleon
himself. It read: *We're losing the war. Sell all that land in the New World.
Get what you can.*

> **Napoleon's Man:** Well, ah weel sell you Florida, Alabama,
> Mississippi, Louisiana, and all other uncharted area around
> there for... uh... 600 million francs.
> **Jefferson's Man:** I'm a little short.
> **Napoleon's Man:** No short jokes! How much do you haf?
> **Jefferson's Man:** 60 million francs.
> **Napoleon's Man:** Sold!
> **Jefferson's Man:** Take a check?

With that purchase, American history began to transform—to change
from mind to muscle. For whatever reason, America liked the *feel* of the
purchase: The extra elbowroom, the bigger size, the concept of expansion.

Jefferson, feeling like a 17-year old boy who's just been asked by
Meghan Fox to stand in for her missing ThighMaster, made his next
move by deploying the Marines across the ocean to kick the stuffing
out of the Barbary pirates on "the shores of Tripoli." At about the same
time he commissioned an exploration of the Louisiana Purchase by two
lunatics named Lewis and Clark, and gave them boats, and guns, and
whiskey, and all sorts of manly gear.

The American people were *giddy*, and Jefferson was swept into office for a second term. Why? Because Americans love spending money on cool stuff. And since that's the case, elected leaders need to exercise fiscal wisdom with the federal checkbook when it comes things like this.

As the American people swept Jefferson into office for a second term, one of America's most hilarious, tragic, and political melodramas began unfolding: Jefferson had more or less dismissed Aaron Burr as his vice president, so Burr was without a real job, an office, or lobbyists kissing his rump and picking up the tab for umbrella drinks at the Capitol Club. It was a humiliating situation for a man who felt he deserved to be leading of the nation.

Fortunately for Burr, a group of Federalists who'd read too many Robert Ludlum books recently devised a conspiracy to break themselves and New York away from the Union. Code-named "Essex Junto," they needed a lapdog serving as the governor of New York when it came time to roll out their finely-tuned plan, and they found Burr trying to invent the unemployment office.

With "Essex Junto" backing him, Burr ran for the governorship, only to find his old enemy Alexander Hamilton acting as the nation's first James Carville, and trashing him in the press. The riff turned into a mudslinging brawl and eventually disintegrated into the two accusing each other of screwing around on their respective wives.

It's hard to pinpoint the moment these two narcissists began this hate-fest, but rest assured each had a boiling, cauldron of abhorrence bubbling down deep in their respective bellies. Hamilton's distain for Burr was so complete, in fact, that when Burr ran for President, Hamilton backed his opponent Thomas Jefferson, *despite the fact* that Hamilton and Burr were members of the same political party. In return, Burr's disgust with Hamilton was so much that he... well, killed him, but I'm getting ahead of myself.

So, let's back up: Thanks in part to Hamilton's mudslinging, Burr lost his race for governor, resulting in his challenging Hamilton to a duel. Hamilton agreed, and the date was set.

Now Hamilton, it would seem, would know more about the "Code Duello" than most, since his son Philip fought in a duel 1801. Prior to that duel, his son came to him and queried, "Well, Pop, how should I play this?"

He told his son that dueling was honorable, but killing someone is immoral. Tracking down *that* particular path of wisdom, Hamilton advised his son to fire his round symbolically into the air, so as to be honorable *and* moral. Hamilton's son followed his dad's advice, and fired into the air—and when the smoke cleared, it revealed that no one provided Philip's opponent, George Eacker, with the same moral compass.

As a result, the younger Hamilton won the "honorable" part of the duel, but lost the "continuing to breathe" part. (And as we all know, it is difficult to stand atop the podium and receive your Honorable Mention award when you are dead.)

Okay, segue back to Papa Hamilton—if you're him, you've probably learned a fairly important lesson here—and not the kind of lesson that slips your memory the following week. We're talking about a *travel the country speaking to high school students about the dangers of wasting your one shot,* level-lesson, no?

It's possible, of course, Hamilton experienced a really early onset of Alzheimer's or something, and just couldn't manage to retain this important lesson learned. However, he did get a very rare "Lesson Learned Mental Post-it Reminder" when, on that fateful day in Weehawken, New Jersey, the referee pulled out the *EXACT SAME* set of pistols used in his son's deadly duel.

Yeah, I know. You're thinking a light bulb would have gone off in the head of the guy on the ten-dollar bill. ("Hey, I recognize those pistols! One of them killed my son! I swear I was supposed to remember *something* about this dueling thing. What is it? What is it? I wonder if they brought donuts for afterwards?")

Sadly, Hamilton's memory failed him, and like his son he wasted his shot; Burr did not, and wasted Mr. Hamilton.

Subsequently, Mr. Burr was charged with murder. Fortunately for him, however, the great, great, great, great, great, great grandfathers of the O.J. Simpson prosecution team stepped up to handle the investigation and prosecution, and the jury gave him a walk. We must take note right here, however, of a critical lesson learned: Disagreements between politicians should be resolved by dueling, because when it's over at least one of them shuts up.

Amazingly, it wasn't enough for Burr to be disgraced as the man who "murdered" Alexander Hamilton. Nope—Bigger, better and more impossibly idiotic plans swirled to and fro in his mind. Before long, he was traveling the west, buying land and making plans to break away from the Union to form a new nation where he would allegedly be crowned Emperor Aaron the First.

He put out feelers to the British Government, and later to the Spanish Government to support him in this brilliant plan. He even developed a scheme to infiltrate disguised men into Washington to kidnap President Jefferson, rob all the banks, and steal all the weapons out of the Federal arsenal (using his army or "*robots*" with "*laser beam*" eyes, one can only assume). He talked of his plans to invade Mexico to add to his new empire, and even promised ambassador positions to those who helped him. Yes, Aaron Burr had plans for going places, and this being America, the place he went was court, to be tried for treason.

Once again Mr. Burr beat the rap, thanks to the partisan antics of Adams-appointee Chief Justice of the Supreme Court John Marshall, who oversaw the trial and saw the perfect opportunity to anger President Jefferson. Burr skipped the country to France until 1812, then returned to New York where he died in 1836. In a leaky van. Down by the river.

Did we learn lessons from the brilliant Mr. Burr, who came within a hanging chad of beating Thomas Jefferson for President? You bet: The political system usually works like a septic tank, allowing the really big chunks to rise to the top. Lessons from Chief Justice John Marshall? Here's a good one: Justices should focus on law, not their personal feelings.

SHOW! ME! THE! MONEY!

Despite Jefferson's popularity, his second term resulted in a violation of some previous lessons learned, the combination of which produced a *new* lesson learned. Here's what happened: The British and French, losers that they are, couldn't strike a decisive blow on one another during the Napoleonic Wars. As bullies are apt to do, they quit fighting each other, and turned to beating up the little kid on his way to the corner drugstore to pick up his mom's prescription. In this case, the "little kid" happened to be America's merchant fleet.

The American people, however, were happy to put up with this because the European Wars made the economy good, and besides—it wasn't *them* out there on the high seas getting pressed into foreign service. Jefferson acted like a leader and refused to fret about the economic impact (because, quite frankly, the economy is *always* good within the world of the President), and thus took action: It was either *war*, or some kind of economic sanctions. After studying the choices, he passed the Embargo Act, which said:

> "The concept of trade is one where we send goods to *you*, and *you* give *us* money. Nowhere in the concept is the idea that we send you goods, and you steal the goods, the ship, and the poor dumb guys sailing the ship. Until you Limeys and Frogs knock it off, we're not gonna send you *any* goods, and you can't send us any either."

That sounds logical, doesn't it? Avoid war by economic means? Wrong. It messed with the economy, Jefferson's popularity plummeted, and we learned another important lesson: When it comes to one's political popularity, there is a sad truth about the American people: If it the average American ain't doing the dying, the economy is more important than the life or death of the nation's warriors.

HERE, LET ME LEAVE YOU A LITTLE SOMETHING...

Despite the fact that Jefferson's numbers were in the dumper due to the Embargo Act, he still held the Bully Pulpit—and he made America bigger, and gave those lunatics all that cool gear, and he seemed like an all-around good guy. So, when it came time to leave after his two terms, he pointed the fickle-finger-of-fate at his Secretary of State, James "Jemmy" Madison, and declared, "You da mahn!"

With that, Jefferson retired to his home, Monticello, where he pursued his personal hobbies, and slowly went broke. (Going broke isn't hard for a guy who ran up a $10,000 wine bill while serving as President).

What hobbies, you ask? Other than drinking good wine? Good question. And the truth isn't too difficult to find—Jefferson was a cross between the Nutty Professor, the Computer Who Wore Cobbled Shoes, and Old McDonald (who had a really, really nice farm). Jefferson's days at Monticello began before sunrise, followed shortly by a "foot soak" in cold water, which Jefferson credited for his good health.

Next on the agenda, some focused puttering and wandering around the nooks and crannies of the home admiring his inventions, and looking for things that could be improved through tinkering. Following the tinkering came–literally–several hours of letter writing, which is a very old-school form of correspondence where a *"writer" "wrote"* a *"letter"* to a friend or colleague, then placed it in an *"envelope"* and *"mailed"* it via the *"The U.S. Mail"* to the recipient.

After a full morning of letter writing, Jefferson would eat a big lunch, then head out on horseback to survey the property, and document/measure/analyze *everything*—from the size of his fruit, to the height of his crops, to the rations being served to the slaves. Why? Who knows? But then again, why do people spend all day tinkering around with the *Excel* program on their computer? *(Come here, Honey! I've set up a spreadsheet to track the baby's doodie trends!)*

It could be argued that the retired Mr. Jefferson had too much time on his hands, given the fact he participated each year in the neighborhood Pea Growing Contest; this electrifying tournament was a hair raising grow-a-thon to see who could bring the first edible peas out of their garden, and the winner "got" to cook dinner for all the participants—with the featured vegetable being the winning peas. The contest was won consistently by a neighbor named George Divers, and the one year Jefferson actually won he kept quiet about it—after all, what kind of prize is "getting" to host a dinner? (I told you Jefferson was smart).

Jefferson's obsession with details and technicalities wasn't, however, something he developed in conjunction with the old man smell; he'd always been that way. Take for instance his response to French naturalist Comte Georges-Louis de Buffon when Mr. Buffon stated that Europe was a *superior* natural environment to the New World. What would *you* do? *You'd* say, "Hey, Buffoon! I got something superior for you!"

Jefferson, on the other hand, responded by writing an entire book entitled *Notes on the State of Virginia*, through which he scientifically proved through charts and graphs and power-less point presentations that Virginia grew things just as big and beautiful as Europe—*better*, even, ya' Frog! To double-dog prove his point, in 1787 Jefferson had some friends back in American mail a moose carcass to him in France, so he could show them the might of our meese.

Now, people, let's get real. Mailed himself a moose? What would it take for you to mail yourself a moose? Short of a winning Powerball lotto ticket tucked into the animal's gut, I'm betting there isn't a single thing under the stars and heavens that could get you to mail yourself a moose—and you have access to UPS! But our man Jefferson? *He mailed a moose to prove a point.* Now *that's* a real commitment to intellectual and scientific achievement.

Also in retirement Jefferson accomplished one of the three things he engraved on his tombstone. The first two noted his writing of the Declaration of Independence, and the drafting of the Statute of Virginia for Religious Freedom. The third? The founding of the University of Virginia. (UVA). It's interesting, of course, that UVA is the place where the history of Thomas Jefferson and I cross.

No, I didn't attend UVA… but I plan to found UVAA, an outreach program to help UVA Grads get over the fact they went there, and to help them break their addiction to bringing up this fact within three sentences of meeting someone.

HISTORY RECAP #2

Well, here's another batch of lessons learned to consider. They aren't difficult to comprehend or learn from—unless you're a sitting president, a member of his/her cabinet, an elected official, a judge, a participant in Big Corporate America, or an American citizen.

> **Lesson:** People really, really dislike paying taxes.
> **Lesson:** You can learn a lot by watching a bad example in progress.
> **Lesson:** Firing into an unarmed crowd makes for bad public relations.
> **Lesson:** Americans are complacent when the economy is good.
> **Lesson:** If a dog is asleep, and you kick him, he'll wake up and bite you.
> **Lesson:** Never underestimate a group willing to die for their cause.
> **Lesson:** Nothing is impossible if you have the right men for the job.
> **Lesson:** A well-communicated message can have a huge impact.
> **Lesson:** Don't get involved in a land war fighting a guerrilla army on their turf halfway around the world, especially if the average American isn't a stakeholder in the ultimate outcome.
> **Lesson:** The majority of the Founding Fathers wanted the people to run the nation, not vice versa.
> **Lesson:** A great president can simply steer the Ship of State, without seeking a legacy or adopting a pretend cause to champion.
> **Lesson:** Many federal appointments are nothing more than ideological abuses of power.
> **Lesson:** Americans love cool stuff, so the people doling out the dough need to be careful not to spend money just making people happy.

Lesson: Dueling between politicians is an excellent idea, because when it's over one of them shuts up.

Lesson: Americans view a good economy as more important than life or death, which clouds their judgment on some really important issues. As a result, our leaders must sometimes make unpopular decisions.

Lesson: A man raised with the proper sense of service and duty can be trusted to accomplish great things.

CHAPTER SEVEN

J AMES MADISON STRODE into office twenty-something years after the conclusion of the Revolution, unaware that Americans insist on fighting a war about every 20 years or so. It's possible, of course, that he was unaware of this tradition—because it wasn't a tradition yet—but it wouldn't take long for him to establish it as one.

In a series of meetings between President Madison and Congressional leaders, the following conversations took place. Although the discussions are paraphrased, the actual reasoning is historically accurate.

> **Congressman Henry Clay:** Has anyone noticed that sliver of Florida we don't own?
> **President James Madison:** I have.
> **Clay:** Well, let's get it!
> **Prez:** But it belongs to Spain.
> **Clay:** No sweat; we'll declare war on Britain!
> **Prez:** What's Britain got to do with our wanting Florida... which belongs to Spain?
> **Clay:** Britain is fighting Napoleon, right?
> **Prez:** Right.
> **Clay:** Britain is kidnapping our sailors and forcing them to serve in their Navy, right?
> **Prez:** Right.

Clay: Well, hell—if they're kidnapping out boys, we have a valid reason to act indignant and declare war on Britain!

Prez: I'm missing something here.

Clay: Aargh—you Founding Fathers are such goody-goodies! Look, Spain is Britain's ally against Napoleon, so if we defeat *Britain*, we can *say* we defeated Spain too, and take Florida as victory booty!

Prez: Good point. Let's run some polls, get a feel for the public's attitude, and make a decision in the next week or so.

Clay: We're a young nation. We're in debt. We're totally unprepared to fight Britain. They'll never expect it!

Prez: Isn't that like a 6th grader attacking the Captain of the High School Wrestling Team?

Clay: Exactly!

Prez: Okay, whatever—I've got a happy hour scheduled with Tommy J. Send out the word.

As a result, Madison got us into "The War of 1812" with Britain. A year into the conflict, Madison received an update on the fighting:

Madison: Well, General... how's the war going?

General: Not so good, Mister President.

Madison: Well, we attacked some British forts in Canada—how'd that go?

General: Not so good.

Madison: The defense of Detroit?

General: Not so good.

Madison: The battle of Queenston Heights?

General: Not so good.

Madison: The fighting on Lake Champlain?

General: Not so good.

Madison: The fighting out west?

General: Not so good.

Madison: Our naval battles?

General: Not so good.

Madison: Good God, General, don't you have any good news?

General: Yes, sir, I do. You know that hot new secretary? The one with the big powdered wig?

Madison: No way...

General: Das right, Playa!

Despite the fact the "1812" part of the War of 1812 did not go well, the British failed to strike a decisive blow to the Americans. Slowly but surely, the Brits got tired and sloppy, and some good things happened for the Americans. You'd likely be bored with the details of who-flanked-who, but the good parts are some things you might actually remember from your history classes.

A) Captain James Lawrence of the American Frigate *Chesapeake*, receives a mortal wound; before dying, he says (remember this?) *"Don't give up the ship!"* Thus inspired, his men get all Rambo, fight back, and win the day.

B) An American Captain named Oliver Hazard Perry engages in a Naval slugfest with the Brits, gets his ship shot out from under him, transfers to another ship, continues the fight, and eventually destroys the entire British squadron. Having done so, he sends a message to his commanding general that says (remember this?) *"We have met the enemy and they are ours."*

C) After capturing and burning Washington, the British attack Fort McHenry in Baltimore and, despite bombing it all night, fail to secure a victory. Observing the fight is a young lawyer named (remember this?) *Francis Scott Key*, who writes a poem called *"The Star Spangled Banner"* in celebration.

D) The British prove that it is, in fact, *possible to learn from history* by referencing a "lesson learned" about fighting wars in a foreign country. In 1814, they sign *The Treaty of Ghent* that says, essentially, "Lesson learned. We're outta here."

SIR, I CAN'T REACH ANDY... THERE'S NO CELL TOWERS AROUND HERE.

Unfortunately for a couple of thousand British soldiers and a handful of Americans, news of the treaty didn't quite reach all the way to New Orleans. As a result, the British attacked, and American General Andrew Jackson *"... fired his guns, but the British kept a' comin', but there weren't 'nar as many as there was a while ago. He fired once more and they commenced to runnin', on down the Mississippi to the Gulf of Mexico. Ho! Ho! Ho!"* Jackson won a pointless victory that made him a national hero, and we the people learned an important lesson from the War of 1812: Decisions made by the government generally have an unspoken, underlying motive.

MEET THE NEW CENTURY. SAME AS THE OLD CENTURY.

All right! We're just into the 1800s, America is 1 and 0 for the century, and the average Joe (who didn't get killed in the war) feels *good*—feels *righteous*—feels *American*!

Sure, we didn't *actually* win, and things remained pretty much unchanged as a result—but we didn't *lose*, either, so it was like a hockey game that ends in a tie, but *your* team won the fistfights with the *visiting* team. Hey, it *feels* like a win! Time to drink beer and tip over a few cows.

Politically, the good feelings generated by the War of 1812 established an American voting tradition of "to the victor go the spoils." The "big government" party, the Federalists, more or less fell to pieces, because they opposed the war, and thus looked more like Frenchmen than Americans. The Democrat-Republicans (huh?), the party of President James Madison, however, frolicked like a Republican Senator on an NRA junket.

As a result, President Madison 'nepotis-onified' the presidency baton to James Monroe, who strolled into the White House in 1816. The era's upbeat feelings followed Monroe into office, and the party continued, complete with economic expansion, growth, index factors, bell curves, market inversion, and all the confusing stuff that economic pundits blather on about on Sunday morning television.

One economic event that *did* occur, which is fairly easy to understand, was the Erie Canal. Here's what happened:

1) Dudes out west declare, "We need an Erie Canal for trade, Mister Prez."
2) President Monroe declares, "Don't have the money, and not my job."
3) State of New York declares, "It's a good idea. We'll raise the money, and we'll build it, and we'll enjoy the economic benefits."
4) They do it; it worked; everyone won, and no one sucked off the federal government's teat.
5) 250 years later, I declare, "What a novel freakin' concept!"

Unfortunately, all that "good feelings" economic mojo led to a situation that was not so simple. Here's a look at the formula that led to the 1819 Economic Instability... Martini, shaken not stirred:

1) The Federal Government, feeling good about the War of 1812, spends money it doesn't have.
2) Bankers, feeling good about the Federal Government spending money it doesn't have, extends credit it doesn't have.
3) Speculators and manufacturers, feeling good about the stupidity of the Feds and the banks, borrow all the money they want.
4) The Federal Government, feeling good about all these good feelings, passes tariffs on imported goods, thus raising money for itself and "protecting" American manufacturers with an artificial price advantage.
5) John Q. Bagadonuts, feeling good that he's not starving, goes to buy a second horse and finds the price has gone through the roof—because the Feds, the Bankers, the Manufacturers, and the Speculators have been playing with money they don't have, and have passed along their economic problems to the price of a horse.
6) I resist the temptation to jump off a freaking bridge and shouting, during my fall, "Why can't we learn **anything**, **ever**, no matter **how** obvious the lesson?!?!?"

President Monroe, however, possessed a keen and rare understanding of history. He looked over the lessons learned from America's history thus far, and uncovered a brilliant-yet-simple formula:

> Economic panic = Unhappy voters.
> *War + economic good times = Happy voters.*
> Economic panic = A divided nation of voters blaming each other for problems.
> *War = Happy voters.*

Although he couldn't think of anyone to attack right then, he did the next best thing: He devised *The Monroe Doctrine*, which put America in a position to always be looking forward to war. The doctrine created a long-standing foreign policy for our United States, which said:

> Dear Rest of the World,
>
> North and South America are now off-limits for future expansion. If you try to expand here, we will kill you.
>
> Love,
> USA! USA! USA!

The American people felt so excited about the prospect of ongoing, perpetual war that they forgot to participate in the economic crisis which, of course, made the crisis evaporate. We the people learned that the economy gets a little weird after a war, and the little guy gets screwed when it happens.

AN ERA OF "GOOD FEELINGS"

The average American -zip-a-dee-doo-dah-ed thru the 1820ish era. Monroe plodded along doing a decent job, starvation ceased being a front-page issue, and if you preferred civilization you could stay in the east, while adventuring types could work their way westward. Unfortunately for President Monroe, however, some constitutional chickens came home to roost.

As best I can figure it, Monroe turned the page in his Presidential Daytimer and there, scheduled between 9:30 and 10:00 a.m. lay the words *"Do something about slavery."* At this point, no doubt, he called in his personal secretary.

> **Monroe:** Have you been messing about with my Daytimer?
>
> **Secretary:** No, Mr. President.
>
> **Monroe:** Then what's this?
>
> **Secretary:** Do you remember, Sir, when you were a Founding Father, and y'all wrote *The Constitution*, and put in writing that you'd deal with slavery *some time later*?
>
> **Monroe:** Yes?
>
> **Secretary:** It's *later*.
>
> **Monroe:** Damn. I was supposed to be dead when this came up.
>
> **Secretary:** Yes, sir. I'm sure you're very disappointed.

America was, as they say, nearing a crossroad.

Sadly, the argument among the power brokers was *not* the morality of the issue, but the fact that slaves counted, population-wise, as only three-fifths of a person—so Southern states enjoyed extra representation in the House of Representatives. When Missouri applied for statehood, a great debate raged as to whether it should be admitted as a slave or a free state.

Unfortunately for the slaves in Missouri, the economy thrived, and by now we all know the stock that voters (and thus vote-*seekers*) place in a good economy. The reason for the good economy related largely to Eli Whitney's invention of the cotton gin, which provided the Northern states with a huge boost in cloth making productivity. *Because* they could convert raw cotton into cotton cloth faster, they wanted more and more raw cotton, which meant that, well, okay, slavery isn't *that* horrible—as long as the Southerners continued delivering the raw cotton... and paying the lion's share of taxes to fund the Federal government... and the economy remains good.

In the end, the admission of Missouri required a compromise (creatively named The Missouri Compromise), but it wasn't, for damn sure, a compromise in any slaves' opinions. It proclaimed that Missouri *could* be a slave state, but there would be no more slave states north of Missouri's southern border.

Confused as to how that's a compromise? Imaging trying to explain it to a slave.

I, however, will have no problem explaining the lessons learned: When push comes to shove and a hard decision needs to be made, politicians will push and shove to avoid making it. As an addendum, let me add that pushing and shoving politicians tend to hurt little people.

CHAPTER EIGHT

T O UNDERSTAND THE next phase of American history, please pay very close to the following analogy. Yes, it's a tad complex, but it works:

An Orphanage for 18-year-old boys is located in the middle of Las Vegas, just off The Strip. The boys living here must march, single-file, past 4 casinos, 6 bars, 3 strip joints, and a massage parlor on the way to their *Gentlemen's Finishing School* every day, then work part-time providing back rubs to Showgirls every afternoon. Unfortunately for these young men, the Orphanage Elders (a professor, a city councilman, and a minister) have a curfew (with breath-a-lyzer) every evening at 6pm.

One day, the Elders come into the dorm and make an announcement:

"Boys," they say, "we Elders have decided to retire to the Bahamas, so we want you to be responsible and behave. Now, if you'll look in the office, you'll find a fully stocked bar, the keys to the Porsche and the Hummer, a bank account with a million dollars, a revolving heart-shaped bed, a hot tub, and a phone system that speed dials every pizza delivery service in Nevada."

(Let us imagine together the silence.)

"Now we don't care *who* takes charge... *but somebody needs to.*"

"Good luck."

And the door closes behind them.

This, my friends, is more or less what transpired when President James Monroe—the last of the gentlemanly, refined, self-disciplined, think-about-others Founding Fathers—left office in 1824.

And as would be the case at the mythical Vegas Orphanage, there was not an "organized discussion" or "rationale debate" as to who could bring real leadership to the table, or who would ensure that everyone received an equal share of the booze, dough, or wheel-time in the Porsche. No, Sir—we're talking about a bare-knuckled fistfight for all the booty. Four candidates strapped on the gloves and got in the ring: Andrew Jackson, Henry Clay, John Quincy Adams, and William H. Crawford.

Crawford struck first by promptly having a stroke. Despite the fact that this strategy *locked* in the mercy vote, he dropped from real contention. Jackson, Clay, and Adams, however, kept swinging—and with the votes tallied, the electoral votes came out as:

> Jackson–99
> Adams–84
> Crawford–41
> Clay—37

Because Jackson failed to capture a clear majority, *The Constitution* threw the decision into the Thunder Dome known as the House of Representatives. Henry Clay (a long-time rival of Jackson, and humiliated that he'd been topped by stroke-boy) lobbied hard for first-loser Adams—and miraculously, Adams got the nod over Jackson. Then, to the shock of everyone (today zero people would be shocked), Adams appointed Clay his Secretary of State.

The fix, as they say, was in.

Adams attempted to make up for his back-door win by proposing lots of "let's share the booze and the Porsche" programs to Congress, but almost none succeeded. The orphaned voters felt the guy in charge just plain didn't know how to party, and decided to wait for the next election to really cut loose. But, his service wasn't completely for naught—We learned a couple of useful nuggets from Mr. Adam's brief but pointless Presidency: Once elected, many politicians think they can get away with almost anything, no matter how blatant. Second, we learned that sometimes they do.

YOU CAN'T HANDLE THE TRUTH, MISTER!!

When the campaign of 1828 rolled around, both Andrew Jackson and John Quincy Adams decided to stress-test the concept of "freedom of speech," and laid the ground work for the political mudslinging we practice today. Check this out:

- Adams supporters decried Jackson publicly as a "Murderer" *(because he had hanged soldiers while in the Army).*
- Jackson supporters accused Adams of loading up the White House with "gaming furniture" at public expense *(because he bought a chess set and a billiard table).*
- An Adams-supporting newspaper reported that Jackson's mom was a hooker, married to a mulatto *(because... because... because, well, they felt like it, I guess).*
- Jackson's people accused Adams of pimping an innocent, young American girl to a Russian Tsar *(because, well, I guess they felt like it, too).*

Unfortunately, the ugliness failed to incite a duel between the two candidates, and the American people went to the polls. When the counting was done, Jackson came out as a clear winner—receiving a mandate that the American public wanted to change from the kinder, gentler way of doing things to a more, uh, *party-on-dude* way of doing things.

This is a fact: Following Jackson's inaugural speech, his supporters stormed the White House and proceeded to trash the place, rock band style. (They found the booze, one would assume).

The Age of Jackson thus enjoyed a very appropriate start.

Andrew Jackson, as President, provides a study in ideological duality, unmatched until the arrival of Bill Clinton. To understand the executive decisions made by Jackson, I resort once again to an analogy to help craft a mental picture, and a psychological mindset:

First, pull out a twenty-dollar bill, and take a gander at that wild-eyed madman. Now envision him sitting atop a stack of beer kegs, half in the bag, in the middle of the wildest Frat party ever thrown. He is a seventh-year senior, having switched majors from frontiersman, to horse racer, to Indian fighter, to war hero, to land speculator. Hanging on with a cumulative GPA of 2.0, he has recently changed his major again—to President. Needless to say, all the other undergrads view him as a god, and feel a constant need for his approval, advice, and assistance:

> **Fratboy One:** Jax! Dude! Wassup?!!
>
> **Jackson:** You, man! You dah playa!!
>
> **Fratboy One:** Dude! Me and the posse don't have any property, so we can't vote! Does that bite, or what?
>
> **Jackson:** Dude! That sucks! You dudes are my posse! I'm Prez, man, and I say *that* rule is history.
>
> **Fratboy One:** Woot! Woot! You da', mahn!
>
> **Fratboy Two:** Jax!
>
> **Jackson:** Represent, Dude!
>
> **Fratboy Two:** The old man cut me off! I got no sizzle—I'm all grizizzle!
>
> **Jackson:** No sweat, Bro! You can help me manage the White House! You're hired!
>
> **Fratboys 3-250:** What about us, Jax??!!
>
> **Jackson:** Duuuuuuuuudes! You mah peeps! You're all hired!

I suppose you get the point: As a President, Andrew Jackson was no Thomas Jefferson. He stayed busy, though, and presided over a lot of change—whether the changes were good or bad depends on whether you like executive decisions issued from atop a stack of beer kegs.

Here's a look at some of the significant events that occurred during the Age of Jackson. It is easier to understand his actions if you mentally put the words, "Dude! Watch this!" in front of his concepts:

1) The virtual elimination of the requirement to own property in order to vote (unless you're a slave, an Indian, or a woman, in which case you could own the Nebraska Territory… and it wouldn't help, anyway.).

2) The policy of unashamedly and publicly giving cushy government

jobs to your buddies (which was always done, but with subtlety... not with all the laughter, tequila shots, and high fives).

3) The institution of a Force Act when South Carolina nullified a federally-mandated import tariff... (which said "We're the Feds, and we'll FORCE it down your throat if you don't like it")–which was a strange stance for an individual liberties guy like Jackson–(unless you remember he was sitting on top of a bunch of beer kegs).

4) The Indian Removal Act—Unfortunately, nothing can be said to redeem or justify the Indian Removal Act. This remains one of the saddest and cruelest chapters in American history, when the Indian nations of the East Coast were rounded up like cattle, and driven west on the "The Trail of Tears" to lands that would supposedly be theirs to keep. It was inhumane brutality, a governmental conspiracy from top to bottom, and a time that will shame our nation forever. Given that virtually no one cared, however, we are offered an insight into the "unenlightened" perspective of this era's view of mankind. In short, racism pumped through every heart—in America and all around the globe.

President Jackson did, however, give us an important lesson for future generations... one that literally rules Washington today: Politicians will do *anything* to keep their voting constituents happy.

OF THE PEOPLE

As the first President who was "one of the boys," Andrew Jackson wallowed in enormous popularity. He opened the bar daily at 9am, bought everyone a Porsche, and started his own casino on The Strip. He was also the last in a line of Presidents who, historically, seemed **bigger** than their nation.

You see, up until Andrew Jackson, Americans spent most of their productive years dying. Sure, life included a certain degree of struggling, starving, and fighting, but for the most part the quest was brutish and short. I've discussed this before, but it's important that you understand that it wasn't until Jackson's time that the *events* of our nation began to overshadow the *leaders* of our nation.

Why? Because prior to Jackson, individual Americans failed to accomplish much, so we can't learn a great deal from their stories. Let's examine a few résumés from those eras:

John Walters, Farmer
Born: 1780
Lay in Crib: 1780-1782
Helped plow Pa's dirt: 1782-1790
Plowed own dirt: 1790-1830
Cut foot on plow, died from tetanus: 1831

Dabney Yarbrough, Trapper
Born: 1790
Lay in crib: 1790-1792
Worked on Pa's Trading Post: 1792-1807
Trapped Beavers & Muskrats: 1807-1819
Eviscerated by Grizzly Bear: 1820

Alton Phillips, Barkeep
Born: 1800
Lay in crib: 1800-1802
Swept floors in Ma's brothel: 1803-1810
Bar Back: 1810-1820
Bartender: 1820-1821
Coughed on by patron with smallpox, dead one week later: 1822

It's quite simple, really: Life in the earlier decades possessed an incredible capacity to stifle creativity (and breathing, too), so the little guy didn't get much notice. As a result, students of history focus on the big picture, and the men moving the chess pieces in the game of nation building.

For some reason—around the time of Jackson—the ingredients for individual achievement trickled down into our Great American

Melting Pot. It's hard to say which came first, the chicken or the egg, but the *people* of our nation rose up, invented, expanded, and overtook the limelight of the presidency.

In short, we spent the previous 150 or so years weeding out the weak among us, and the strong were ready to reap some goodies.

1831—NAT TURNER

Speaking of strong, an African-American fellow in Southampton County, Virginia by the name of Nat Turner held some fairly strong opinions about slavery. Suffice it to say he didn't care much about the South's economic need for slaves, or Missouri Compromises, or whether Massah's woman needed a new pair of shoes: Slavery sucked, and he set his mind to do something about it.

As a slave himself, he couldn't write his congressman (primarily because he didn't have a congressman), and there was no local television station "Action Line" to call to complain, so he did what he could: He got some equally pissed-off buddies, and they killed a bunch of white folks.

In my humble opinion, this was a perfectly reasonable thing to do—I'd have done the same thing myself; unfortunately for Nat, Southerners in the 1830s found this entirely unacceptable, and retaliated by killing him, most of his friends, and lots of other slaves who were sleeping at home minding their own business.

The rebellion of Nat Turner gave slave owners throughout the South the willies, and served as fuel for the fire being stoked by the very few actual abolitionists in the north. The tip of the iceberg broke through the choppy waters of public opinion, and bobbed around dangerously. And it taught us the obvious: A person can only take so much.

SPEAKING OF SLAVES

As the nation grew Westward, the settlers made a startling—albeit fairly obvious—discovery: This country is one *big* S.O.B. This proved to be problematic when thousands of pioneers migrated to a "better life" out west, but upon arrival encountered a number of challenges they couldn't overcome using only their two hands, three sons, and a mule.

Consider the quandary:

A) The desire to *claim* lots of land, but the inability to *plow* lots of land.
B) *If* all the land got plowed, the inability to reap all of what was grown.
C) If it *got* plowed, and *got* reaped, and the settler was rolling in cash, the inability to call back to the East Coast and rub it into their know-it-all brother-in-law's face.

Three dilemmas? No problem—three inventors stepped forward. John Deere invented a new, superior plowing system; Cyrus McCormick invented an automated, horse-drawn reaper; and a few years later, Samuel Morse invented a telegraph receiver and transmission code.

Total federal funding? Zero.

Total problems solved? All.

The expansion westward blasted forward. And Americans learned again that they don't need the government to solve all their problems.

1836–THE ALAMO

In the 1830s, the Texas territory belonged to Mexico, thus the Americans there were... anyone? Yes, illegal aliens or undocumented settlers, depending on your political views.

Unfortunately, no one took the time to explain to the Mexican president Antonio López de Santa Anna that Americans didn't lose a lot of sleep over taking land from its rightful owner. Relations between the Mexican government and American settlers finally reached a breaking point, and Texas revolted.

Santa Anna decided he'd better do something about this growing problem of illegal immigration/undocumented settling, so he gathered

5,000 soldiers and rode north. In January of 1836, they arrived at an old Spanish mission called the Alamo, where they encountered 187 frontiersmen dug in for defense, among them Colonel William Travis, Davy Crockett, and Jim Bowie. Hoping for reinforcements, the 187 held off the 5,000 for 10 days. None came, unfortunately, and even the Mexican Army couldn't manage to lose with those odds.

Santa Anna continued his march into Texas, and pursued Sam Houston's retreating army. In April found himself outside San Jacinto. Military genius that he was, he did not figure out Houston was leading him into a trap, and thus he granted his men permission to take their afternoon "siesta," while failing to post security well outside his lines. (Military Axiom: The road to hell is paved with the bodies of officers who failed to post security.) It was during their siesta that Sam Houston and his forces launched a surprise attack, shouting "Remember the Alamo!" and devastating the Mexican Army.

Shortly thereafter, Texas declared its independence, made Sam Houston president, and petitioned for annexation into the United States. America remains perplexed as to whether they ever actually joined.

MANIFEST *WHAT?*

This general era of America unfolded as a little nuts. Not bad, bad nuts like, say, Idi Amin-style where the president was eating his citizens—but pretty sociopathic, nonetheless.

Case in point: Journalist John O'Sullivan wrote in his magazine of "the fulfillment of our manifest destiny to overspread the continent allotted by Providence."

Come again?

Manifest Destiny? Allotted by Providence?

Everyone out there thinking God in His Heaven looked down and said, *"Hey, I never noticed that continent before—that's pretty cool. I better get some white guys there fast,"* please raise your hand.

It boggles the mind. He created the Indians by accident? He realized He'd given them too much room? Changed His mind? Look, you and I (and hopefully the Indians) can make peace with the fact that we plain old *stole* all their land because we wanted it, and they were basically unarmed. This was the way of the world at the time, and still is in many third world nations. But to bring God into it?

Amazingly, Americans bought into it. Embraced it. Manifest Destiny—God is insisting we continue westward. As strange as it seems, I guess it made sense at the time.

SAY HELLO TO MY LITTLE FRIEND—

While the concept of Manifest Destiny made settlers feel better about themselves, and new passages opened to the west coast, America ran into a problem when they completed a title search on California. Namely, it also belonged to Mexico.

God, it seems, failed to inform the tan guys about his Manifest Destiny masterplan for the white guys, and as a result the Mexicans retained a rather inconvenient claim to all that American-esque property along the southwest coast. Americans shouted from atop purple mountain majesties and fruited plains for California's acquisition, as no one wanted to sing, about a country that spread "from sea to within-a-days-ride-of-another-shining seeeeeea." The acquisition options for the States were limited, especially since God seemed unwilling to send forth an Arch-Agent to handle the closing.

President Polk decided *action* was necessary, and deployed a small army to camp out on the border of the Rio Grande, where they challenged the Mexican troops in the area to a grown-up version of "Red Rover, Red Rover, send a patrol, right over." One morning one of the American soldiers turned up dead, and America declared war.

Many historians express disgust at the Mexican War. They proclaim it didn't involve true global politics or struggles for righteousness, and was nothing more than a blatant land-grab from another nation. And I say, "Damn straight! Right on!"

The Mexican War was a *good* war as far as wars go. It was what it was. We didn't hide behind false pretenses, and speeches, and hollow declarations of outrage from politicians: Mexico had something we wanted, and we decided to take it.

Hell. we *offered* Mexico $40 million for California, and back in those days $40 million bought a lot of *chalupas*. Mexico not only said "no," they refused to even see the President's bagman. Decisions *that* stupid are usually prefaced by the words, "Hey, hold my beer—I wanna try something."

Is this our fault? Okay, yes. It is. But we did offer, and they failed to counter-offer. There are rules, Smokey. After they failed to respond, we hand-delivered the offer right through the gates of Chapultepec Palace in downtown Mexico City. Shortly thereafter, sea to shining sea became a reality.

NEXT STOP, FREEDOM.

A cool little land-grab from Mexico just didn't have the juice to distract many educated Americans from a most divisive issue: Slavery. Debates, declarations, and Congressional Compromises on the subject made less sense than an Oliver Stone conspiracy theory. As best I can decipher, the debating unfolded something like this:

> **Northern Politician:** Youse guys can't have slaves.
> **South Politician:** Y'all ain't the boss of us.
> **North:** Okay, let's compromise—youse guys *can* have slaves, but no slaves in the *new* states that come along. Youse gets extra representation because of 'dem.
> **South:** Okay, but let's change the wording a little: We *can* have slaves, and new states get to *vote* on whether they want slaves.
> **North:** Okay, but only if California is exempt and it comes in as a free state.
> **South:** Okay, but only if y'all agree not to give shelter to our runaway slaves.
> **North:** Okay, but if you land on Boardwalk or Park Place, then—
> **Harriet Tubman:** You honkies call *this* crap a *compromise*?

Harriet Tubman, in case you didn't know, is the African-American woman who helped orchestrate the Underground Railroad, a brilliant and secret network of safe houses and trails that led from Southern slave states to the freedom of the North. It was not a big favorite among rich Southerners when it came time for year-end giving, and the fact that many Northerners assisted with its operations rubbed salt in a growing wound.

The iceberg loomed on the horizon. And our lesson for the timeframe is that even a really cool war that you win quickly won't keep Americans distracted for long.

IS THERE A SPIN DOCTOR IN THE HOUSE?

Just about every American knows of the Gold Rush of 1849. You might even recall something about a guy named Sutter who found gold at his mill, and within a week Yosemite Sam and Bugs Bunny were brawling over bags of the stuff.

Like much of what you were taught, this is "kinda" true.

Yes, gold *was* found at Sutter's Mill and, yes, it *did* get people excited, but that occurred in January of '48. America's first spin-doctor actually drummed up the rush.

Here's the rub: Just outside San Francisco lived a Mormon named Sam Brannon, who just happened to own a newspaper. Like Bill Gates, he understood that the *real* money isn't in the *commodity*—it's in *supplying* the *needs* of those using and pursuing the commodity. He figured he'd leave the prospecting to the mouth-breathers, but sell them their shovel, pickaxe, booze, tent, lantern, and L.L. Brannon waterproof boots. Instead of digging for gold, he'd have the gold delivered right to his store.

Now, where would he find a few million prospectors? Just sit around and wait for someone to strike gold?

Or, perhaps, print the proverbial "I heard from a friend of a friend's friend" type story in his very own newspaper about how someone had *already* struck gold—**big**—just a short distance from the Sam Brannon Prospectors R' Us Shoppe. Media spinning was born, and the rush was on. The rest is history. And thus we learned the lesson that states, "Don't believe everything you read."

I'M MAD AS HELL, AND I'M NOT GONNA TAKE IT ANYMORE!

The iceberg moved a little closer as the 1840s progressed, thanks to the public arrival of escaped slave Frederick Douglass. A powerful public speaker, a self-taught writer/author, and a regular-old genius, Douglass spoke loud, long, and clear on the evils of the "peculiar institution" called slavery. Although no other historian will state this (because no other historians dare offend your politically correct sensibilities), the reason for Frederick Douglass' unbelievably important part in shaping our nation is simple: Before him, lots of amply-racist Northerners couldn't have cared less about slavery.

In fact, in the 1840s only 10% of Northerners even considered themselves "abolitionists."

After encountering Douglass's writings and ideas, it dawned on some of these people for the first time that "Hey, that fellow isn't simply a *black man*; he's a *man*, like me. And if *he*'s a man like me, maybe the *rest* of them are too."

Douglass was no shrinking violet, or political "yes man." He proclaimed, in no uncertain terms, that you can't be *pro*-slavery and *anti*-conflict—choose sides, people! Frederick Douglass stirred the hearts of the political and societal leaders up North through his brilliant writings in his autobiography *Narrative of the Life of Frederick Douglass,* his establishment and publishing of an abolitionist paper (The *North Star)*, and through widespread speaking engagements.

MORE PESKY IDEAS?

While Frederick Douglass argued logically and decisively, Harriet Beecher Stowe brought emotion, family, and humanity into the equation. She accomplished this by writing a book called *Uncle Tom's Cabin*, a novel of the slave experience that explored the tragedy and pain of families ripped apart, individual heroism, and dignity in the face of terror.

Stowe's novel struck a chord among tens of thousands of (literate) Americans, and slavery morphed into an issue discussed at dinner tables.

When an issue works its way *that* deep into Americana, it's an issue that needs to be dealt with. And from virtually everyone involved and every angle of the issue, we learned the lesson you can't understand another man until you've walked a mile in his shoes.

As America staggered into the 1850s, the issue of slavery overwhelmed much of its political dealings. Granted, it had zero effect the lives of the average Joe, but it gridlocked the work of a congress trying to oversee the growth of a nation.

In modern times, gridlock is *good*. Today, if congress is gridlocked, they can't create new taxes, stupid laws, and additional unenforceable regulations. In the 1850s, however, new states were trying to join the Union, new industry rose from the fertile soil of capitalism, and growing commerce needs called for new roads to be built—I know it's hard to imagine, but the life of a congressman didn't exist entirely around cocktail parties, VIP dinners, and free vacations disguised as fact-finding trips.

Eventually, it became obvious that Congress and the President (being political bodies) couldn't arrive at an answer or a solution; this wasn't due to a lack of trying, but more an issue of two entirely different cultures (North and South) trying to get one government to represent *both*. As a result, when James Buchanan was inaugurated in 1857, he said he hoped the Supreme Court could help resolve the issue.

The Supreme Court did, in fact, give its opinion in the matter, just two days later. The case centered around Dred Scott, a slave suing for his freedom because his owner kicked the bucket when they lived in Illinois, which was a free state.

Chief Justice Roger Taney's ruling stated: Dred Scott, being a slave, wasn't a citizen, and as such retained no right to be suing in the first place. (The old "lack of standing" bit.) In fact, Dred was nothing more than property, and property is protected from federal fingers by the *Bill of Rights*, meaning the United States Congress passed illegal compromises that rendered some states free, because only *states* could make the decision about their own destiny.

In hindsight, it's horrible that a man as educated as a Supreme Court Justice ruled a human to be nothing more than property.

COULD SOMEONE TAKE CHARGE, PLEASE?

It has been my observation that, in times of crisis, people invent answers to fit the problem. This is most frequently seen among people in their mid-twenties when, upon graduating from college, encounter a spiritual crisis—usually brought on when they discover that "real life" involves working all day, but doesn't include professors that "respect their opinion," or Christmas Break, Spring Break, and Summer Vacation. Lord knows the graduate-crisis is understandable, but it fails to rise to the level of "big concern" for the new graduate's boss—the Bossman believes he's overly generous with the one-week vacation, plus Thanksgiving, Christmas, and New Year's off.

Analogy: The spiritual crisis of these young adults is typically resolved with the invention of a coping-religion that combines seven or eight religions, and sounds really cool and deep: Karma is involved, and there's some sort of good/evil mojo, and animals are held up as more in tune with the Great Spirit. When fully morphed, these coping-religions end up a bit like the religion of that dude on that old show *Kung Fu*, but they require far less effort, plus it's okay to get drunk and hook up with your ex.

Segue out of analogy: This crisis of faith reaction pretty much sums up the tact taken to deal with the issue of slavery in American politics: In fact, the Crisis gave birth to lots of new McParties: The Republican Party, Democratic Party, Whig Party, Free-soil Party, Liberty Party, Southern Democratic Party, Constitutional Union Party, and a Party At My House This Weekend, BYOB.

Each of these parties offered a different solution to the issue of slavery but, since Dr. Phil wasn't born yet, no Deus Ex Fat-Bald-Guy solution materialized. With all the foot-dragging inside the Beltway, the people of Kansas devised their own solution: Start killing each other, and whoever is wiped out first, loses.

Bloody Kansas really had no other choice, and in reality these killing fields served simply as a microcosmic view of the overall United States: Two cultures, pro-slavery and anti-slavery, were attempting to coexist in the same space. This is like trying to live in a state where half the residents are pedophiles, and half are parents with lots of kids. This isn't a political disagreement—it's a **cultural canyon.**

It doesn't work. Two diametrically opposing cultures cannot coexist peacefully. It has never happened—*never*—anywhere in the world throughout all of recorded history. (And that's a big world with a lot of history.) Bloody Kansas earned its name and reputation, and foretold America's future.

JOHN BROWN

Helping to make Kansas bloody was an Abolitionist madman named John Brown. The father of 22, only his potency rivaled his fanaticism, and he and some of his sons hacked five pro-slavery settlers to pieces with machetes alongside the Pottawatomie River. One might surmise he felt strongly about slavery.

Feeling boisterous and brave after murdering five unarmed settlers, Brown put together a plan to free all the slaves. He secured some financial backing, and gathered together a band of like-minded nutcases, and captured the federal arsenal in Harper's Ferry, W. Va—from there the plan was to establish a stronghold, battle the slaveholding South, and offer refuge to runaway slaves.

Anyone who disagrees that John Brown was a barking lunatic need only do what I have done, which is to visit Harper's Ferry. If you hired a thousand military generals to search the earth for a million years, they'd find no place more indefensible than Harper's Ferry, and nowhere in Harper's Ferry was there a building more indefensible than the federal arsenal. In tactical terms, they chose to establish their HQs at the impact end of a shooting range.

After blasting their way into the arsenal as "Step One," Brown's plan faltered, mostly because he had no "Step Two." The local militia surrounded the place and kept Brown and his merry band of maniacs bottled up, awaiting the arrival of federal forces. In short order, Colonel

Robert E. Lee and some Marines arrived, stormed the building, and captured Brown and eight followers.

In the six weeks that followed, during the trial and conviction of Brown, a metamorphosis occurred. Somehow Brown, the butcher of unarmed settlers, went from Ike Turner to Barrack Obama: A man of vision, courage, conviction, and dignity. Two of the biggest celebrities of the day—Henry David Thoreau and Ralph Waldo Emerson—jumped on the bandwagon, and portrayed Brown as a Christ figure (assuming of course that when the Disciples weren't looking, Jesus Christ took a machete and hacked up people who disagreed with him). When federal authorities planted a freshly-hung John Brown six feet deep, they buried not a murderous psychopath, but a martyr.

At this point, the lookout quit swigging on his flask and screamed, "Iceberg! Dead ahead!" And perhaps we should consider this lesson: A celebrity's fame causes constipation, which eventually backs up so badly it fills their brain.

CHAPTER NINE

W HY THE UNITED States erupted, shortly thereafter, into a war for Southern Independence is a complex issue. These days we want to divide it cleanly between the "honorable, humanitarian North," and "cruel, racist South." The legend goes that the North wanted to free the slaves, and ensure they are treated as equals, just as the South wanted to keep their slaves, so they can continue livin' *la vida plantationa*.

Reality check: This was the 1850s. Virtually every person in America was racist as hell. There was a tiny sliver of Northern residents that cared about slavery, but the institution is what offended them—anyone thinking they viewed Blacks as equals or were willing to have Blacks move into their neighborhood is badly mistaken.

Were the Southern states wrong to own slaves? Duh. But America today is trying to overlay 21st Century morals onto a 175-year-old culture. Very few Southerners thought about slavery, because it was legal, and had "always been there." Hell yes they were racist and viewed Blacks as little more than highly intelligent pets—*exactly* like whites in the North.

Is there anyone so woke they think 150 years from now America's residents won't be looking back at us as abhorrent? We eat meat. We abort babies. We pollute. We fight wars, and argue politics on Facebook. We allow old people to die because we allow them to get sick.

The War Between the States occurred for the same reason all wars happen: Power and money.

The rich Southerners wanted to keep their slaves, and decided to leave the Union because Northerners were raising hell and taxing the hell out of them—in fact, the overwhelming majority of federal taxes and tarrifs were paid by the South, while the overwhelming majority of those funds were spent improving Northern states. The North couldn't allow the South to secede, because it would literally bankrupt the Feds.

No one cared about the plight of the Black slaves. Abraham Lincoln himself said publicly, "If I could preserve the Union without freeing a single slave, I would do so." Is there something ambiguous or confusing about his words? How did he earn the moniker "the Great Emancipator" when he didn't emancipate anyone until it became a politically expedient to do so?

Does anyone believe hundreds of thousands of Southerners died so the very rich could own slaves? The top 10%, who lived a life of total leisure? Does anyone believe hundreds of thousands of Northerners died to free people they viewed as sub-human?

It's a very complex issue, and there are several viewpoints that must be considered, each as important as the other.

Northern Politician—This guy views slavery as fine as long as it continues to make the South rich and productive. After all, almost all Federal taxes collected are paid by Southern states, and the South continues to send raw cotton up to Northern mills, which employs his voting constituents, which ensures his re-election. However, as soon as newspapers begin writing about it... which causes his constituents start discussing it, he goes full woke. "I'm against it!" he proclaims. "Sure, no one in Congress has ever put a bill forward even hinting slavery should be abolished, but I'm so against it that... that, I'm willing to die to end it. Sorry, I mean I'm willing to let *the white immigrant trash* go die to end it!"

Southern Politician—This guy, since birth, has lived a pretty good life within the good-old-boy network of his area. His big donors and supporters thrive in a slave-based economy, and said economy pays for all his mint juleps, dove hunts, and Pookum's hoop skirts. Owning slaves, to him, seems as much a part of life as humidity, gnats, and mosquitoes—in short, a necessity to life in the South. "Look, we'll pay your damn taxes," he says, "but don't be thinkin' that you can tell me how to run my state. Me and my constituents consider this to be a matter of honor, and you probably know where we stand on stuff like that. If you don't, you will."

Northern Joe Twelvepack—This guy owns a factory, and his life is pretty good. He couldn't care less about slavery, and would probably own some if he could—because *he* has to *pay* his workers upwards of 4¢ a day, and sometimes when he beats them, they quit. He is delighted to discover that, if shooting commences, he can legally buy his way out of military service.

Southern Joe Twelvepack—This guy owns a plantation and slaves. Freeing the slaves means he's got to do more than sit on the veranda drinking bourbon. This, of course, will not do. He's happy to find that if war comes he can buy a Regiment, which means he gets a cool title, and a badass uniform, and can shout orders from the rear… while the white trash does the actual dying.

Northern Joe Sixpack—This guy works in a factory, has a first-grade education, and his life sucks. He has never seen an African-American, but his life sucks too much to give it much thought.

Southern Joe Sixpack—This guy rents a little land and owns a mule, and his life sucks. He's never owned a slave, and never seen a Yankee, but he keeps hearing that the Yankees "are gonna come down here and tell you how to live your life." He begins cleaning his gun.

Northern Joe Emptycan—This guy barely speaks English, and doesn't give a crap about slavery, one way or the other—he just wants to avoid dying of disease in a gutter. When he finds out Army enlistees are fed moldy bread and worm-filled meat, he sprints to the recruiting office to sign up.

Southern Joe Emptycan—Born and raised in the sort of rural poverty that breeds true meanness, his guy survives day to day, and his life really, really, really sucks. For the most part, slaves live a much more secure and better-fed life than he, and only by looking down on them can he take any comfort in their presence. Like a drunken roofer on payday, this guy is *always* spoiling for a fistfight... and loud-mouthed Damn-Yankees are as good as the next guy.

These different points of view *did* play a role in the War for Southern Independence, but the real problem was this: Two cultures with opposing views were attempting to occupy the same space, and this does not work. Whether the issue was slavery, or states' rights, didn't matter—the truth is that these issues are, upon close examination, the same thing. Let's examine an easy-to-follow example:

> Dude #1 is wearing a T-shirt that says,
> "Free Northern Ireland: Kill an Englishman."
> Dude #2 is wearing a T-shirt that says,
> "Make the Queen Happy: Kill an Irishman."

You put these two dudes in a prison cell with one bunk. Do you think they're going to talk it out? Share the bunk? Open new lines of dialogue, maybe? No, they are going to resort to physical violence, one of them is going to force his will on the other, and the stronger of the two will get the bunk. This, of course, is what the ugly concept called "war" is all about, and the "bunk" in question is the right to pursue "life, liberty, and happiness" without interference.

Think of the situation in employer/employee terms: The company's president, Billy Yank, is powerful, well-connected, and educated, and for several years he has been evaluating the performance of one of his managers, Johnny Reb—the guy who is responsible for 80% of his company's profits.. Every Monday, Billy Yank calls Johnny Reb into his office and says, "I disapprove of the way you do your job—I might fire you on Friday. We'll see how I feel at the end of the week."

One day, Billy Yank brings on a new foreman, Abraham Lincoln, and calls Johnny Reb into his office.

"Johnny" he says, "Meet the new yard boss, Abe Lincoln. Needless to say, since I hired him it stands to reason that he and I think alike, but I wanted you to get a good, hard look at him... wonder what he's like... and be afraid while you're out there trying to keep your job."

Johnny Reb snaps.

"Screw that," Johnny says, "I quit."

"You can't quit," Billy Yank replies.

"The hell I can't."

"You can't," Billy Yank insists, "we have a contract."

"Yeah," Johnny says, "that's right—and the contract says I can quit same way I was hired."

"No," Billy replies, "the contract says you can never quit."

"That so?" Johnny asks. "I tell you what: I *quit*, and you just try to make me come into work."

"If that's what you want," Billy says.

"Yeah... that's what I want."

And guess what happens next?

A MAN OF DESTINY

It was, in fact, the election of Abraham Lincoln that served as the straw that broke the mule's back. Lincoln was an enigma to the Southern states, and they assumed he stood for immediate abolition. Nothing could have been further from the truth; Lincoln's vision centered on preserving the union. Period. Was it for the lifeblood taxes the South paid? That doesn't matter—he was willing to kill to keep the union together.

The South, however, violated a previously discussed lesson, by jumping to conclusions, and pulled out of the Union without further discussion. The die was cast.

The Starting Lineups

The Northern Yankees
Head Coach: Abraham "Abe" Lincoln
Quarterback: A new one every season, eventually settling on General U. S. Grant.
Game Plan: Utilize depth of lineup to wear down the opponent.
Offensive Game Plan: Run the ball up the middle, and rely on the mathematical certainty that the other team will run out of players first.
Eligible Players: 4 million
Number of Fans: 18 million
Team Bankroll: $240+ million

The Southern Rebels
Head Coach: Jefferson "Jeff" Davis
Quarterback: Robert E. Lee
Game Plan: Utilize the smarts of the Southern generals, who were arguably the best group of generals in history.
Offensive Game Plan: Do the unexpected.
Eligible Players: 1.2 million
Number of Fans: 5.3 million
Number of Residents Pulling for the Opposing Team: 3.5 million (remember to divide by 3/5)
Team Bankroll: $74 million

Pre-Game Color Commentary

> **Frank:** Well, I'll say we've got a helluva match-up for this one. We've got the incredible size and resources of the Yankees versus the raw talent and back-against-the-wall-attitude of the Rebels. Should be a great game!
> **John:** What about those that say the Yankees' size will immediately overwhelm the Rebels?

Frank: Not gonna happen, John. These Southern boys show a lot of character just staying alive in the humidity down there. I think they've come to play ball.

John: Do you think team leadership will play a big role?

Frank: Well, let's look at the offenses—the Rebs have Bobby Lee, Jeb Stuart, Stonewall Jackson, George Pickett, Nate Forrest, an' Jim Longstreet; but who's leading the Yankees—McClellan? Hooker? Meade? They're a bunch of girly-men who don't like to get dirty. I think leadership is gonna be big, and it'll be a contest of brains versus brawn.

John: What about special teams?

Frank: The South is weak on that one, John, and the North has this kid Billy T. Sherman who everyone's talking about—a real psychopath—he could be a player.

John: What about the experience of the individual players?

Frank: Good question, John.

John: Thank you.

Frank: You're welcome.

John: And?

Frank: Ah, yes, individual experience. John, it's like this: The average Yankee player is a city boy; works in a factory, or in a store, or on the docks. Life is pretty crappy, but it's 'three squares and a roof' type crappy. Not a lot of luxury, but not a lot of violent danger, either. They're hard men, but only as hard as they gotta be.

The Southern boys, on the other hand—most of them were born and raised in *hard* poverty: The kind of life that makes pain take a back seat to survival. Those fellas are rock-hard from the inside out, and I'm glad I'm commentating and not fightin 'em myself.

John: One last thing: Motivation; Who has the edge?

Frank: That's what's gonna make this war long, brutal, and ugly. Some of the Yankees enlisted to free the slaves, but most joined because it's a job better than working in a factory 14-hours-a-day. The Rebels mostly joined because the recruiter told 'em Yankees were invading his homeland, and that doesn't sit well in Dixie. After a couple months of the horror of war, none of the enlisted men will even remember what they were thinking originally... they'll be fighting for the man on their left and their right, and to avenge the lives of his fallen buddies. If we've learned anything about Americans thus far, it's that all of us are ornery and tough—the mutts of the world. This is bad day for America.

John: Well said, Frank.

Director: Cut! Segue to commercial! We're off the air.

AS BLOODY AS IT GETS

Hundreds of thousands of Americans are fascinated by the War Between the States, although I must admit I am not one of them. My lack of fascination stems from my military training, and my studies of combat and the art of war—there are good wars, and bad wars, and then there is the War Between the States.

This was a war as bloody, and as ugly, as they get. More Americans died in this war than in all other American Wars combined, from 1755 to 1970. Families split apart, and brothers fought brothers—this is not noble, this is horror—this is the worst fate a fighting man can imagine. This is, indeed, hell come to town.

The weaponry of the War Between the States also provided a source of horror. The huge muskets fired large, clumsy rounds that impacted like a freight train, ripping flesh and pulverizing bone. To be hit in a limb meant, also certainly, the loss of that limb, or a slow, agonizing death by infection.

Medical treatment around the battlefields rated as practically medieval, especially for the Southern Army. Casualty treatment consisted primarily of amputation, and pain medication consisted of a couple slashes of whiskey. When flies landed on the open wounds they were allowed to remain. Why? The flies would dine on the flesh and lay their eggs simultaneously, and upon hatching the maggots ate the rotten flesh, thus helping ward off gangrene.

To make matters as bad as possible, the Confederate Army ranks arguably as one of the greatest armies in history (behind only the army of Alexander the Great and the German Army of WWII), and thus pressed the war years longer than they should have. In addition, once U. S. Grant took over the Army of the Potomac, the strategy became one of "Hey, diddle-diddle, straight up the middle," with a goal of making the Confederates simply run out of living soldiers.

Saddest of all, perhaps, is that the war was unnecessary. If the Southerners had waited to hear about Abe's plans, they would have seen him as a good and decent man. Lincoln's goal was to preserve the Union: Period. In fact, in his first inaugural address he said, "I have no purpose, directly or indirectly, to interfere with the institution of slavery in the States where it exists. I believe I have no lawful right to do so, and I have no inclination to do so."

Like many historians, Lincoln knew slavery was on the way out—yes, at that time the rich folk in the South were up to their necks in the sin of slavery, but public sentiment and education were working against them. When your church starts pointing out that it's wrong, and the kids come home from college feeling it's wrong, something's going to give. The elites in the South were just plain-old furious—they were using slave labor to pay the vast majority of the federal taxes, yet the nation was slowly beginning to view them as the bad guys. Were they? Certainly by today's understanding of morality and equality. By the standards of 1860? No… but here in the early 21st Century, we sure do love to look back and judge the morality of our forefathers.

Anyway, as depressing as I find the War, I will nonetheless provide you with a synopsis. If you want to learn more, there's plenty of literature out there.

Note: The Confederate Army referred to battles via land masses or town names; the Union Army used names of rivers. The trick to remembering? Lee's army was the Army of *Northern Virginia* and the Union army was the Army of the *Potomac.*

1860
December 20– South Carolina leaves the union.

1861

January 9–	Mississippi secedes
January 10–	Florida secedes
January 11–	Alabama secedes
January 19–	Georgia secedes
January 26–	Louisiana secedes
February 1–	Texas secedes

April 12– South Carolina orders the Yankee soldiers at Fort Sumter, a federal fort in Charleston Harbor, to *vamoose*. This is because South Carolina has officially declared they are no longer a part of the United States, thus their fort is being illegally occupied. When they refuse, Charlestonians deliver a bomba-gram to the Fort. Charlestonians are so excited and happy they open the bar, start drinking and don't stop until... well, actually, don't stop. It's still going.

April 15– Lincoln decides this attack demands a reaction—despite the fact there were no casualties and the Union soldiers were treated as gentlemen by the Charlestonians. He asks for 75,000 volunteers for three months service.

April 17– Virginia secedes, followed by North Carolina, Arkansas, and Tennessee

April 20– Robert E. Lee resigns his commission in the United States Army, and joins the Confederate Army. In fact, almost all of the U. S. Army's Southern officers leave to join the Confederate forces, as the thought of fighting against their home states is too much to bear. Pick-up wagons with gunracks begin appearing all over the South.

July 21– The First Battle of Manassas [town name] / Bull Run [a stream running through the battlefield] in Virginia. Ladies and Gentlemen arrive from Washington and set up picnics to watch the "fireworks." Their pleasant afternoon is interrupted by bombs exploding in the chicken salad, followed by Yankee soldiers stomping across their blankets as they retreat from the battlefield.

August 5– U. S. Congress passes the first income-tax to pay for the coming war, and advises all those 90-day volunteers that, oops, their enlistment just became two years.

August 10– Union forces defeated in Oak Hills (Wilson's Creek), Missouri.

October 21– Union forces defeated at Ball's Bluff, Virginia.

November 1– Lincoln begins a game of Musical Generals that will last throughout the war. General Winfield Scott is fired, and replaced with George B. McClellan.

1862

February– General U. S. Grant captures Fort Henry and Fort Donelson in Tennessee. This gives the Union some important control of both the Tennessee River and, of course, country music distribution channels.

March 11– Lincoln fires General George McClellan as General-in-Chief, and replaces him with General Henry W. Halleck; McClellan isn't *completely* fired, however, and is given the Army of the Potomac.

April 6–7– Battle of Shiloh (Pittsburg Landing) in Tennessee. Union Casualties -13,000, Confederate–11,000.

May– McClellan drives his Army of the Potomac to within 20 miles of the Confederate capital city of Richmond, but for some reason loses his nerve and stops to await reinforcements. The fact that he's attacking the most pissed-off (and one of the best-led) armies in history might have had something to do with his nervousness.

June 2– Robert E. Lee assumes command of the Army of Northern Virginia.

July 2– The Seven Days' Battles. Robert E. Lee chases McClellan away from Richmond.

August 30– The Second Battle of Manassas (Bull Run) in Virginia. Robert E. Lee chases a *second* Union Army out of Virginia.

September 17– Robert E. Lee goes on the offensive, and smashes into Union forces at the Battle of Sharpsburg (Antietam) in Maryland. In a *single day*, casualties of exceed 23,000.

September 22– Lincoln issues *Emancipation Proclamation* which frees ONLY the slaves in the Confederate States. Strangely, the Union discovers that many of their volunteers enlisted only to preserve the Union. In fact, the Emancipation Proclamation generates a backlash, when enlistments decline because the Northerners don't want free slaves to move up North and take their jobs. The decline in enlistments causes the Conscription (drafting) Act of 1863, and when Joe Sixpack and Joe Emptycan find out that Joe Twelvepack can buy his way out of conscription, riots begin and a "White Lives Matter" movement emerges for the first time. Blacks are lynched throughout New York City.

November 5– Lincoln decides that General McClellan is a lousy McLeader, and replaces him with Ambrose Burnside. ('Sideburns' got their name from Burnsides' ridiculous sideburns)

December 13– Battle of Fredericksburg in Virginia. Robert E. Lee stomps Burnside. Union Casualties—12,000, Confederate—5,000.

1863

January 25– Lincoln fires General Burnside, and replaces him with General Joseph Hooker. ('Hookers' got their nickname because General Hooker allowed ladies of the evening to follow his troops, and provide professional services)

May 2-4– Battle of Chancellorsville in Virginia. Confederate forces defeat General Hooker, but both sides suffer over 10,000 casualties. General Stonewall Jackson is accidentally shot by one of his own men while riding into camp. He dies May 10th, a devastating loss to the Confederate Army and to Robert E. Lee personally.

May 14–   Battle of Jackson in Mississippi. Union General William T. Sherman defeats Confederate forces. Satan cackles.

May 22–   General U. S. Grant begins a siege of the Confederate position in Vicksburg, Mississippi, a location vital to controlling the Mississippi River. Because things are going so poorly in the east, these western victories bring notoriety to Grant and Sherman.

June 25–   Lincoln fires General Hooker, replaces him with General George Meade.

July 1-3–   Some Confederate troops walking through the town of Gettysburg, Pennsylvania stumble into a group of Union cavalry. Insults about each other's mothers are exchanged, shots are fired, and an impromptu skirmish leads to reinforcements and quickly becomes the bloodiest battle of the war as both sides pour in from the surrounding area. Confederate casualties reach 28,000, while the Union loses 23,000 men. Robert E. Lee tells his badly bloodied army they've got to "rub some dirt in it and walk it off," and leads them back to Virginia.

July 4–   General U. S. Grant's siege of Vicksburg results in victory, and 29,000 Confederate soldiers surrender. The Union now controls the Mississippi, and has split the Confederate states into two sections. To a military strategist, this is a very big deal.

September
19 & 20–   The Battle of Chickamauga in Georgia. The Confederates chase the Union out of Georgia and back to Tennessee, but it hardly seems worth it: Confederate Casualties—18,000, Union—16,000.

October–   U. S. Grant receives an 'attaboy' from Lincoln, for having actually won some battles; he is now in charge of the Union's western forces.

November 19–   Lincoln delivers the Gettysburg Address, one of the few speeches ever given by a politician that does justice to the sacrifices made by a nation's warriors.

November 23–   U. S. Grant chases Confederate forces out of Chattanooga, and is now in a position to further slice and dice the Rebel states into sections. (The old divide and conquer bit.) Country music access drops to zero.

1864

January 14–   General William T. Sherman begins his march through the South from his position in Mississippi. His plan is to "bring the war" to the civilians of the South, and break their will to continue to fight. Excited about the news, the Devil whips up a batch of sweet tea, throws another log on the fire, and begins to prepare a special room for Sherman.

March 10–   Lincoln fires General Halleck as General-in-Chief, and replaces him with U. S. Grant, now promoted to Lt. Gen.

May 5–   Battle of the Wilderness in Virginia. Grant understands that he was promoted to Top Dawg because Lincoln wants aggressive tactics. This is his first chance to show he understands the concept, and attacks not to take a strategic objective, but to kill Rebel soldiers.

May 8-12–   Battle of Spotsylvania in Virginia. Grant continues to attack.

June 3–   Battle of Cold Harbor in Virginia. Grant continues to fight like a parent trying to score Taylor Swift tickets for Muffy's Sweet 16. His losses are horrific during the last three battles, but mathematics are on his side—he can lose five men for every Rebel killed, and still eventually win.

June 15–   U. S. Grant begins a siege of Petersburg, Virginia.

August 5–   Admiral David Farragut successfully bottles up the port of Mobile, Alabama. During the battle one of his ships is sunk by a mine, and Farragut yells "Damn the torpedoes! Full speed ahead!" Even a Southerner like me must admit this is an exceptionally studly sound-bite.

September 2–   Sherman takes Atlanta, and burns it to the ground. Bravely, his men beat up the women and rape the cattle.

September 19–   Union General Philip Sheridan continues Grant's tactics, and slugs it out with Confederate General Jubal Early. Despite heavy losses, he eventually chases the Confederates out of the Shenandoah Valley in Virginia.

November 8–   Lincoln is reelected.

December 22–   Sherman takes Savannah and bravely kicks the local street urchins in the ribs.

1865

January 15–   The Union Navy bottles up another Southern port— Fort Fisher, N. C.

February 17–   Sherman burns Columbia, S. C., and passes an order to his men that residents of old folks' homes should be punched in the face. Letters recount his men throwing early hand grenades into huddles of crying women and children.

February 22–   The Southern port of Wilmington, N. C. falls.

April 1–   Robert E. Lee launches a desperate offensive at the Battle of Five Forks in Virginia. When it fails, he sends word to Jefferson Davis to get the hell out of Richmond. On April 3rd, Richmond falls.

April 8–   With the Army of Northern Virginia in tatters, Lee surrenders at Appomattox Courthouse in Virginia. Lincoln orders that the terms of the surrender be merciful. The Union band plays Dixie as Lee rides away from the scene, and the quest for Southern independence dies.

And from Abraham Lincoln and General U. S. Grant, we learn a lesson that serves our nation well until 1950: War works, but only if you're willing to go all the way to the point of acting like a rabid animal.

SO WHAT HAVE WE LEARNED, CLASS?

Let's take a quick look at some of the Lessons that have come to light since the War of 1812. A lot of blood, tears, and national treasure were expended providing us with these nuggets of wisdom, so analyzing them is the least we can do, right?

> **Lesson:** Decisions made by the government usually have an ulterior motive.
> **Lesson:** The economy always gets a little weird after a war, and voters are always worrying about the economy.
> **Lesson:** When push comes to shove, politicians will push and shove to avoid making a hard decision.
> **Lesson:** Pushing and shoving politicians tend to hurt the little people.
> **Lesson:** Politicians think, upon achieving power, they can get away with anything.
> **Lesson:** Politicians will do anything to keep their constituents happy.
> **Lesson:** A person can only take so much.
> **Lesson:** Americans don't need the Federal Government to solve all their problems.
> **Lesson:** Don't believe everything you read.
> **Lesson:** You can't understand another man until you've walked a mile in his shoes.
> **Lesson:** Diametrically opposed cultures cannot coexist peacefully.
> **Lesson:** A celebrity's fame causes constipation, which eventually backs up so badly it fills their brain.
> **Lesson:** War works, but only if you're willing to go all the way.

CHAPTER TEN

THE CIVIL WAR was won by the North for one simple rea-son: Abraham Lincoln was 100% committed to winning. The Confederate Army outfought and out-thought the Union at almost every turn, yet they won battles by their willingness to send men to their deaths.

Think how easily Lincoln could have ended it all with a speech that said, *"I'll sacrifice not another life to force a partnership on those who seek to leave us."* Or *"Their cause is wrong, and in time they will come to see this, and the Union shall be restored stronger than ever, without this needless violence."* Or *"Hey, I feel your pain."*

But he didn't.

He believed in the sanctity of the Union, and ordered to their deaths over 350,000 free men, pursuing a vision that Lincoln felt worth the horror it spawned. And just as he served as the keystone for winning the war, so the Union needed him to serve as the keystone for winning the peace. Consider the circumstances: The South was defeated in battle, and disarmed by the victorious Northern Army. The Southern male popu-lation was, uh, dead, their railroads were torn up, their ports destroyed, their crops pillaged, and their major cities burned. To top it off, all of their Confederate money turned into, well, Confederate money.

It was worse than having dirt on the Clintons.

But as Lincoln's willingness to bring total war on the South arose from his commitment to a unified America, so his vision for rebuilding the South included a plan for unity. He advised his cabinet that it was his plan to engage the South with a moderate and healing approach, and that the Southern states would be reunited with the American dream quickly and efficiently. After all, the point of the war was to preserve the Union, not stomp out all life below the Mason-Dixon Line.

Unfortunately, no one explained this to ass-monkey John Wilkes Booth. Booth is described by history as a "fanatical Southerner," but rarely is it pointed out that he wasn't "fanatical" enough to actually join the Confederate Army and risk injury to himself. If anything, he was a "fanatical coward," and proved himself so when he shot an unarmed Abraham Lincoln in the back of the head at Ford's Theatre on Friday, April 14, 1865.

Booth's bullet did several things:

A) Killed Lincoln.

B) Ended the South's chance of merciful post-war treatment.

C) Wrecked the play's chance for good reviews.

PLEASE PASS THE SPOILS...

With Lincoln dead, his vision for a healthy, unified nation vanished. You might say Congress couldn't see the forest for the (smoke of the burning) trees. We won! We won! You're screwed! They were giddier than Jeffrey Epstein at the closing of a new home in Mister Roger's neighborhood. You can almost hear the dinner conversations they were having:

> **Congressman:** Uh, Sweetie, please pass the spoils of war.
> **His Wife:** Sure, darling—Say, how are plans shaping up for the re-admittance of the South to the Union?
> **Congressman:** *Heh-heh.* We whupped them Rebels good, didn't we?
> **His Wife:** Yes, dear. The men actually fighting the war did. So what now?
> **Congressman:** Screw 'em!

His Wife: But didn't we just fight a war to keep them *in* the Union?
Congressman: Nah, we fought to whip some ass! Getting' to kick 'em while they're down is just a little icing on the cake.
His Wife: Well, aren't we bringing them back in?
Congressman: What's your point? *They* lost!
His Wife: Yes, dear, that's my point. They lost.
Congressman: And *we* won!
His Wife: I know, darling. We won the right to keep them in the Union.
Congressman: Right! *We* won!
His Wife: And the plans are?
Congressman: Whupped 'em good! That's what I'm talkin' about!
His Wife: Sweetie? Plans?
Congressman: Land a' Dixie, my ass! Heh-heh!

What followed entailed the creation of a wide variety of Congressional policies known to history as Reconstruction. Calling the policies "reconstruction" is not unlike an HMO administrator listing an autopsy after a patient dies as "follow-up treatment." The South during Reconstruction, some believe, served as the birthplace of the chaos theory. Consider the sequence of events, policies, and human dynamics all at work at the same time:

- Confederate money suddenly became useless paper—and "Sorry, I'm being reconstructed" didn't cut it as an acceptable excuse when the tax bill arrived.
- The region's leaders had all, naturally, been officers in the Confederate Army, and were stripped of the right to hold elected office under the rules of Reconstruction. When educated experienced leaders are prohibited from leading, then... I think you get it.
- Newly-freed slaves comprised a vast section of the region's population, but unfortunately they could not read, write, or do mathematics.

Now, take those dynamics, and mix them with the rest of the Reconstruction Ingredients:

- In order to protect the newly-freed slaves, the Federal Government maintained control of the South through armed, military occupation.
- They then orchestrated "elections" which turned the Southern state governments over to newly-freed slaves, both in elected and appointed positions. There's no doubt these freedmen were fine folks, but—well, there's that pesky issue of not being able to read, write, or do math. Even given the low opinion I have of elected officials, I *do* think it's better if the members of the State Budget and Control Board can do a little basic reading and third grade arithmetic.
- They allowed "Carpetbaggers" to come south with real American money and bribe their way into positions of power, or even bribe their way into winning a congressional seat (the freed slaves were fine for governing Southern states, but Federal Congress didn't want any of "them" up in Washington, for goodness sake).
- They raised taxes to… to… to more than zero, which was exactly how much money the average Southerner had.

Please note: One must also view this era *in the context of its historical, sociologic time.* Most Americans in this era, North and South, grew up being told—from birth—that Blacks were an inferior race. No matter how morally repugnant this idea may be today, it is what they were told by their parents—and now the Blacks were in charge. To the average Southerner, the Federal government embodied pure evil.

Were they truly evil? Perhaps not. But they were certainly jerks. Here's an example: Lincoln's successor, Andrew Johnson, embraced Lincoln's vision of bringing the South mercifully back into the fold. This made your average Congressman madder than a skinhead watching *Malcolm X*, and when their anger reached a pinnacle, they struck.

How? When Johnson fired his Secretary of War (a member of *his* own cabinet), Congress said "you can't do that, because *we* okayed his appointment." Next step? They *impeached* Johnson, and failed to convict him of his "crimes" by a single vote. The impeachment was, of course, utterly unconstitutional, and threatened to destroy the government's system of checks and balances—but the Congress of 1868 was so drunk with power, they couldn't be bothered with something as mundane as The Constitution.

SPEAKING OF DRUNK...

Fresh off the hero circuit for winning the Civil War, Ulysses S. Grant stepped into the role of Consumer-in-Chief in 1868, and proceeded to oversee the most corrupt administration in history. This is not entirely Grant's fault, of course—you try drinking Jack Daniels for breakfast, then govern America.

Historical accounts of Grant's presidency are almost always unintentionally funny—he's treated a bit like the Soccer Mom driving a Chevy Suburban: Everyone knows she can't see a damn thing, but no one wants to be rude by asking her if it wouldn't be safer to drive a vehicle that isn't 65% blind spot. *"It's not polite to poke fun, dear—let's not discuss it over history."* It should be noted, however, that although Grant was a drunk, he never drove his buggy off a bridge and drowned a girl he'd just met.

THINGS GO MESSY...

Almost as soon as the Civil War ended, American history got messy. What I mean by "messy" is this: Up until the late 1860s, American history was very organized and linear:

> A happened,
> so B happened,
> which caused C to happen…
> which resulted in D.

Post-Civil War, however, America exploded with growth and ideas, and the place grew so big so fast, with so much going on in so many places, with so many significant people doing so many significant things, that history (like this sentence) got messy:

> A happened,
> while B was price-fixing with C,
> while D was snatching land from E,
> while F was inventing G;
> which H stole, to force I,
> to give J L, M, N, O, & P,
> in exchange for K.

Sadly, I am not the first to consider this era of history messy. The United States Senate and House of Representatives also decided it was messy, and opted to break for cocktails for the next 50 years while the mess sorted itself out. As a conservative libertarian, I would normally be thrilled with this idea, but given the coming madness, it would have been nice if they'd popped in to check on things between vodka gimlets every decade or so.

NO COUNTRY FOR OLD MEN

Just after the Civil War the famed American Cowboy arrived on the scene—tanned, tough, armed to the teeth, and usually found in the saddle, drunk or badly hungover. For some reason, most historians feel a great calling to pooh-pooh the cowboy myth, spending entire pages harping on their low wages, grueling work, and high mortality rate.

Well, duh—

That's what makes the cowboy such a great symbol! Is America a nation of blue-bloods, and ballet? Hardly! This nation—since day one—has been about sweat, and blood, challenges, and sucking it up when the going gets tough! The cowboys lived life as real American junkyard dogs—Confederate veterans, freed slaves, Mexicans, the occasional

Indian—to a man they were served the proverbial doodoo sandwich, without pickles, for their meal of life, and had no choice but to munch away!

> **Confederate Veteran:** No land, no money—this sucks.
> **Freed Slave:** Oh, boo-hoo, dude. My family was sold off to another master.
> **Mexican:** Hey, my entire country was stolen.
> **Indian:** Money? Land? Family? My country was stolen; my family was slaughtered; my people don't even have a *word* for *money*; and they're still after me.
> **Confederate/Freed Slave/Mexican:** You win.
> **Indian:** Oh, that does me a lotta good—what do we do now?
> **Confederate Veteran:** I guess I'm gonna have to sign up for welfare and disability.
> **Mexican:** I think I'll hold a march in front of the White House.
> **Freed Slave:** I'm gonna move back in with my parents and go to Law School.
> **Indian:** Good thinking! And maybe I'll catch the tornado express to the Land of Oz!
> **Rancher:** Hey! You fellas want a crappy job that'll keep ya' from starving to death?

And thus the American Cowboy was born.

A Cowboy's life centered around the pushing of Texas longhorn cattle from the pasturelands of Texas to the railroad junctions in Colorado, Missouri, Kansas, and Wyoming. After a successful drive (which meant you weren't dead), the Cowboys would kick it in towns like Tombstone, Dodge City, and Deadwood—just the names alone conjure up visions of Spring Break, no? For the most part, they behaved like you would expect men with nothing to live for and a wad of paycheck cash to behave: They spent it on booze, hookers, and poker... and the rest they blew, foolishly.

This post-Civil War Cowboy Heyday also provided us with all the cool good guys and bad buys. Even World Wrestling Entertainment couldn't top this lineup: On the side of mayhem stood Jessie & Frank

James, Cole Younger and his brothers, Billy the Kid, Butch Cassidy, the Sundance Kid, the list goes on. The side of law and order was equally filled with testosterone—Wild Bill Hickok, Pat Garret, Wyatt Earp & his brothers, Doc Holiday, Judge Roy Bean, that list goes on, too!

I ask you: Does it get any better than this? Guns, leather saddles, horses, whiskey, cigars, hookers, poker games, blood, sweat, and well, more sweat, dressed in a full-length duster and a low-slung holster tied to the leg? Men of black, white, red, and tan, all swaggering out into the high noon sun to "do whatta man's gotta do?" Is this America, or what?

Sadly, the era of the cowboy lasted only from about 1865 to 1890. First some spoilsport figured out that the Longhorns could live quite fine, thank-you, up near the rail junctions year-round, thus eliminating the need for the cattle drive. Then another spoilsport invented barbed wire, which allowed ranchers to fence-in their cattle over vast areas, thus eliminating the need for men to cow-sit the heard.

And that was that. If a problem needed a better solution, some brilliant American rose to the occasion, and labor costs were slashed. The American Cowboy rode off into the sunset, but left us with a symbol that survives—globally—to this day. I for one laugh when I hear Europeans refer to us as "cowboys," because we are, down to our DNA.

AAAAAARMY TRAINING, SIR!

Following the Civil War, while the Cowboys and Lawmen and Outlaws drummed up material for Larry McMurtry, the Federal Government found on the payroll a victorious, albeit bored, army. Since the Southerners were essentially disarmed, it only took so many troops to menace them, so what to do? What to do?

How about a mission for the good of humanity? A mission to help spread opportunity and prosperity across the land? A mission of thanksgiving for that Manifest Destiny thing? Here, let's study together the words of General William Tecumseh Sherman, that brave Union General who tore through the undefended South:

> "*The more Indians we can kill this year, the less will have to be killed the next year, for the more I see of these Indians, the more convinced I am that they all have to be killed or be maintained as a species of paupers.*"

Yes, gentle reader, I'm afraid that—once again—the American government is back to killing Indians.

I know, I know—you're *tired* of hearing about it. You *agree* we were perhaps a little misleading by breaking, well, every treaty we ever signed. You *know* killing women and children like they are rabid dogs isn't exactly compassionate conservativism.

But—darn it—it's hard to avoid the facts.

So that's why I'm afraid it's time we discussed the Indian situation in blunt terms. Why? Because to discuss the issue merely through apologies and gnashing teeth serves no better purpose than self-assuring ourselves we *know* we were bad, and feel bad about it. (*Not bad enough to give them back the land we stole, but, hey—pretty darn bad.*) On the other hand, a full discussion of the issue can provide us with useful date for the future.

For further insight on the issue, I spoke with a Marine buddy and Montana Indian reservation resident named James Raymond. He is attorney of unsurpassed reputation, an expert in tribal law, a member of Mensa, and looks so much like former Wrestler-turned-Governor Jesse Ventura that people buy him beers. Except for his time at the Naval Academy and in the Corps, he has spent his entire life on the reservation—he has numerous Indian friends, colleagues, and clients, and has regular dealings with the Tribal government. His studied analysis of the situation is thus: White Europeans came to America as a conquering tribe. They came here to expand—just like the Egyptians, Greeks, Romans, Mongolians, French, Spanish, and British did for thousands of years before them. And when one nation conquers another, there are only four options in dealing with the conquered:

1) Kill them—A specialty of the Mongolians and the Spanish.
2) Enslave them—The Egyptians often chose this route.

3) Assimilate them—The Romans (and the Brits) preferred this route, as it yielded productive citizens within a generation or two.

4) Place them on a welfare system, and make them wards of the state. This concept was so stupid that no one had ever tried it.

Anyway, white Europeans arrived in this new land, and discovered the Native Americans—an almost-Stone Age people, to a tribe. Yes, they were peaceful, and spiritual, and excellent farmers, and connected to the earth, and loving parents, and—fill-in-the-compliment here—but technologically, they were in the Stone Age, and this makes defending your way of life against people with gunpowder a little tricky. In the 200 years that followed the Europeans early settlement, the people of European descent invented things like railroads, telegraph communication, repeating rifles, and, well, a self-governed nation. The Indians' advancements were few. (Again, this is simple fact, not an analysis of intellect.)

A conquering nation, of course, always kills people when they *initially* arrive, because the Home Team doesn't want to give up what they've got. Next step, the Home Team analyzes the situation and, once they realize the fight is hopeless, surrenders. The problem with the American situation was two-fold:

1) America is really, really, really big, and the Native Americans had no system in place for communicating with each other, thus coming to a collective agreement on the hopelessness of the situation.

2) The Indian tribes were culturally built on courage and honor, and they weren't the types to give up easily. This resulted in the killing phase of the formula going on for centuries (which is *exactly* what would happen if some UFOs tried to invade the United States in this day and age).

Eventually, the surviving Indians surrendered, and threw themselves on the mercy of their conquerors. (Big mistake coming up.) What the American government *should* have said was: *Look... we're sorry about all the violence, but that's the way it goes. You're one of us now, and that means you're a U. S. citizen and you have to live by the rules. Now learn a trade, and get out there and pursue some life, liberty, and happiness along with all the other Joe Emptycans. We know you'd prefer a home where the buffalo roam, but, well, we won, and these are our rules.*

Had we done this, of course, these very capable people would have risen to the occasion, retooled and retrained, and gone on to be productive, successful members of their new United States tribe. For some reason, however, the American government chose an entirely untried approach: The "wards of the state" system. This involved placing the Indians on a valueless piece of land called a reservation, and saying, "Sit. Stay. Good Indian."

Wherein lies the possibility of success? Of life, liberty, and the pursuit of happiness? The Indians were allowed to live neither like Indians nor their conquerors—simply thrust into a netherworld, enabling the Whitemen of the era to ease their guilt over brandy and cigars, pontificating that the reservations "allowed the Indians to retain their simple culture and native tongue."

It was a bad idea in the 1800s, and a worse idea in the 2000s. We picked the worst option available *then*, and for some reason stand by that decision *today*, as generation after generation of our original residents are raised in a Twilight Zone existence that reminds them every day that they are too different to be treated as equals.

The one thing the Indians *do* have going for them today is a government that allows them to (at least) live. Indian Wars raged during this period of history—terrible, bloody, and lopsided events completely lacking in mercy. Eventually the Indians vowed "to fight no more… forever," and the conquering nation created the reservation system. One wonders if the Great Chiefs would have ever surrendered if they had a way to see into the future. And one also wonders about the lesson that, sometimes, it's just best to get the hell out of the way of the authorities.

CHAPTER ELEVEN

TAKE OFF THE GLOVES... PUT ON A TIE?

ONCE AGAIN, AMERICAN history turns another corner, and comes into the world of *recent* history. If you're 30, anything before 1900 probably seems like caveman times—but if you're 60, your grandparents actually *lived* through this exact era. It's pretty amazing, actually—we came out of the Civil War, and, voila, recent history.

For good or bad, once the Cowboys rode off into the sunset, America changed from a nation where muscle mass mattered to a nation of business—and it became the playground of a group of business thieves called the Robber Barons. The best way to understand the Robber Barons is to first understand that there are people out there smarter than you and me. Not rocket-science smarter, but smarter in a way that enables them to see "the entire playing field."

Most of us see the world as I described it just a few pages ago, in **Things Go Messy**... "If I do A, B will happen, etc., etc., etc."

Some smart people see that "If I do A, then B and C will happen, which will result in D, and then I can accomplish E." The brilliant guys—like the Robber Barons—can see that "If I do A, then B and C will happen, which will force D to join forces with E and F; the result of which will be G, which I can acquire by lending H to I through a merger with J, then increase stock profits by unloading K, L, and M, and then take N public and use the cash to form O&P Equities… etc., etc., etc."

This is not Econ 101!

These guys are very, very, very rare, and their rise to the top of the business world is virtually certain. Their brilliance and their internal drive forces this success. As you will see, however, they are not choirboys. In fact, they are almost always greedy, power-hungry, fame-seeking, self-centered bastards, but this combination of characteristics is a de facto standard for lying, cheating, and stealing their way to the heights they reach.

THE PLAYGROUND OPENS FOR BUSINESS…

During any given generation, the United States has maybe 25 of these business geniuses moving and shaking—today we have Rupert Murdock, Bill Gates, Warren Buffett, Richard Branson, Jeff Bezos, Elon Musk, the Google dudes, and so on—and their success is often attributable to the same thing that made the Robber Barons insanely rich:

- An industry exploding with growth
- A government entrenched in bribery (although now it's "legal" because we call it campaign contributions).
- A media too afraid to cross them.

For a business genius, this set of circumstances made making money as easy as taking a lollipop from a baby, then beating the baby's skull in with it.

THE FORMULA…

The real formula for the arrival of the Robber Barons was approximately this:

A) The country wants to grow westward.
B) Politicians keep their jobs by keeping people happy, so they make it clear they want railroads built.
C) Building railroads and new industry requires *someone* to build and own the railroads, someone to make steel, someone to provide fuel, and someone to finance the deal, and... and... a gazillion workers bees to do the work.
D) Ta-daaaaaah, Robber Barons.

The story of the Robber Barons is, unfortunately, as complex as it is depressing. I remember as a kid learning about these dirtballs and being troubled, but I also remember the teacher being fairly uncritical of them. I think this was because, until recently, criticizing the free market or any form of capitalism was bad form: There simply wasn't any middle ground. Choose your team—full-blown capitalist, or full-blown communist.

Having learned from history, I now believe a very thin sliver of middle ground runs between the two, but it's hard to stand there: It's a slippery slope in both directions. My analysis is a scratch in the surface, but it will give you a feel for why completely unchecked, unregulated, Darwinesque capitalism (devoid of basic human ethics) is not, in fact, a good thing:

An unlevel playing field—Although the Robber Barons would disagree, their success hinged on one essential fact: Politicians and appointees of this era were for sale. Not kinda/sorta for sale like a Mississippi Sheriff in 1965, but *totally* for sale like a Mexican border patrol cop with a cocaine habit and two wives. When the men who *make* laws, *enforce* laws, and *rule* on laws are *all* on the take, you no longer have a democracy: You have fiscal anarchy, where money (instead of muscle) determines who runs the show.

Railroads—The two men who built and controlled the railroads of the era were Jay Gould and Cornelius Vanderbilt, and although they worked as competitors, each had to be impressed with the other's use of wholesale bribery, kickbacks, and stock fraud to build their respective empires. They hated each other—naturally—because each wanted the *whole* pie, but their rails ran in different parts of the country. Someone call a Whaa-mbulance.

Steel—The man to see for steel during the era was Andrew Carnegie, who unlike the others lived a true rags-to-Robber-Baron story. He made a legitimate rise up a corporate ladder, but his genius for bare-knuckled "business" didn't shine until Texas Tea turned up on some land he owned. He parlayed this newly found money into a steel production empire, which he ran very efficiently by having workers who attempted to strike murdered by none other than the Pennsylvania State Militia. *("Hey, Governor, it's me, Andy. Remember that million-dollar bribe? Yeah, I need to borrow the militia.")*

Oil—John D. Rockefeller owned the proverbial gas station during this era, and his first company proved so blatantly corrupt that it bit the dust. His do-over, Standard Oil, ran more smoothly, as John bought off entire state governments, then developed a system of end-user kickbacks so complete that all of his competitors withered on the vine. By the early 1880s, Rockefeller's monopoly of the oil refining business was so obvious and destructive that something had to be done: Did the Feds step in? No, Rockefeller used his army of lawyers to invent the concept of a "trust," which enabled him to be a monopoly without being a monopoly, because his *big* monopoly was broken out into *smaller* monopolies. It worked great—the smaller monopolies all ate dinner with the big monopoly, but they didn't put out after three glasses of wine. This plutonic affair appeared so innocent that other Robber Barons began using trusts.

Financing—The man with the most fun tickets during this era was J. P. Morgan, son of J. S. Morgan (who'd made a fortune brokering deals between the U. S. and Britain, then the U. S. and France). As the son of a rich guy, J. P. managed to avoid fighting in the Civil War, and instead spent the years cutting deals and making money. He eventually accumulated so much dough that he became the banker's banker, then really got into every pie when the stock market crashed in 1869.

How? He used the financial problems brought on by the crash to lend everyone money, and suddenly he owned a piece of everyone's company. Before long, Morgan ceased being just the banker's banker—He was into steel, railroads, and generally being a full-time, big, fat, rich pain-in-the-ass.

ALL WORK AND NO PLAY MAKES JACK A RICH BOY—

Understandably, many Americans struggle to understand why the Robber Barons are such a big deal—a bunch of grouchy old farts rolling in dough? Man, we got 'em by the tens of thousands, these days.

Well, actually, we don't.

You see, the Robber Barons were **all** Jeff Bezos-style rich. Huge, huge, huge, unheard of wealth (The Vanderbilt's had parties where guests dug in troughs of food for jewels). They owned *everything*, and shared nothing.

Minimum wage? Overtime? Benefits?

These guys would wet themselves from laughter if someone even pitched them on the idea. Factory workers labored a minimum of 12 hours a day, for pay that barely kept them from starving to death. Farmers fared just as poorly, as price-fixing and corruption screwed them on the cost of the machinery, the cost to ship their crops to market, and the price they received for what they sold. Coal miners died in droves, and railroad workers were getting blown up or maimed on a daily basis. The government, of course, was of no help, because they were all on the take.

GOOD, MUTT BLOOD

As so poetically stated in the motion picture *Stripes*, Americans are the mutts of the world. We're a big melting pot of races, creeds, and colors, and the result is the blood of a truly unique junkyard dog. And like a junkyard dog, Americans will only take so much before they fight back. This was the case in the "Robber Barons vs. Everyone Else" dilemma.

The workers began to revolt against their lot in life, demanding such rights as the right not to die on the job. The steel workers struck, the railroad workers struck, coal miners struck, and machinery builders struck. In virtually every instance the government sided with the Robber Barons, even as striking workers lay murdered in the streets by their boss's henchmen.

Despite the odds, the workers of the nation pressed the fight for their right to be treated like human beings, but the fight cost them dearly—and there is quite literally no way to know how bad it could have gotten, save for the arrival of a group of writers known as the "muckrakers" and a truly great president named Teddy Roosevelt.

ANY GOOD NEWS, HEREABOUTS?

Okay, here's a quick recap of American history following the Civil War:

A) Federal government kicking the reconstructed South in the nuts.
B) Federal government slaughtering Indians.
C) Robber Barons kicking working class America in the nuts.
D) Federal government giving Robber Barons a foot massage.

Fortunately, however, it wasn't all bad news—some pretty good stuff happened as well:

- Alexander Graham Bell invented the telephone, which at the time did not include text messaging, so it could still be considered a good thing.
- Thomas Edison invented the light bulb, which made it easier to see at night, which enabled telephone users to see the phone when they dialed.
- Edison invented the phonograph, an invention he had no idea would one day lead to hip hop music, so at the time it was a good thing, too.

- The Federal Government opened up vast tracts of land in the west to those who had the settler bug, and allowed people to rush out there and strike a claim.

WOW, I'M CHEERING UP...!

Unfortunately, the land the government was giving away belonged to—you guessed it—the Indians. In addition, the U. S. Supreme Court upheld the decision in a case called Plessy v. Ferguson, which created the "Jim Crow" laws, which said "separate but equal" segregated facilities would be A-OK. This meant equality for black Americans was put on the backburner (again) for a very long time to come.

Sorry, Gang, the last half of the 1800s wrapped up much the way it started: Depressing. We did, however, walk away with a couple of valuable lessons. First, corruption in politics can cause the downfall of a nation, so penalties should be so harsh that they are a deterrent. Next, the Federal government should do something about a monopoly *before* it gets out of hand.

CHAPTER TWELVE

AS ALWAYS, AMERICAN history brightens up with... anyone? Anyone? Bueller? You in the back? Very good! A war. Here's what precipitated the situation:

1) America had been at the gym everyday doing industrial revolution pushups, and spent a lot of time looking in the mirror and feeling very buffed.

2) The older kids in the class—mostly the newspaper moguls Hearst and Pulitzer—were teasing President McKinley that "all the other nations are growing. Why aren't we? Ya chicken? Hey, you're chicken!"

3) McKinley ignored the teasing until the older kids said "Hey, Spain is bullying Cuba, and Cuba wants to be *free*, like us—*do* something, ya chicken. Chick, chick, chick, chick-kennn!"

Of course, a President can only put up with this sort of teasing for so long, then somebody's getting a smackdown. McKinley knew better than to get in a fight with newspaper magnates who bought ink by the barrel, so Spain got the *"You talkin' to me?"* method of American diplomacy.

In a perverted sort of retrospect, the Spanish-American War provided a few laughs, assuming you didn't get dead during the telling of the jokes. The story is probably best told through the conversations between the Spanish president and his press secretary:

January 25, 1898
Spanish Press Secretary: Mr. President, the Americans have dispatched the battleship *Maine* to Havana Harbor!
Spanish President: Why?
Press Sec'y: They say they are here to protect the Americans we've been brutalizing.
Spanish Prez: *Have* we been brutalizing Americans?
Press Sec'y: I think our desire to avoid genocide has prevented that.

February 15
Press Sec'y: Bad news, Mr. President. The battleship *Maine* blew up in Havana harbor.
Spanish Prez: Castro's Cojones!! What happened?
Press Sec'y: The American newspapers are howling that we blew it up with a mine.
Spanish Prez: Well, *did* we?
Press Sec'y: I think our failure to develop mine technology yet has prevented that.

March 27
Press Sec'y: Uh, sir, the Americans have given us a list of demands.
Spanish Prez: Agree to them all.
Press Sec'y: Well, actually, sir, they're quite difficult to live with.
Spanish Prez: Living is also difficult when a United States Marine's bayonet is jammed through your lungs.

April 11
Press Sec'y: Well, sir, we agreed to everything.
Spanish Prez: Splendid. So we will enjoy peace?
Press Sec'y: I think President McKinley's declaration of war has prevented that.
Spanish Prez: What do I do now?

Press Sec'y: Call your bookie—take America, minus
the points.

And so it went.

The United States let slip the dogs of war on May 1st, and began a lop-sided fight that included attacks on Spanish holdings in the Philippines, Puerto Rico, and Cuba. In less than three months, the war was over, and just like when the class bully beats up a younger kid, not much was accomplished—save for one small issue: Teddy Roosevelt emerged a war hero, a fact that would soon save our nation from itself.

And what did we learn from this war? Here's a good one: With the emergence of large-scale newspapers (and true, mass communications) the President must have the moral courage to resist having his policies shaped by the men who control the press.

CHAPTER THIRTEEN

FOLLOWING THE SPANISH-AMERICAN War, everyone felt good for a short while, then remembered that the Robber Barons still ran the show: Think of it like the entire nation is enjoying a long recess on a warm spring day, when the teacher sticks her fat, horrid mug out the window and snaps them back to reality by shrieking, "Children! Children! Recess is over! Back to your pointless, crappy lives!"

Then, something fortunate happened (provided, of course, you weren't President William McKinley).

An anarchist assassinated President McKinley.

And that put Teddy Roosevelt in the seat of National Hall Monitor, complete with really cool hat and official-looking armband.

This was a true, divine irony, as war hero Teddy Roosevelt was a rising star in the Republican party, but the elders didn't like the lad—it appeared young Theodore had the nerve to care about the little guy, and didn't spend nearly enough time giving backrubs to big business. Their solution? Get him elected as vice president, and after four or eight years of obscurity and ribbon cuttings he'd fade away as an irrelevant has-been. But a single bullet changed all that, and suddenly Mr. Rough Rider had an additional weapon in his arsenal—Namely, the Big Stick.

So, Teddy and the Big Stick. How does one best describe it? Okay, try this: If you've ever read anything about prison, you know the biggest man is a man to be feared—and doubly so if he has "a big stick." Well, you don't get much bigger than having the entire federal government at your beck and call, and the Robber Barons soon found themselves in a symbolic jailhouse, with Mr. Big Stick in the mood for some lovin'.

Teddy selected as his first "girlfriend" John D. Rockefeller and Standard Oil, and the noise from that encounter inspired the other Robber Barons to start sleeping with one eye open. Teddy, of course, didn't seize Rockefeller's money—this is, after all, America, not Bolshevik Russia. But what he *took away* was what Robber Baron Rockefeller valued most: *His unlimited power.* Just like multi-billionaires of today, the Robber Barons no longer hopped out of bed in the morning for *money*—they couldn't spend all their money on themselves if they tried. Nope, their buzz came from their power, and their ability to act as God to millions of people.

From there, Teddy Roosevelt moved on and quickly developed the nickname "Trust Buster." Quite simply, he broke up the "trusts" the Robber Barons hid behind, which exposed their monopolies, which meant they could keep Boardwalk but had to unload Park Place and turn in their *Get Out Of Jail Free* card before they could pass "Go" and collect their 200 million dollars. They remained stinkin' rich, of course, but TR made sure that said Robber Barons weren't the guys wielding the big stick anymore—and *that* power was a Robber Baron's reason for living.

WELL, THE WORLD NEEDS DITCH-DIGGERS, TOO

Once Roosevelt set the wheels in motion for sticking it to the monopolies, he decided he needed some new challenges—and what could be more challenging than digging a ditch between the Atlantic and the Pacific? Teddy, however, faced a dilemma: The best route to build a canal across Central America was through the Isthmus of Panama, but the Isthmus of Panama belonged to the nation of Colombia—and the Colombians listed the property at a price normally reserved for oceanfront land... with a view of a nude beach... that allows only 25-year-old female aerobic instructors to frolic. After studying the issue, and weighing his options, he came upon an answer that worked beautifully—an answer utilized to this very day by suburban towns looking to grow their tax base: He rezoned the property.

Of course, Teddy's rezoning wasn't simply a small-town issue concerning strip malls and developers in slick suits—it involved financing a revolt by the native populace against their mother country, whereas most small towns' rezoning issues just pisses-off a few old-timers. In the end, the result was the same: Panama became Panama, with a strip of land from coast-to-coast that was zoned "Uncle Sam's Canal."

GO AHEAD... MAKE MY DAY

Under Teddy Roosevelt, the American government adopted a new attitude towards foreign policy, most likely because of the way Teddy thought, spoke, and lived his life. You see, Teddy felt A-OK about doling out an ass whuppin' to someone who needed it, and there were lots of loud-mouthed, bad complexion, adolescent countries around the world who needed it—probably not as bad as all the loud-mouthed, deodorant-challenged European nations needed it, but Teddy had been taught to respect his elders.

As a result, America enjoyed its first taste of being a *Team America World Police,* with its rookie beat being the western hemisphere. And we the people learned that Presidents who don't suck up to the rich and glamorous are more effective.

A SAD EPILOGUE

It is with heavy heart that I must tell you that one of our four, great, heavyweight presidents behaved—in the end—like a... well, a heavyweight.

After two brilliant terms, Teddy Roosevelt left the office to his handpicked candidate and good friend, William Howard Taft. With that—poof!—he orchestrated the world's coolest disappearing act, heading off to Africa to do a year's worth of big game hunting. Like many great men, however, a life out of the spotlight (even one that revolved around drinking booze, shooting guns, and romping with voluptuous starlets) somehow wasn't enough. (One would assume you have to be great to understand what is lacking in the described lifestyle.) Roosevelt returned to the states and got re-involved in politics, then ran for president as a third-party candidate, and caused Taft (the Republican incumbent) to lose to democratic challenger Woodrow Wilson.

Is there a lesson here. Methinks so. When you retire, please, just shut up and retire.

PERHAPS WE WERE DRUNK...

As you are no doubt aware, the near future involves a discussion of prohibition, the Federal Government's attempt to outlaw alcohol. I believe I now know why prohibition occurred: The Feds thought the entire nation was out-of-their-mind, spring-break, "hey-let's-make-a-sex-video" drunk. There can be no other explanation for why, in 1913, the states did not revolt over a constitutional amendment (#16) saying, "Yes, Federal Government, we would be pleased to have you create an income tax."

The Feds were thrilled by the decision, but so are most people when they find a one-night stand just as the bartender shouts "last call!" The problem arises when you wake up in the morning, and wonder if that anonymous person next to you who is snoring and hogging the covers has a drinking problem. Clearly the Feds woke up, and decided that—yes—we the people *must* have a drinking problem if we'd agree to an income tax.

STILL CRAZY AFTER ALL THESE YEARS

In 1914, in the Balkan capital of Sarajevo, a young Serbian national assassinated the visiting Archduke and Duchess of Austro-Hungary. Why? Who knows—probably Austro-Hungary-phobic. Then, like a trailer park game of Quarters that somehow dissolves into a full-scale gunfight, Europe managed to take this fairly insignificant incident and turn it into The Great War... [later to be known as World War I.]

HEY, IT'S YOUR FIGHT...

America of the early 1900s had little interest in going to Europe and doing the dirty work of a bunch of nations who still had Lords, and Dukes, and Queens, and the inbreeding that comes with such titles. Sure, there were *some* American warhawks, but as is always the case, said warhawks wouldn't be the ones doing the actual fighting. It's easy to be a rhetorical tough guy when you have the U. S. military to back up your play.

Woodrow Wilson, however, acted wisely, and kept his weapon holstered, and let the Euro-weenies spill their own blood. This decision was so popular it won him a second term. The Germans, however, failed to learn from history—after all, it doesn't take a room full of Ph.D.'s doing all-nighter research to discover that Americans *do* like to fight if the fight seems righteous.

In February of 1917, German U-boats sank the *U.S.S. Housatonic*; then in March, it was revealed that Germany was attempting to form a Mexican-German alliance against the U. S., a move America considered... well, pretty funny.

Unfortunately for Germany, once the laughing subsided, America declared war.

THE BIG DOG EMERGES

After four years, and about a gazillion dead and wounded, the European countries found themselves mired in a trench warfare stalemate. The Great War was getting uglier by the day, and no one had a solution for ending the fighting.

Segue: World War I and World War II are *not* good subjects to discuss over beers in any British or European pub. Why? Because Team America won them, of course. And in June of 1918, the Krauts got their first taste of Americana, apple pie, and baseball when they tangled with the U. S. Marines in a place called Belleau Wood, France.

Were the Americans really tougher than their Euro-weenie allies? How can we ever tell? Hey, here's an idea—let's compare them side-by-side: As the newly-arrived Marines advanced on Belleau Wood, they were practically trampled by the retreating French soldiers. When told he'd be wise to have his Marines join the retreat, Marine Captain Lloyd Williams announced "Retreat, hell! We just got here!" The Germans who survived their encounter with the Marines, which lasted two weeks and ended with knife fighting in the trenches, stated that the Marines fought like "hounds from hell," and thus gave the Corps its beloved "Devil Dogs" nickname. From there, it's academics.

American soldiers and Marines kicked ass and took names. That's all there is to it. Of course, the Limeys the Frogs and Russkies still boo-hoo-hoo about how the war was "almost won" when America arrived, and they'd already sacrificed so much, and blah, blah, blah. The dog ate their battle plans, one supposes.

But here's the real fact: A bunch of kids got into a big brawl out on the playground, and it took the global Football Coach to come out and break it up, dole out the spankings, and point out the lesson that sometimes the best diplomatic message is delivered from the business end of a rifle.

SO, LET'S REVIEW OUR LESSONS...

It's been quite some time since our last lesson review, so let's take a look at where we are. Perhaps since these lessons aren't such ancient history, we will have learned *something* from them, right? (Of course we haven't)

> **Lesson:** Once you win the war, it's a good idea to win the peace.
> **Lesson:** Sometimes it's just best to get out of the way of the authorities.
> **Lesson:** Dishonesty and corruption in politics can cause the downfall of a nation, and punishments should be punitive.

Lesson: The Feds should do something about a monopoly before it gets out of hand.

Lesson: With the emergence of a large-scale press and thus the ability to communicate with the public at large, the President must have the moral courage to resist having his policies shaped by the men who control the press.

Lesson: Presidents who don't suck up to the rich and famous are better leaders.

Lesson: When you retire, shut up and retire.

Lesson: Sometimes the best diplomatic message is delivered via the business end of a gun.

CHAPTER FOURTEEN

AFTER WINNING THE Big One over in Europe and carving up Germany and Austro-Hungary for a Legion of Nations all-you-can-govern buffet, Americans wondered "what now?"

Let's recap: They chucked the British out of America, killed the Indians, stole Mexico, expanded coast to coast, killed the remaining Indians, dug a hole through the continent, now run the Western Hemisphere, and just saved the world—hey, seems like a good time to break for cocktails! While folks all across the fruited plain hoisted a glass to being the best, our history got as messy as some Delta Tau Chi parties. Consider some of the incredible occurrences that rolled out in the early 1900s:

- Automobiles revolutionized the nation, as Henry Ford's Model T became affordable to the middle class, and grouchy old men discovered yet another reason to hate teenagers.
- Electric lights flooded the nation, which may have led to the heavy drinking that brought on prohibition, as spouses had to look at each other an additional 4 to 6 hours a day.
- The Wright Brothers went from inventing the airplane in 1903, to manufacturing and selling them seven years later, an idea that causes safety bureaucrats to have panic attacks this day. ("Timmy, if you don't behave, the unregulated man will get you when you sleep.")

- Motion Pictures exploded into Americana, as spouses scrambled out of the house to find a place without all that damn electric light.
- Immigrants poured into America with a hope for a better tomorrow, somehow drawing a feeling of hope from sailing past the Statue of Liberty (mostly because they couldn't read English and didn't realize Lady Liberty called them "huddled masses" and "wretched refuse" as they steamed by).
- Telephones worked their way into the world of mainstream business, enabling employees across the nation to call their bosses and say they'd be out on client calls for the rest of the day.

The nation was, as they say, a-twitter.

The post-war economy and stock market rocked, the 18th Amendment to the Constitution which prohibited alcohol offered a joke with an endless punch line, and there were piles of immigrants pouring into the country to do all the really hard work.

Think of the life of a forty-five-year-old man or woman. *Just twenty-five years earlier*, life entailed working sunrise to sunset, then collapsing exhausted into bed. In the Roaring '20s, the end of the day meant hopping in the "automobile" with the one you loved, catching a "movie," drinking at a "Speakeasy," dancing the Charleston on the tables, then using the "telephone" to call your spouse and say you were tied up with the "stockbroker." This was in one-third of a lifetime!

If that wasn't enough, the women of the era dumped their petticoats, cut their hair, invented the diaphragm, got the vote, and discovered that pre-marital sex did not result in a life of prostitution and drug addiction. In historical terms, we're talking about a nation-wide game of naked twister with free Tequila shooters and 10-cent Buffalo wings.

Everything, it seemed, conspired to cause a national good mood: The celebrities of the day—Fitzgerald, Hemingway, etc.—were all writing books about how life sucks, which meant they were personally troubled, and everyone's happy when a celebrity's not. Charles Lindbergh flew solo across the Atlantic, offering an airmail delivery of the message, "We're

#1", to the European countries. And Jazz music exploded onto the scene, providing white folks with a sense of rhythm for the first time in history.

Yes, in the Roaring '20s the nation was a-twitter. And we learned that if bankers and stockbrokers are giddy, something's amiss.

NOTHING FOR SOMETHING

In terms of the stock market, the American people were enjoying something for nothing during the Roaring '20s, and it's a bit baffling (once you understand what happened) how things were allowed to get as screwed up as they did. An analogy is perhaps appropriate:

You are the milkman, and your business acumen is commensurate with that of most milkmen. For your labors, you are paid $2,000 a year, and over the last ten years you've saved up $1,000, which you keep under the mattress. One day, down at the ABC milk bottling plant, one of your buddies claims that he heard from a friend of a friend's cousin's ex-step brother-in-law (twice removed) that the cows over at XYZ Dairy all have mad hoof disease, and will all have to be killed. This will, of course, reduce supply, and make the milk at the ABC Dairy much more valuable. You rush home, and get your $1,000, and sprint over to the stockbroker to buy $1,000 worth of ABC stock.

"No, no, no," says your stockbroker. "Don't buy $1,000 worth—buy it on margin for 10 cents on the dollar, and get $10,000 worth."

"Cool," you say.

"But," the stockbroker says, "if you've got your hands on $1,000, it's obvious you're a man who knows business. Why don't you go see the banker next door, show him the $1,000—impress him—and borrow another $1,000. Then come back here, and we'll put you into $20,000 worth!"

"Wow," you say, "That sounds brilliant!"

You do the deal.

Unfortunately, your friend of a friend of a friend's cousin's ex-step brother-in-law (twice removed) made a boo-boo. Turns out he heard XYZ's cows **don't** need to be killed: Now that he *really* thinks about it, he remembers he heard XYZ was going to make a *killing*, because it's the ABC cows that have mad hoof disease. A week later. your stockbroker margin-calls you to say ABC Dairy needs to buy a new herd, and could you please send in the nineteen thousand dollars you have outstanding.

Your milk, as they say, has curdled.

Now, take this analogy, replace yourself with every person who has a job, replace the dairy with every business that issues stock, and the bank with every bank.

Next, fire off a press release that mad hoof disease is sweeping the nation.

Then, dump your stocks, and watch out for falling stockbrokers.

Oh, and burn this lesson into your brain: What goes up, must come down.

WHAT A HANGOVER

That is more or less what happened. Things looked good, the nation cruised along on economic cruise control, and the little guy was finally, finally, finally, finally getting a break.

Then, on Black Thursday—October 24, 1929—word leaked about the possible mad hoof disease, and insiders dumped their stock. On Black Tuesday, just five days later, the bottom fell out. (Not only are you now bankrupt, Mr. Milkman, you're *throw yourself off the top of the barn* bankrupt—to the tune of 19 large. Of course, you and all of the other milkmen can't pay ABC Dairy *or* the bank you borrowed from, so they bite the dust along with you.)

11,000 banks failed, and—POOF—two Billion dollars in deposits vanished, because banks don't keep your dough under the loan officer's mattress. Industrial stocks lost 80% of their value, and because no one had any money, farm prices dropped 50%. The only thing that went up in value was "Life sucks and then you die" bumper stickers.

The genius at 1400 Pennsylvania Avenue presiding over all this was one Herbert Hoover, who felt it would appear socialistic to provide a governmental solution to the situation—never mind that the government had failed to regulate scumbags like Joseph P. Kennedy, who helped drive the market to collapse, then lived in luxury while the nation starved. Hoover felt it was a "private sector matter," much like O. J. Simpson was involved in a "marital matter."

By 1932, somewhere between 25 and 40% of Americans had no job, and this was back before people were *trained* to have no job. For these Americans, no job meant no food—*not* no cable TV and no Christmas presents this year—but no *food*, as in starve to death.

Are you hearing me, here? Food stamps, low-income housing, free medical care in the ER—these things didn't exist. Black, white, yellow, red, tan, it didn't matter. No job equaled boot hill for you and the kids, and there were no Zippy Marts or Burger Worlds to toss you a minimum wage job on 45 minutes notice. I know this is depressing to think about, but your Grandparents weren't lying—it *was* that bad.

EVERY GOOD COMES WITH BAD

Although they had little else, Americans still had two feet and two hands, and used their feet to walk to the voting booth, and their hands to vote Hoover out of office. The new president, Franklin D. Roosevelt, did what he had to do, and what he was elected to do—unscrew the situation.

FDR's plan for unscrewing things revolved around growing the federal government to stimulate, regulate, create, orchestrate, confiscate, stipulate, and fornicate every aspect of Americana. In short, he sent out an EmploymentGram to every citizen that read "You're hired." Within a couple of years, you either worked for the Feds, answered to the Feds, were regulated by the Feds, got welfare from the Feds, or gave pedicures to the Feds. Slowly but surely, America clawed its way out of the economic septic tank, as FDR's New Deal stimulated the economy.

Unfortunately, FDR failed to install an internal thermometer to pop out when the programs were through working, thus indicating it was time to take the whole mess out of the oven. As a result, the federal entitlements turkey continues to cook to this very day. And together we learned that all Federal programs should be required to have a termination date.

WHAT COULD BE MORE DEPRESSING THAN THAT?

As America crawled and clawed its way out of the Great Depression, it seemed that things could only get better. The Twenties had been a party, the Thirties had been a hangover to beat the band, and the Forties would be—well, who could tell?

FDR had an inkling, as a German guy named Adolph Hitler rolled through half of Europe in the fall of '39. Overcome by the belief that only *he* could lead America through the coming crisis, Roosevelt ran for a third term in 1940, and being the incumbent, won easily.

Soon, we found ourselves fighting World War II. And the service of the American men and women—of every age, race, creed, and color—in the coming war is perhaps the greatest testament to our nation's strength ever produced. It is decidedly unfunny, as somewhere in the neighborhood of 292,000 brave men (and thousands of women) lost their lives defending our shores from Japan, and fighting to preserve democracy for the people of Europe. Back at home, civilians bought war bonds, and grew victory gardens, and rationed goods, and worked in war machinery factories. It was a team effort like never before. However, before I discuss some of the fundamentals of the Big One, there are a couple of "You Suck" awards I'd like to issue:

1) To all the wealthy, able-bodied men who failed to volunteer for service, but instead stayed home and made money.
2) To all the Europeans who—to this day—claim America waited too long to join the war effort—*their* war, on *their* continent, against *their* enemy, who'd already kicked *their* asses when *our* servicemen arrived to save the day. (The French who live near Normandy and treat the American graves with reverence are exempt).

A PAIR OF VERY BAD MISTAKES

On December 7, 1941, Japan sneak-attacked the American battleship fleet while it was snoozing in Pearl Harbor. The Japanese government prepared a long and—at the end of the day—pointless list of reasons why they did this, but suffice it to say they considered the U. S. as a bad guy. Hey, the gazelle considers the lion to be a bad guy, too, but that doesn't give him permission to run up and hoof the lion in the nuts during a nap. Japan would come to understand that Americans do not abide this sort of behavior.

Adolph Hitler also considered the U. S. to be bad, because the U. S. was providing beans, bullets, and Band-Aids to the countries he was invading. He, too, took to sneak-attacking Americans with his U-boat submarines by sinking supply ships bound for Europe. Very poor long-range planning, Adolph. It's time for you to learn that the real master race consists of a melting pot of mutts.

The good news, however, was a lesson that surely we'd never forget: Other countries do not apply rules of "fair play" when it comes to war.

AGAIN, THE MUTT SHOWS HIS PEDIGREE

If nothing else, this book should have made one thing abundantly clear: Only the toughest, most adventurous risk-takers from around the world came to live, survive, and thrive in America. From every culture on the globe, the people who immigrated here were the type to volunteer to go out and kill the saber-tooth tiger. The ones who *didn't* immigrate here were the "I'll stay behind and protect the women and children and maybe do a little gathering" types. In the case of those who were forced to come here as slaves, who survived that brutality? The toughest and smartest.

Result? You're sitting in it. A nation of wealth and success like nowhere in history. The world, however, did not yet realize what sort of large-scale *military* occurs when you unify the world-tribe's bravest, toughest gene pool.

They would soon, though.

The gene pool lifeguard was now on duty.

CHAPTER FIFTEEN

AMERICANS ARE ACCUSED by most of the world of thinking life is one big John Wayne movie. There's a reason for this, however: It's because *that's* exactly how World War II played out—like a John Wayne movie. Our fighting men *deserve* the comparison to the Duke, because they kicked ass like they were following a script. In the event you are a doubter or a Frenchman, let's take a look:

Act 1, Scene 1—Because the Japanese knew about the war before we did, they used their built-in Pearl-Harbor momentum to take the Philippines. Douglas MacArthur was stationed in the Philippines at the time, but President Roosevelt decided that he was too big a star to be an extra on the Bataan Death March, and ordered him to fly to the safety of Australia. "I shall return," MacArthur announced. ("Once you people get some Marines in here to clean this mess up.")

Act 1, Scene 2—Losing the Philippines made the good guys mad, especially one Major General James Doolittle. Doolittle devised a plan to fly a bunch of B-25s off the cramped flight deck of a U. S. Aircraft Carrier, without catapult assist, bomb Tokyo, then… then… well, then came a problem, because the B-25s wouldn't have enough fuel to make it back to the carrier—and if they did, they weren't designed to land on a carrier anyway. Doolittle told his group of volunteer pilots that they would ditch the planes in China, and hookup with Chinese friendlies.

Needless to say, it took several days to reconfigure the seats in the planes to allow for the size of these pilots' balls, but once done, the mission proved successful, and most of the airmen made it to China.

Japan got its first "Uh-oh" wakeup call.

Act 1, Scene 3—In this scene, the Japanese find that they failed to do quite enough damage to the American Fleet at Pearl Harbor. They engage the American Navy in the Battle of the Coral Sea and the Battle of Midway, and get their Samurai swords jammed up where the Rising Sun don't shine. In essence, the Japanese *Naval* threat is eliminated, and the war is just getting started. (Can you say, "Please pass the hara-kiri knife?")

Act 1, Scene 4—U. S. Marines land on Guadalcanal and undertake a bloody, nasty slugfest. Unfortunately for Navy-Marine Corps relations, the Navy claimed to have a brunch appointment or something, and left the Marines on the island without re-supply. By the time the Marines finished kicking ass six months later, they were gnawing on roots for dinner. Victory was theirs, nonetheless, and Japanese troops who managed to survive and retreat from Guadalcanal nicknamed it "The Island of Death."

Act 2, Scene 1—After several years of stomping all over the European allies, German Field Marshall Erwin "Desert Fox" Rommel runs into General George Patton and his 8th Army in the sandy clime of North Africa. Rommel receives a quick lesson in how mutt-blood deals with master-race blood… primarily by shedding it.

Act 2, Scene 2—Despite being warned by Rommel that "those dudes are serious," Hitler commits more troops to North Africa, most of whom come to understand what Patton meant when he said, "You win wars by making the other poor dumb bastard die for *his* country."

Act 2, Scene 3—Allied forces under the leadership of General "Ike" Eisenhower invade and capture Sicily. Feeling decidedly less tough, Mobsters stay indoors baking pizza to feed the troops as the tanks roll by.

Act 2, Scene 4—Allied forces land at Salerno, Italy. The Germans are dug in deep, and the fight is brutal. The Americans win (of course), and eventually drive the Germans out of Italy. In the wake of the American victory, the Italians (get this) declare war on Germany. This Italian threat causes, no doubt, nights of real sleepless fear among the German SS Storm troopers.

Act 3, Scene 1—As the Marine Corps' island-hopping campaign to take all Japanese-controlled islands moves forward, the island of Tarawa stands in the way—so well fortified that the Japanese commander proclaims it would take "a million men a thousand years" to defeat it. Unfortunately for the Japanese, this information was not shared with the Marines, who took the island in four days.

Act 4, Scene 1—The Allied invasion of Italy continues, as troops land in Anzio. Heavy fighting follows, without a clear victory.

Act 4, Scene 2—Allied forces break through the gridlocked areas in Italy, and for the first time German soldiers begin practicing their Swiss Accent. *(Ya, ya! Vee love der Von Trapp family! Goot friends, actually! Me Swiss—yeah base-a-ball and Meeky Mouse!)*

Act 4, Scene 3—Germans find out more about mutt-blood, as U. S. soldiers (and some tag-along allies) invade Europe on D-Day. Although not shown in Steven Spielberg's *Saving Private Ryan,* many of the American soldiers find they can take cover behind their own huge, steel gonads. It takes four days of bloody combat, but the Germans are displaced by the invading forces. The beginning of the end begins.

Act 5, Scene 1—U. S. Marines continue the greatest military campaign in history by taking Saipan, Tinian, and Guam. Japanese soldiers adopt a new tactic in producing casualties by killing themselves when defeat is imminent. (Marines wonder if the Japanese could be convinced to execute this concept at the *beginning* of a battle, instead of at the end.)

Act 6, Scene 1—Allied forces invade Europe from a second front in Southern France, and quickly retake Paris. Frog Fact of the Day: The French surrendered to the Germans *so quickly*, and became such efficient lapdogs, that Paris appears untouched by war. In fact, the retaking of Paris *hurts* the Parisian economy. U. S. soldiers subsequently drink all of the city's booze and sleep with all the women.

Act 6, Scene 2—The Germans, being German, counter-attack and generate the Battle of the Bulge. Military historians claim the battle got its name from the "bulge" created in the allied line, but another theory states this: When the 101st Airborne Division found themselves surrounded by German forces, the German commander sent a message demanding their surrender. The Division Commander, General Anthony McAuliffe, responded to the demand for surrender with a message that said only **"Nuts!"**

When word of the message spread to the American troops, a frightening and motivational "bulge" appeared in their pants, and the end result was yet another American victory.

Act 6, Scene 3—Americans deliver a Say-Uncle-Sam-Gram by firebombing Berlin and Dresden. Hitler begins to rethink his idea to bring America into the war, and asks aides if they think we will give him a "do-over."

Act 7, Scene 1—Marines storm the shores of Iwo Jima. Despite suffering massive casualties, the Marines take the island in a month-long slugfest, and bring home as a souvenir the most recognizable military photograph ever taken—the five Marines and a Navy Corpsman raising the flag over Mount Suribachi. It's worth noting that the fighting was brutal; three of those flag-raising Marines would die before Iwo Jima was secured.

Act 7, Scene 1—Marines land on Okinawa. In a battle that lasts three months, Americans suffer 80,000 casualties, 12,500 of whom make the ultimate sacrifice. The Admirals and Generals and Washington politicians confer, and realize that a mainland invasion of Japan will likely result in the *total* loss of the United States Marine Corps, and will require a follow-on invasion by the United States Army. American casualties are estimated at 1 million, with Japanese suffering 10 times that. Marine Corps troops pray for a miracle to spare them from the coming horror.

Final Act, Scene 1—With Berlin under attack, Adolph Hitler marries his girlfriend in his fortified bunker. Then (realizing what he's done) kills himself. Even Satan himself is surprised at how quickly Hitler's soul is delivered to the Gates of Hell. Hitler is assigned to spend his first gazillion years in a cell with a 6'8", 300-pound, Hell's Angel named Hyman Goldstein.

Final Act, Scene 2—Germans surrender, May 7, 1945.

Final Act, Scene 3—The Marine troops' prayers are answered. A miracle falls on Hiroshima, then again on Nagasaki. The world is spared the butchery that would have come with a mainland invasion of Japan. The Japanese surrender, September 2, 1945.

Curtin Call—The gene pool lifeguard has restored order. And we the people learn that by pulling together, Americans can accomplish anything.

FUMBLING ON 4TH AND GOAL

World War II makes for a pretty good football analogy: The Global Goodguys were locked in a tight and ugly World Championship Game with The Hitler Henchmen, and at the beginning of the 4th Quarter it was anyone's game. Both sides felt exhausted, and the veteran ballplayers were getting carted off by the team trainer after every play.

Suddenly, the Global Goodguys make a surprise announcement: They've signed Team America, and these brash and brave young studs take the field. They successfully execute drive after drive, touchdown after touchdown. Their defense is flawless, and Hitler's Henchmen can do little more than punt. The tides turn, the Global Goodguys pull ahead, and finally secure the win—now, there's only one thing left to do: *Cover the spread!* One last touchdown will do it!

Then, the unthinkable happens: The agent for the Team America players—Franklin D. Roosevelt—trips while pacing the sidelines, falls and smashes his head open on the Gatorade cooler—and suddenly believes he has all the answers. He rushes onto the field, and joins the huddle:

> **FDR:** Alright, men! It's been a real team effort! Now we need to share the glory, and give away our signing bonuses—that'll make everyone happy.
>
> **Churchill:** Listen, man, in case you haven't noticed, the Russians on our team are actually a bunch of commies. We shouldn't give them squat.
>
> **Patton:** I agree, Mr. Prime Minister. In fact, we should keep the drive going, and now that we're through whipping the Germans, we should make the Russians get on their team bus and go home: All the way home.
>
> **Ike:** Gee whiz—I agree with FDR. How's that, FDR? Can I have your job when you retire?
>
> **FDR:** Okay, then we all agree: I have the contract for all the Team America players, *and* control what happens to their salaries and bonuses, *and* I'm smarter than all you. So, here's the game plan—*I'll* score the final touchdown on a Quarterback Sneak.
>
> **Patton:** For the love of Pete, you're in a wheelchair!
>
> **Churchill:** And your head is half caved in from the Gatorade cooler.
>
> **FDR:** I know, isn't it great! On two! Break!

The quarter back sneak that FDR orchestrated was complex, but for the most part culminated at the Yalta Conference, which was a "what-now?" meeting between FDR, Churchill, and the head Russian Commie, Josef Stalin. The meeting was, at best, a "strange bedfellows" scenario because FDR and Churchill were democratically elected leaders, and Stalin was a hard-line, homicidal maniac, dictator. In many historians' opinions, the following is, more-or-less, what *should* have happened:

> **FDR:** Okay, we've just about defeated Germany. Mr. Stalin, you guys lost 22 *million* civilians and 7.5 *million* soldiers. That's a bummer. Unless you want to lose 22 million more, you'll pack up the gang and go back to Russia. Team America will sort things out, and we'll pick up the tab—you just go home and have a few vodkas. I'll send you a picture postcard when we get things wrapped up."

Unfortunately, what happened, was more along these lines:

> **FDR:** Okay, I've got a plan, and it's based on the fact that I'm nervous about the fact that Japan hasn't surrendered—sure, I admit it, I'm admitting my fears at the bargaining table, but—hey, you guys should see those little Japs! Man, they can fight! Reminds me of this guy in the 6th grade who –
> **Stalin:** Meester President—your proposal?
> **FDR:** Ah, yes. Anyway, I'm really worried about these Japs, so if you would agree to declare war on them, too, well, that would make me real happy.
> **Stalin:** Zis is all?
> **FDR:** Oh! One more thing! I want to create a real nice United Nations where everyone will work together and use arms for hugging.
> **Churchill:** Waiter? Could you bring me a shotgun? I want to blow my brains out.
> **Stalin:** Hokay, let's review der facts.
> a) Team Amereeka von de var for us.
> b) You could kick our asses if you vanted.
> c) You've nearly got zee atomic bomb invented.
> d) You know vee are commies, and that communist doctrine demands vee orchestrate a global revolution against countries like yours.

e) My nation is starved, and my people are about to revolt.

FDR: (Cough, cough) That sounds about right.

Stalin: And you vant us to declare var on Japan and partic- ipate in your United Nations?

FDR: (Wheeze, cough, gasp, hack) Yes.

Stalin: Okay—but you are asking a great deal. Here's our offer:

a) Ve'll participate in the United Nations, but it has to be structured so vee can veto any significant decisions.

b) Ve'll declare var on Japan as soon as it's conveen-ee-ent.

c) Vee vant all of eastern Europe and Eastern Germany, and Poland added to our communist empire."

FDR: Wow, that sounds very reasonable! Anything else?

Stalin: Else?!! Ah, yes… *else*. Of course there is else! Once vee even *say* vee'll fight Japan, vee vant Manchuria, and Mongolia, and—uhhhhh, the Northern half of Korea.

FDR: Splendid!

Churchill: Waiter? This is birdshot. I requested buckshot.

FDR: (Whispering) Winston, don't sweat it. I know something Stalin doesn't—

Churchill: Which is?

FDR: I'm really smart.

Churchill: Waiter!

FDR: No, listen, dude. I'm really smart and everyone loves me. After we defeat Japan, I'll get all this worked out. I'll make really friendship speeches and stuff… trust me.

Churchill: You're a sick, old man! What if you die?

FDR: Hmmm… gotta admit I hadn't thought about that.

And guess what?

FDR kicked the bucket, and left his Vice President, Harry Truman, holding the bag… and the bomb.

MR. PRESIDENT... WE NEED TO TALK

Narcissist that he was, FDR told his "veep", very little about the Administration's covert operations. Why bother? FDR figured he could keep things ticking by himself. The one thing, however, FDR *couldn't* keep ticking was his heart, and the end result was *President* Harry Truman.

Truman moved into the White House blissfully unaware of what was brewing in the War Department, and one can almost imagine the excitement of the move: Beers in the Rose Garden, big maps in the briefing room, all those cool paintings—maybe even a little nookie in the Lincoln bedroom. You can almost see him in the Oval Office—feet all propped up, big cigar and glass of scotch, congratulatory letters from the world's power brokers... and then... then... then a knock on the door.

> **Military Aide:** Mr. President? You have some decisions to make.
> **Truman:** No problem. I've already decided.
> **Aide:** Sir??!!
> **Truman:** Yup—I'll have the Cornish game hen, mashed potatoes –
> **Aide:** Uh, no, Sir. These are different decisions. Much bigger decisions.
> **Truman:** Okay, heh-heh—drop the bomb on me, Colonel.
> **Aide:** Well, for some reason, President Roosevelt gave away Eastern Europe, and we're pretty sure the commies will turn it into a police state. Next, there's been a secret effort called 'The Manhattan Project' to build an atomic bomb. It can blow up a whole city, and it appears we now have a couple in stock. Third, it looks like we'll have to invade Japan, and it could cost a million American lives, and 10 million Japanese lives.
> **Truman:** Didn't you say something about a decision?
> **Aide:** Yes, Sir—If you drop the atomic bombs on the Japanese, they might surrender. You'd save millions of lives and scare the goosecrap out of the Commies, to boot. But,

of course, you'll have to go to sleep every night knowing you
nuked a city or two full of civilians.
Truman: Whoa...
Aide: What do you think, Sir?
Truman: I think I'd like to swap that Cornish game hen
out for a bottle of scotch.

As we all know, Truman decided to drop the bomb, and historians have been boo-hoo-hooing about it since the instant the bomb
was dropped.

Was it the best option?

Was it the only option?

Would the Japanese have surrendered once the Russians declared war?

Was the Japanese military about to revolt against the emperor?

Was it necessary?

Hey Gang, do the words Kamikaze and hara-kiri mean anything to
you? Pearl Harbor? Bataan Death March? This was a nation of people
whose culture and heritage included "suicide to save face" because they
forgot to send a thank you note after a dinner party. These were *hard*
people—records show that residents of *Hiroshima itself* were *angry* that
the Emperor surrendered.

So was the bomb necessary? Maybe not to some milquetoast historical
nabob sitting in his cushy office passing judgment on the men who make
the hard decisions, but to the simple rifleman (and his family)—the grunt
who was going to invade Japan and have no chance of surviving—to
that guy, Harry Truman was an Angel of Mercy.

As for the Japanese... well, nobody made them sneak attack Pearl
Harbor. No Pearl Harbor, no atom bomb on their cities. I believe the
concept is captured nicely by the idea, "You mess with the bull, you
get the horns."

And from Harry Truman's decision, we learned that the century-old
words of Napoleon were 100% accurate: ***"If you're going to take Vienna,
then TAKE Vienna!"***

CHAPTER SIXTEEN

WHO'S GONNA CLEAN THIS MESS UP?

THE POINT OF a war is to hurt people and break stuff, and WWII stands a solid example of a war's war. Europe looked like the gods came down from Mt. Olympus and launched a two-month tequila bender, complete with Gatling guns and chainsaws. Not only was all the stuff broken, but the stuff that *makes* stuff was broken, too.

It was a mess.

The priority of the average GIs, as we all know, revolved around getting home and getting back to bidness with their special lady friend—the baby boom bears witness to that. The priority of the government, however, was less about soldiers procreating and more about institutionally un-procreating the pathetic decisions made by FDR at Yalta.

Here were the issues:

- Almost immediately, the "Iron Curtain" descended across Europe, and the Commies commenced to rule with torture, murder, and imprisonment.
- The destruction of free Europe's economy and infrastructure added up to such a mess that the concept of a communist group-hug might begin to look appealing to the average Ian,

François, Hans, Zorro, and Guido . (Note: Communism always sounds appealing to the masses when it's explained in theory. When your family is being bulldozed into a mass grave— not so much.)

The U. S. government, in a rare flash of intelligence, actually thought the problem through, and developed a good (albeit expensive) solution. The solution came to be called The Marshall Plan, and it was based on this idea:

- Europe is capitalist, and America is capitalist.
- Europe is so blown up that capitalism may have a very hard time getting jump started again, thus communism may look good. And if Europe becomes communist, who's gonna buy all our manufactured stuff?
- We need to help them back onto their "capitalist feet."

We did so by providing Europe with $12 billion dollars in aid over a four-year period, and this was back when a billion dollars actually bought a more than a Condo in Aspen. In fact, it bought so much stuff that Europe got nicely reestablished, copped their crappy attitude, and failed to say, "thank you." Despite their thankless attitude, we did learn a lesson: You can influence people and governments by getting them addicted to "the good life."

DOES NOT PLAY WELL WITH OTHERS

One group of people the U. S. and allies felt did *not* deserve to be "killed with kindness" was Hitler's cadre of high-ranking officers. Instead, they were tried in Nuremberg, Germany, then regular-old killed. And another easy lesson popped up from the annals of history: If you put a homicidal maniac to sleep, he can't kill ever again.

AMERICA GETS WHAT IT DESERVES

Japan was defeated. Germany was defeated. Italy was defeated. Europe was knocked on its ass. And America—who hadn't asked for any of it—was standing tall, proud as a game rooster. We'd done the right thing—we helped everyone back on their feet. Some historians whine that our decision to help the world recover was self-serving, and that we did it to "spread capitalism." According to that logic, giving away the Polio vaccine to the world was also self-serving because we were trying to "spread shoe sales."

Whatever.

The fact is this: After generations of the average Joe fighting for survival against nature… fighting for freedom against enemies the government fingered… fighting for their families by working sunup to sundown in some crappy factory or on a farm… finally, the average Joe *was getting some deserved payback.*

A good mood spread from sea to shining sea. There was reverence for those who'd fought and died in the war; the economy boomed; America was a Super Power; and everyone knew that the Average American Joe was **the** world's toughest warrior on the battlefield; oh, and everyone was making babies.

Sadly, this is where it all started to unravel.

We the people achieved our high-water mark: Combat tested, hard-working, and proud. This generation provided an example *extraordinary enough* to serve as a role model for many generations to come. But we all know how children act towards the things their parents hold dear.

There is an old saying that describes the next 75 years in America: Hard times make for hard men; hard men make for easy times, easy times make for weak men; weak men make for hard times. And we've gone from D-Day and Iwo Jima to safe spaces and crying rooms at universities.

Pretty sure we've got some hard times coming.

COMMUNISM DOES ITS THING

It doesn't take a Ph.D. in political science to know that the communist doctrine is based on one primary goal: A global revolution where the "workers" overthrow their "bosses," and everyone sits around wondering why everyone's sitting around and not working.

WWII was hardly over when the Soviets made their first attempt at global expansion by blockading the West from re-supplying the free city of Western Berlin. Their argument was that *all* of Berlin was on *their* side of the Iron Curtain, and our game of "Red Rover, Red Rover, send Capitalism Right Over" was mucking up their Utopia. This was, of course, a fairly gutsy move, as the President was still Harry "I used the bomb" Truman.

Truman opted, however, for a non-nuclear solution by airlifting supplies to Berlin, a tactic that caused the Soviets to eventually grow bored and lift the blockade. The airlift was important, however, because it drew a line down the center of the global backseat: *You* stay on your side, and *I'll* stay on mine. NATO was then formed to ensure the Commie brats did just that.

MCCARTHY ARRIVES... JUST A FEW DECADES TOO SOON

In 1950, Senator Joseph McCarthy caught wind of the concept that Americans hated communism. Communism stood for fewer vacations, fewer cars, fewer fluffy couches, less fun, damn it—and we'd just fought a war to defeat... well, to defeat fascism, but all those "isms' are pretty much the same if they don't have the word *capital* in front of them.

Anyway, old Joe perceived that communism was a voter hot button, and decided to howl about it, long and loud. Although most Americans don't realize it, McCarthy's actions resulted in what I have dubbed the "McCarthy Formula," and 50 years later it is the formula by which virtually all our "news" is generated. See how many news stories of recent years fit this formula:

1) A nobody—usually a well-positioned nobody—has an agenda they want to further. In this case, it was McCarthy and communism, but it could be anything.

2) The nobody announces a list of groundless, malicious accusations against the people or company they don't like.

3) The media falls all over themselves printing the accusations, and bragging how they've spoken with an "informed source" or an "investigator close to the case," or "a friend of the accused's mother-in-law's cousin."

4) The nobody is thrilled with all the coverage, and rolls out more accusations and proclamations, usually more groundless than the ones before.

5) The media continues to cover the story, and hides behind their insidious role in the scheme by claiming *the accusations and proclamations are news.* They never stop to consider the idea that the accusations *aren't* news unless the media reports them.

6) The nobody continues to plow forward.

7) The media trails behind, feeding on the scraps.

8) The media coverage provided to the nobody makes the nobody some sort of de facto authority or leader, and thus the nobody becomes somebody, and in a bizarre "who's on first" sort of way the story becomes even more important. (In McCarthy's case, he became the Chairman of the Subcommittee on Governmental Operations, having done nothing but lather and lie about Commies in our midst.)

In our current day and age, the McCarthy formula usually ends here, because some other nobody is shouting new accusations, and the media leaves to go report on them. (Their audience demands breaking news, they explain.) Tail Gunner Joe wasn't so lucky, and his story stayed in the news long enough to be proven a bunch of bull.

These days, of course, that part of the story would run in section Z, page 214, just behind the legal notices, with a headline that reads "McCarthy Allegations Untrue." But in his disgrace, Tail Gunner Joe did give us a lesson about newspapers: Virginia's dad was wrong—just because you read it in the *Times* **doesn't** mean it's true.

AT LEAST TRY TO ACT SURPRISED...

The American people, at this point, still remembered good-old FDR as a wonderful, caring guy—blissfully unaware of the long-term effects of his social welfare state, and how long it would go on. As a result, no one wanted to defile his memory or embarrass Eleanor (Bless her heart), so everyone agreed to act surprised when the Communist government of North Korea invaded democratic South Korea at 0400 on June 25, 1950.

Let me digress to an analogy, which some folks do not like because it insinuates that humans are base and predictable, which is precisely why I like it:

> A fox comes to a river, and prepares to swim across it. Before entering the water, a scorpion crawls up and asks if he might catch a ride on the fox's back; scorpions, he explains, cannot swim.
>
> "Do you think I'm a fool?" the fox replies. "You might sting me enroute, and I would grow weak and drown."
>
> "Then I would drown, too," the scorpion explained. "That doesn't make much sense does it?"
>
> The fox reflects for a moment, then agrees to give him a ride. Halfway across the river, the scorpion stings the fox, and immediately the poison goes to work. The fox knows he is done for, but does not want to die without understanding his folly.
>
> "Why?" he asks, unable to go any further. "Now we both will die."
>
> "I am sorry," said the scorpion, as the water sucked them under. "But I could not help it. I am a scorpion, and it is my nature."

Let's face it: When you have a militaristic dictatorship using the Communist Manifesto as a road map, it's *not* difficult to understand where the train is headed.

WE DON'T NEED NO STINKIN' MILITARY

At this time in America's history, some strange mechanics began to unfold. It went roughly something like this, with my own theories injected:

a) America had won the Big One just a few years earlier.

b) Although we'd won it through the tenacity and courage of the American fighting man, the Atomic Bomb stole much of the glory. Americans felt "We got the bomb, and we'll use it—so everybody *back off.*"

c) The President and Congress capitalized this feeling of security to dismantle the world's greatest fighting machine, then used that available money to send home the pork to ensure they'd get elected again.

d) To further foster the feelings of public security, the Army Air Corps became the United States Air Force, who remained on-call around the clock to drop atomic bombs from B-29s.

THE CATCH 22...

The American people didn't have the bomb, and *Congress* didn't have the bomb. The *American military* didn't have the bomb. Harry S. Truman *alone* had the bomb. And because Harry dropped the bomb before, he alone had to lie awake at night pondering the ramifications of the Big Bang II. This likely caused him to toss and turn a bit, because Harry wasn't a career soldier, and thus didn't have the defense mechanisms in place to block that guilt from his mind.

And in my (insightful, brilliant) opinion, that key fact unlocks a vault of explanations: Truman felt guilty about nuking Japan, and—although he never said so—had no intention of nuking anyone else. Thus, he didn't nuke the North Koreans who attacked South Korea. And the unused nuke is the reason we didn't have a military in place anymore to respond quickly. To a military man, this would be a classic SNAFU (Situation Normal All "Fouled" Up).

WHO YA GONNA CALL?

The United State had, literally, a handful of military men in Korea when the Commies came south.

> **Lieutenant:** Uh, Sir? I think that's a division of Commies coming our way.
> **Colonel:** Yup, right on schedule.
> **Lieutenant:** What should I do, Sir?
> **Colonel:** Our orders are that we try our best to look surprised.

The Communist Forces plowed through the barely-defended South Korea like Hillary Clinton through special investigations. The advance continued towards the southern port of Pusan and disaster appeared possible—until the 1ˢᵗ Provisional Marine Brigade sailed into town, deployed, and stopped the advance in its tracks.

With a Pusan perimeter now established, and neither side making any progress, something had to be done. General MacArthur decided to attempt a nearly impossible maneuver by landing an amphibious force at Inchon—behind the enemy's lines—then attacking them from their rear.

He gave the job to the Marines, who made it look easy. By October, the Communists were repulsed from South Korea, the capital of Seoul had been recaptured, and things were looking good.

COMBAT... MEET THE GROUP HUG

From here—for the first time ever—the United States military machine went absolutely upside down. But not for the reasons you'd think. You see, the American military had a formula down pat for winning wars. It was a formula they'd been perfecting since 1775—a formula that had won, well, *every* war they'd ever fought in. It was this: *Break things and kill people until the other guy gives up.*

That's it.

And it *worked.*

Every time.

After the war was won, you'd provide a courtesy heads up to the President and Congress that their approval ratings were about to go up, but that was about all the role politics played.

Korea, however, was different.

First of all, it became a U. N. operation, and every nation with a Boy Scout troop glommed on to show how tough they were. Shortly thereafter, the place was filled with men armed to the teeth, none of whom could speak the language:

> **U. N. Soldier**: Resnik mach fein der omelette por la vrik en du nos a la jeheen ole! *(You go ahead, and we'll cower back here in a group hug!)*
> **U. S. Lieutenant**: What the hell did he say?
> **U. S. Sergeant**: I think he said, 'You go ahead, and we'll provide covering artillery fire!
> **U. S. Lieutenant**: Cool. Men! Fix Bayonets!

As any moron can figure out, the American fighting man counts on support from his fellow American fighting man, and the 24th French Croissant & Merlot Battalion just doesn't quite measure up to American standards (unless, of course, the French Battalion is there to fix brunch). The resulting "partnership" is not good, as Americans were crippled by their allies' inability to keep up with the pace of the plan. Let's call this interesting little factoid problem number one.

The second problem, I believe, came back to the bomb.

The President, for the first time ever, had a weapon that only *he* could fire—He alone called the shots on that bad boy. Somehow, however, Truman came to feel that he called the shots at other times, too, and the advanced communications of the 1950s enabled him to voice his opinion (orders) to the commanders on the scene. This became a *huge* issue, as the Chinese entered the war shortly after the North Koreans had been beaten back, and Truman created extensive "rules of engagement" about fighting the Chinese.

The insanity of it was breathtaking. Think of it like this: Your child—your own flesh and blood—is out in the front yard in a fight with the neighborhood bully, and teaching the guy a long-overdue lesson. In fact, he's beating the tar out of him. Suddenly, a pickup truck full of the bully's cousins pulls up, they jump out, and start stomping your kid.

Do you worry about getting involved? Do you ponder the fact that the gang may throw rocks through your window that night after you intervene? Do you fret that their Dad might beat you up for getting involved?

Hopefully not. Your child is being ganged up on by a bunch of bullies who shouldn't be involved, so you get out there and start stomping some bully-butt.

Truman, however, fretted about the bully.

The Chinese were pouring across the Yalu River with the express purpose of killing Americans, then did so—by the hundreds of thousands. In response, did we bomb their bridges? Did we bomb their supply lines? Did we bomb their homeland? No, *we did not want to confront them directly, for fear of angering the Soviet Union.* Say what? Come again? Confront them directly? What are *they* doing? Sending us mean tweets with a 'smiley face' at the end? If you're *not* going to *fight* the bully's cousins, for God's sake at least go get your kid, and bring him up on the porch, and get him away from the fight that you're afraid to participate in!

Somehow, this line of reasoning failed to occur to Truman. Somehow, it did not dawn on him that American doctrine since day one entailed providing every available resource to our fighting men. Somehow, it did not occur to him that if a war is worth *fighting*, it's worth fighting *viciously*. And this from the man who had the moral courage to save millions of Americans (and Japanese) by dropping the Big One.

It is a puzzle that will be pondered forever.

LET'S NOT GET ALL DEPRESSED, HERE...

Although the Korean War was not destined to provide a victory on par with WWII, it did prove one thing for damn sure: We still got it. The soldiers, sailors, airmen, and Marines were nothing less than glorious, and fought with courage and distinction befitting of the uniforms they wore.

The conditions were as brutal as any our military had ever faced, yet our men fought with valor, often with feet so frostbitten they would never again support their owner properly. One obvious example of their courage was demonstrated by the 1st Marine Division, who fought a Chinese force twice their size as they moved from the Chosin Reservoir to the sea. Despite sub-zero temperatures, despite being massively outgunned, outnumbered, and surrounded, despite horrendous casualties—they crushed the Chinese aggressors, and left behind not a single Marine, and not a single usable piece of equipment. In short, our nation's warriors served with all the distinction of their World War II predecessors… but without the nationwide support and adoration for their efforts.

Did they win? Lose? Tie?

Let's look at the body count.

North Koreans & Chinese—1.5 to 2 million dead.

Allied Forces—88,000 dead.

You decide what column it goes in.

WHEN 1 + 1 DOESN'T EQUAL 2

To a simple guy like me, those numbers make clear who won the Frozen Foray into Korea. But old math no longer applied to combat, because of the rules of combat mathematics underwent a massive overhaul when FDR gave away the farm. The math before the Korean War went like this:

$$\begin{array}{r} \text{Army of Goodguys} \\ + \quad \text{Army of Badguys} \\ \hline \text{WAR} \end{array}$$

$$\text{War} \times \text{Battles} \div \text{Casualties} = \text{Victories}$$

$$\begin{array}{r} \text{Lack of Victories} \\ \text{Lack of Resources} \\ \text{Losing Army} \\ + \quad \text{Angry Public Back at Home} \\ \hline \text{Demands to End War} \end{array}$$

$$\begin{array}{r} \text{Demands to End War} \\ - \quad \text{Waning Resources} \\ \hline \text{Surrender} \end{array}$$

The Korean War mathematics, however, took a turn for the strange, and resulted in mathematics becoming a liberal art:

$$\begin{array}{r} \text{Communist Dictatorship} \\ + \quad \text{Communist Doctrine} \\ \hline \text{Communist Expansion} \end{array}$$

$$\frac{\text{Communist Expansion}}{\text{Nation Next Door}} = \begin{array}{r} \text{Unprovoked Attack} \\ \text{Bordering Nation} \\ \text{Cries for Help} \\ \hline \text{U.S. Intervention} \end{array}$$

$$\frac{\text{U.S. Intervention}}{\text{Politics}} = \frac{X \text{ [Rules of Engagement]}}{Y \text{ [Presidential Involvement]}}$$

$$\begin{array}{l} \text{U. S. Military} \\ \text{U. S. President} \\ + \ \underline{\text{Rules of Engagement}} \\ \text{Ineffective Tactics} \end{array} \qquad \begin{array}{l} + \ \underline{\text{Calling Military Shots}} \\ \text{Ineffective Strategy} \end{array}$$

$$\begin{array}{l} \text{Bad Strategy} \\ + \ \underline{\text{Bad Tactics}} \\ \text{No Way to Win War,} \\ \text{Despite Winning Every Battle} \end{array}$$

As an added problem, there was "Red's Law of Combat Numbers," which stated:

$$\begin{array}{l} \text{Communist Philosophy} \\ \text{Ruthless Homicidal Leader} \\ \text{Poor, Uneducated Populace} \\ \underline{\text{Complete Martial Law}} \\ \text{Endless Numbers of "Volunteers" to} \\ \text{Fight for the Cause} \end{array}$$

As one can see, the new mathematics no longer results in an equation where the basic rules of math and political science apply. The result is an unacceptable outcome.

BUT, BUT, BUT—WE ALWAYS WIN...

The Korean War ended where it started: At the 38th Parallel, with pissed off commies to the north, and pissed off free men to the south. Nothing was gained, the borders were unchanged, and a lot of people got dead.

The question now is, "Was the Korean War Winnable?"

Yes.

Virtually any war is winnable, if you're willing to go all the way to win it.

Let's analyze the situation confronting the U. S. and the Allied Forces:

1) The North Korean population lived as virtual slaves. Ruled by a dictator, they had no access to any information other that what he provided. If he told them, "The round eyes are invading to rape Korean babies," the North Koreans had no counterpoint to consider.

2) The North Koreans' opinion about the war or serving in the military did not matter. (*Don't want to serve? Here, we'll murder your family and see if that improves your attitude.*)

3) The Chinese Communists supported The North Korean cause, and sent men and arms across the Yalu River to join in the fight.

4) The Soviet Communists supported the idea of global communism, and now possessed the atomic bomb. At any point, escalating the war could result in the Soviets jumping in, and nuking some cities in the old US of A.

I think that just about any historian will support these facts. Now one must ask "What could you do in order to win a war with these facts surrounding it?

Well, if you accept the assumption that the North Korean and Chinese troops had no choice or free will in the issue (serve and fight, or face execution), the traditional war method of killing lots of enemy soldiers couldn't work. The communists could always send more unwilling fighters, and with the Chinese involved that means a *lot* more.

So could it be done?

A) *Cut off the enemy from their leadership*—This would involve vicious, ongoing aerial attacks on the cities where the North Korean leaders were holed up drinking their Russian vodka and smoking their Chinese opium. The bombing would stop when:
   • Everyone was dead
   • The War was over

- The commie leaders started sharing their vodka and opium.

B) *Cut off the enemy from their re-supply*—This would start with blowing up every bridge across the Yalu River, then blowing up every staging point in Manchuria. If the Chinese kept coming, the bombing would continue into China and stair-step its way until the last bomb landed on Mao Tse Tung himself.

C) *Strap on a sack and stand tall*—This tactic would involve announcing to the Soviets that "this is none of your concern, and if you get involved you will die, too... nukes, or no nukes."

WELL, THAT DOESN'T SOUND NICE

Granted, the plan outlined above is messy. A lot of civilians, pilots, and approval ratings would get dead. But that, dear friend, this is how the game is played. And if you are not willing to do what is necessary to win, then how dare you send our fighting men into harm's way? To a man in a foxhole, there is no such thing as an "acceptable level of casualties" if the potential for victory doesn't even exist.

And in Korea, that was the case.

So, what did we learn?

First, fighting one Communist Regime means potential war with another. Second, some wars cannot be won unless we are willing to fight with a very un-good-guy like viciousness. And third, before committing to a gunfight involving American troops on the ground, there must be a plan for ultimate, military victory.

RECAP TIME

Once again, it's time for our dreaded analysis of "lessons we should have learned." Am I the only one who thinks that history is a good tutor? That perhaps we should consider the pain and suffering of those who stepped into the hornets' nests so long ago? Maybe this batch will convince you:

Lesson: If bankers and stockbrokers are giddy, something's amiss.

Lesson: What goes up must come down.

Lesson: Federal Programs should be required to have a termination date.

Lesson: Other countries do not apply rules of "fair play" when it comes to war.

Lesson: By pulling together, Americans can accomplish anything.

Lesson: If you are going to take Vienna, then take Vienna.

Lesson: You can influence people by getting them addicted to the good life.

Lesson: If you put a homicidal maniac to sleep, he can't kill ever again.

Lesson: Virginia's dad was wrong—just because you read it in the Times doesn't mean it's true.

Lesson: Fighting one communist regime means a potential war with another. This lesson also has a corollary, which states the same holds true for fighting Muslim regimes.

Lesson: Some wars cannot be won unless we are willing to fight them with a very un-good-guy-like viciousness.

Lesson: Before committing to a gunfight, there should be a plan for ultimate victory.

CHAPTER SEVENTEEN

RITCHIE, FONZIE... LEROY—

FOR MUCH OF America, the decade following the Korean War was the American Dream. The economy grew, folks worked hard, the suburbs flourished, and the daily challenges inspired enlightened, brilliant conversation:

> **Mike**: I sure like life here in the suburbs.
> **Joe**: Yup.
> **Mike**: Hear we might get rain.
> **Joe**: Yup.
> **Mike**: That'd help the lawn—get a little grass growin'.
> **Joe**: Yup.
> **Mike**: You get a new lawnmower?
> **Joe**: Yup.
> Mike: It one of them new John Deere's?
> **Joe**: Yup.
> **Mike**: Think I oughtta get one?
> **Joe**: Yup.
> **Mike**: I'm ready for a beer. You ready?
> **Joe**: Yup.

It was, indeed, the best of times for some… and the worst of times for others.

Why? Because as the white community thrived, most of the black community struggled—struggled against a system that would not let them get ahead.

This was nothing new, of course—treating black Americans poorly served as a de facto standard since the day they were brought to America in chains. Their treatment, however, felt comfortably invisible to white America, as blacks moved through life utilizing facilities that were supposedly "separate but equal." Separate but equal felt good, because they were equal, but enjoyed their equality in… well, *separate* facilities. (It is, indeed, difficult to have a lunch meeting with a potential client when you're not allowed to eat in the same restaurant.) Their treatment nationwide was inexcusable, but their treatment in the South was particularly bad, because in the South the treatment was encouraged and protected by law.

The nation took its first baby-step forward in addressing race relations with a Supreme Court ruling in the case *Brown vs. Board of Education of Topeka, Kansas*. Argued before the court by later-Justice Thurgood Marshall, the case proved that segregated facilities were, by definition, **un**-equal. The ruling meant integration for schools, a decision that did not sit well with white trash.

Interestingly, the first big step forward in the Civil Rights movement—the step that launched a thousand marches—was taken by a mild-mannered, working-class woman, Ms. Rosa Parks. Uncontrolled by any organization, Ms. Parks took a seat at the front of a Montgomery, Alabama bus after putting in a full day's work. Sadly, it was illegal for a black to sit in the front section of a bus, and Ms. Parks was told to move. She said, "I'm-a-person-too-and-I'm-not-moving," and the cops applied the handcuffs.

It was the arrest heard 'round the nation, and caused blacks to boycott the city's bus system. Suddenly, America's "ugly little situation" could no longer be ignored.

A LEADER EMERGES

The boycott of the Montgomery bus system caused some ugly responses. Much of the less-educated and rural white population of the South felt angry and indignant, as they felt the blacks were treated "pretty well." This feeling, of course, was based on the concept that they'd "always been treated this way, and didn't complain before."

Times, as Mister Dylan wrote, were a-changin'.

The Rev. Martin Luther King, Jr., Ph.D., emerged as the leader to guide the African-American populace through the potentially dangerous times of the boycott. King devised a brilliant concept for advancing the cause, despite the tightrope of challenges confronting the black population. I believe he arrived at his plan through logic something like this:

- The natural, human response to oppression is violence. Violence, however, will not work for our cause, because:
  - a) We cannot win an intellectual argument through un-intellectual actions.
  - b) It would give bigots another reason to distrust blacks.
  - c) Once started, it may never end.
- The Christian response to oppression, however, is forgiveness, and peaceful resistance. This *will* work for our cause, because:
  - a) It will show us as compassionate, moral humans to those who observe our actions.
  - b) It will provide a shocking backdrop to the unprovoked violence we will encounter.
  - c) Once started, it has the potential to draw other compassionate humans to our cause.

Voila. King created a way to show the injustice being done to our nation's black citizens *without* violent revolution, *without* bringing the blacks down to the bigots' level, and *without* frightening the "undecided" population into thinking that someday they might be subject to black violence. From the very beginning, King was destined to prove his point.

THE WINDS OF CHANGE

With the recent wars in the past, and the Civil Rights Movement show-
ing promise, and white America feeling good about life in general,
American politics took a swing to the left. Enter John F. Kennedy, Jr.,
the young, dashing, bright, good-looking, sexy, war hero son of Satan
himself, Joseph Kennedy. JFK was perfectly packaged for the times,
and with funding from his dear old dad, offered a hopeful, idealistic
alternative to the stoic old WASPs who'd been running the show since
George Washington. Jack showed his stuff exceptionally well during a
debate with Republican candidate Richard Nixon that was "broadcast"
on a kinda-newfangled contraption called television. Although most
historians who *read* the transcripts of the debate considered Nixon the
winner, the American people—for the first time—got to *see* the candidates
in person. JFK's combination of good looks, just-back-from-the-
regatta-haircut, and concerned, caring expressions won them over; lock,
stock, and lower-lip-bite.

JFK's election produced America's youngest president ever—age
43—in 1960.

DON'T GET ME STARTED

The baggage that JFK, the Kennedy family, and his father, Joe, brought
with them to the White House required the National Guard to unload.
Quite frankly, the old growth forests of the Pacific Northwest would
require logging to generate the paper needed just to draft an outline.

Fortunately, you and I aren't bothered with such facts when we read
the history of JFK's days as president. After all, who really wants to know
that JFK didn't write a word of *Profiles in Courage*, the book that won
him a Pulitzer Prize? Not you and me! We want to read gushing prose
about the "magic of Camelot," and the "dignified beauty of Jackie,"
and… and… sorry, I just need to stop for a bit and have a good cry.

THE POWER OF WORDS

Love him or hate him, JFK could do one thing like nobody else: hire a great speechwriter. His inaugural address ranks way up there for inspirational prose, and has stirred the passions of Americans ever since:

> "Let the word go forth from this time and place, to friend and foe alike, that the torch has been passed to a new generation of Americans…"

Oddly enough, this is when the wheels came off.

CURLEY, MOE, AND FOREIGN POLICY

When the Russians launched a silly little satellite called *Sputnik* into space in 1957, Americans kicked into Chicken Little overdrive. We were space racing, digging bomb shelters, overhauling our education system, and generally worrying ourselves silly about the Red Menace. So instead of worrying about communism, the CIA and JFK launched a plan to do something about it—and pulled it off with all the precision and brilliance of Dr. Jethro Bodine in brain surgery.

The setting: The Oval Office, after 14 martinis and a handful of Cuban cigars.

> **JFK**: Can you believe those damn commies? They got Cuba, damnit. Cuba! I *like* Cuba. Damn good cigars, damnit.
> **CIA Director**: Wouldn't it be cool if we could, like, do a revolution to **un**-revolution Castro's revolution?
> **JFK**: Who says we can't? Dude, I'm President.
> **CIA Director**: Hey, why don't we get a group of pissed-off exiles, get 'em all trained up like ninjas or something—then, you know, invade!
> **JFK**: Yeah, invade! What do ya need? Navy? Marines? Fighter jets?

CIA Director: Naaaah! We like to be all triple secret and stuff; we'll put it together, and then call if we need something.

The plan came together like something out of an Ed Woods film.

On April 17, 1961, the CIA dumped 1,400 clueless Cuban exiles on the beaches of the Bay of Pigs with the instructions, "Go in there and shoot your guns, and get all the people likin' you and stuff, then, then... you know, get everybody to be on your side and overthrow Castro!"

Things took a turn for the bad very early on when the CIA discovered that the Bay of Pigs, which was supposed to be deserted, wasn't. In fact, an entire beach resort—complete with a new home for Castro himself—was under construction. Shortly after the invading force arrived, Castro had several thousand troops inbound. The CIA wasn't foiled yet, however—they had an ace in the hole!

The Setting: The Oval Office. The phone rings.

Ring. Ring. Ring.

JFK: Ohhh, yeah, Marilyn... ohhhh, that's it... *Ring. Ring. Rin –*

JFK: What, damnit!

CIA Field Operative: Mr. President! *The raven is in the nest.*

JFK: Huh?

Operative: *The raven is in the nest.*

JFK: Teddy? Quite screwin' around; I'm busy.

Operative: Sir! It's Momma Bear! *The raven... is in... the damn nest!*

JFK: Eunice? Are you drunk again?

Operative: Oh, for the love of—this is Momma frickin' Bear—we're invading Cuba, and the invading force is on the beach, and—Holy Moses, Mr. President, does this sound familiar?

JFK: Oh, yeah! Man, I love all this codeword stuff! How's it going?

Operative: Bad. We forgot to plan for what to do if our 1,400 untrained guys encounter several thousand trained troops.

JFK: Bummer.

Operative: It's okay, Sir. We've got a bunch of Navy ships just offshore, and fighter planes in the air. We'll just blow the Cuban forces to pieces! All we need is your permission to fire.

JFK: Hmmm, let me think. Gotta think—damn these painkillers make me foggy. Think! Okay... when Truman was in this situation in Korea, he was worried that bombing the Chinks might piss off the Russians, so bombing the Cubans might piss off the Russians, too. Gotta learn from history, that's my motto. So... the answer is no.

Operative: But Sir, we put them on the beach!

JFK: Nope. Don't wanna be perceived as being aggressive.

Operative: Aggressive? We gave them guns and grenades! We dropped them off! Our friggin ships are practically in plain view!

(Click) Hello? Hello?

The Bay of Pigs, of course, was a complete SNAFU. The entire invading force was captured, then ransomed back to the U. S. for 53 million bucks in food and medicine. Kennedy's first 100 days in office made Bill Clinton's first 100 days seem like a non-stop honeymoon. And we learned a lesson, which is: When you learn a lesson from history, make sure you learn the obvious.

A MAGICAL DO-OVER

As Hitler learned after picking a fight with the USA, history doesn't give do-overs. Once you've blown it, that cat known as "consequences" is out of the bag and looking for a cashmere sweater to pee on. And Kennedy had blown it hard. The homicidal maniac running the Soviet Union at that point was Nikita Khrushchev, and he perceived two things:

1) JFK was an Ivy League wuss-boy.
2) Cuba was a nifty, safe launching pad for atomic missiles.

The Russkies shipped in some missiles, set up some launching sites, and settled in for a few vodka margaritas. Legend has it that their presence was discovered when some American spy planes noted something funny on the ground—namely soccer fields. Cubans didn't yet play soccer, so the analyst made the assumption that there were some palefaces prowling around the island. Further inspections found the missile sites, and the president was notified.

And JFK got one of those very, very rare do-overs.

Acting very un-politician-like, JFK stepped up to the plate and became, well, a leader. He announced to the world that, nuclear war or no nuclear war, the Soviets had to get the hell out of Cuba. To back up his demand, he ordered the U. S. Navy to enforce a total blockade of Cuba, and prepped the military for a full-blown amphibious invasion.

Khrushchev sweated… and sweated… and sweated… and then… he blinked.

Khrushchev ordered the missiles removed, and got busy building a massive Soviet navy to make damn sure he'd be ready for "next time."

JFK was once again da' man.

AND IN THIS CORNER…

It was about this time that a strange pair of competitors squared off in the global ring, in a bout that would come to be known as the Cold War.

It was the Capitalist Free World versus the Communist Soviet Union. Our way versus their way. Freedom versus Bondage. The individual versus the state.

The stakes, of course, were high—namely, life on the planet earth. And for the next 30 years, the two heavyweight contenders stood toe-to-toe with sweat pouring down their faces, ready to deliver a death blow if the other guy so much as cocked back.

As we know, the Free World won.

And not with a knockout punch, but a kiss.

In reality, *they* should have won. After all, their fight was controlled by a handful of mouth-breathing, psychopathic dictators. They weren't burdened with things like elections, and free press, and an exchange of opposing ideas. Their people were nothing more than body-baggage, waiting to fill their place in destiny. Their leaders enjoyed taxation without representation.

And yet, we won.

How?

Because stealing around the globe at the same time as the Cold War was the concept of the American Dream. The concept that it *is possible* to have a nation where all citizens can vote. A nation where every generation can pass along more to their children. And this idea, for some reason, moves more easily than fear and hate. The *war* may have been strangely absent from Saigon in the years ahead, but Jesus Christ, Coca Cola, and Carrier air conditioning were not.

Consider the proverbial parable: Give a man a fish, and you feed him for a day. Teach a man to fish, and you feed him for life. Show a man an EZ Boy Recliner, TV, and a pizza, and he'll fish his ass off earning the dough to buy them. And *that*, is what changed the world, and ended the Cold War. Not politicians. Not speeches. Not treaties. Not news coverage. Not the hippies or Hanoi Jane. Not even threats and violence.

It was the Big Mac… Rock 'n' Roll music… Blue Jeans… Pantyhose… Canned beer … the Frisbee… T-shirts with logos on them… and Mickey Mouse. We made it, and the world wanted it—everyone! Even the Commie dictators. And a nuclear war would have screwed up the party, so it never came about.

I HAVE A DREAM…

The Civil Rights Movement played an important role in the events, and realities, of America in the 1960s. The treatment our black citizens suffered while seeking simple equality *should* be taught in our history classes—not as a mechanism to open old wounds, but to serve as a backdrop to what can be achieved, despite overwhelming odds.

In August 1963, Martin Luther King gave a speech that ranks in the top five ever given in this nation of free speech. His words, although not yet realized, give us something to strive for:

> *I say to you today, my friends, that in spite of the difficulties and frustrations of the moment I still have a dream. It is a dream deeply rooted in the American dream.*
>
> *I have a dream that one day this nation will rise up and live the true meaning of its creed: "We hold these truths to be self-evident; that all men are created equal."*
>
> *I have a dream that one day on the red hills of Georgia the sons of former slaves and the sons of former slaveowners will be able to sit down together at the table of brotherhood. I have a dream that one day even the state of Mississippi, a desert state sweltering with the heat of injustice and oppression, will be transformed into an oasis of freedom and justice. I have a dream that my four children will one day live in a nation where they will not be judged by the color of their skin but by the content of their character. I have a dream today. I have a dream that one day the state of Alabama, whose governor's lips are presently dripping with the words of interposition and nullification, will be transformed into a situation where little black boys and black girls will be able to join hands with little white boys and white girls and walk together as sisters and brothers. I have a dream today....*

ELVIS DID IT...

On November 22nd, 1963, John F. Kennedy was assassinated while riding in a presidential motorcade through Dallas, Texas.

Who did it? Castro? The Mafia? Lyndon Johnson and the CIA? Elvis?

I have done a fair amount of reading on the subject, and of this I am certain:

Lee Harvey Oswald fired at least one shot.

CONSPIRACY FODDER FOR YEARS TO COME

Lee Harvey Oswald, who could only be described as one really, really, really weird cat, was arrested later that day. For two days Oswald was interrogated, but denied everything. When he was being transferred between jails, however, some guy named Jack Ruby stepped out from the crowd and shot him at point-blank range, then made no attempt to escape.

Why? Ruby said he felt sorry for Jackie and was mad. If you read about Jack Ruby, you'll find he spent most days mad at everything and everybody, and always carried a gun in case someone made him super-duper-uper mad. I guess Oswald did.

TV NEWS IS BORN

In the wake of JFK's assassination, America experienced one of the most profound social changes it would ever know: Television news discovered itself, came to recognize its power, and liked what it found.

For days, the networks went live, offering up every scrap of unsubstantiated news they could find. The funeral was covered in agonizing detail, with camera work orchestrated like a motion picture drama. All the while, commentators told us how the First Family felt... how the world felt... and how America felt.

And Americans ate it up.

No reading the paper, then thinking through the details. No introspection or conversation. No long confusing explanations filled with "boring" facts and information. No, it was a pure emotion buffet, served up piping hot and spoon fed to Americans in their living rooms.

And what did TV learn about itself? That a *story* isn't what people want—*feelings* and *emotion* are what they want. And with this knowledge, they came to understand that power is not about slanting facts in a story, it's about building a story around an emotion.

Why? Because people don't act on facts, they act on feelings. And if you can show and tell someone how to *feel* on a topic, well, then you're not covering *news;* you're shaping opinion, and inspiring the very actions of the American people. Sadly, you are in charge.

THINGS FALL APART

JFK's assassination was something akin to the murder of Santa Claus. In short, what do all the elves do now?

JFK represented the Santa of the era's warm, gooey, group-hug atmosphere, and—poof—he was gone. Things fell apart. The first problem—Santa's replacement, the Grinch himself, V. P. Lyndon Baines Johnson. Having been chosen by JFK to deliver Southern votes, LBJ was the Al Gore to JFK's Bill Clinton.

Johnson did, to his credit, push forward with some of the issues dear to JFK, and led the passing of the Civil Rights Act of 1964, followed by the Voting Rights Act, followed by the creation of a number of social programs like the Job Corps and Project Head Start. The U. S. finally declared, in law, that our black citizens were human beings, and deserved to be treated as such. As a result of these accomplishments, we mostly skip over the fact the LBJ was a bone-deep racist.

Unfortunately, Johnson's crowning achievement was the development of the welfare system we still provide today, which is designed in an insidious way to trap the poor in a never-ending cycle of poverty by providing them with financial scraps and food stamps… which ensures they will vote Democrat out of fear the scraps will cease coming. LBJ knew exactly what he was doing, and it was his devious plan that, 60 years later, still has millions of Americans imprisoned by generational poverty.

It was meant to do exactly that, and LBJ should be having daily workout sessions with Satan for the damage he did to America.

WOULDN'T IT BE EASIER TO JUST BRIBE THE VOTERS?

Lyndon Johnson was running for re-election against Barry Goldwater, who claimed Johnson wasn't tough on communism—tough like himself, one supposes. Johnson thus needed to show his toughness, and 'carpe-ed his diem' when an "incident" occurred in the Gulf of Tonkin, halfway around the world, in a country no American had ever heard of. Here's the Reader's Digest version:

The U. S. was advising a democratic country called South Vietnam on how to avoid being overrun by their communist neighbor, North Vietnam. In fact, the U. S. had 15,000 advisors in-country, which seems like a lot of folks to teach marksmanship, hand-to-hand combat, and camouflage 101. We also had, it seems, a Navy destroyer full of advisors, operating 10 miles off the coast of North Vietnam, in the Gulf of Tonkin, well within North Vietnamese waters. (They had to be close in case they needed to dispense advice quickly, I suppose.) The North Vietnamese didn't want any advice, and sent three patrol boats out to let the advisors on the destroyer know as much. For their troubles, the destroyer blew them up.

President Johnson seized the opportunity to react to the North Vietnamese "aggression", an idea not unlike suing your neighbor when *your* Pit bull chokes while eating *their* kid. This time, Johnson sent two destroyers into the Gulf of Tonkin, which resulted in the destroyers firing on some "suspicious radar blips." Johnson decided those "blips" equaled "further attacks," and launched air strikes into North Vietnam. (Now you're not only suing your neighbor, you're sledge-hammering his wife in the forehead.)

Johnson whipped Congress into a frenzy, and convinced them to pass the Gulf of Tonkin Resolution which said:

Dear Mr. President,

You're in charge, no questions asked.
    If you need anything, we'll be curled up in a cowardly fetal position, here feeling important and entitled.

Love, Congress.

LBJ now had the tough guy image he needed to get reelected, and the power to do whatever he wanted in Vietnam.

THE VIOLENCE BEGINS

The coming war in Vietnam would not be America's only taste of violence in the sixties... as I said earlier, the entire nation was going insane. JFK was assassinated... then an NAACP leader named Medgar Evers was murdered... then a church in Birmingham was blown up... then three civil rights workers in Mississippi were murdered—it was White on Black, Black on Black, White on White, Black on White—it was madness. Amidst the violence, a new variety of black leadership evolved, claiming that Martin Luther King's nice-guy approach to be a losing proposition, and declaring it was time to fight with violence.

The fight-back concept erupted first in a Los Angeles suburb named Watts in 1965, when White policemen arrested a young Black man for suspicion of driving under the influence. A crowd gathered, bottles flew, and a riot erupted. The riot segued into a battle, which raged for days. When it was over, Watts lay in ruins. Some theorize that this was the beginning of the end of Martin Luther King's role as the leading spokesman for the Civil Rights Movement. When King toured the devastated area, residents taunted him. Many Blacks of the era viewed Watts as some sort of "victory," which spawned riots in other urban areas in years to come. Blacks and Whites moved farther apart, and racial tension and distrust became even more poignant. What tens of thousands of Black and White Civil Rights workers managed to achieve in previous years, a handful of people undid in a matter of months—and King's brilliant plans of peaceful integration fell apart.

ARE YOU LESS DEAD IF IT'S CALLED A CONFLICT?

The War in Vietnam remains one of the great riddles of American history. Almost nothing about it made sense. Virtually every lesson learned about "big-blue-arrow" strategy was violated, while American boys found themselves shipped overseas by the tens of thousands. The enemy lurked everywhere, as hundreds of thousands of South Vietnamese fought American troops as Viet Cong—some by choice, and some who were kidnapped by active-duty Cong and told "Fight, or we'll slaughter your entire family."

On dozens of levels, American policy prevented the winning of the war: Rules of Engagement, Rules of Pursuit, Rules of Conduct, Rules for Creating New Rules. North Vietnamese Army troops enjoyed the ability to fight, then run away to places like Laos and Cambodia, which were off-limits for American action. Locals often refused to help the effort, as to aid the Americans offered a sure-fire way to get hacked to pieces by a Viet Cong machete as soon as the Americans moved on to the next village.

For the most part, the American troops on the ground had no desire to be there. Unlike the volunteers who normally filled the ranks, most of these troops were drafted, and were well-aware that rich kids were able to avoid service by going to college. The result added up to somewhat "less than ideal" morale.

Speaking of morale, suffice it to say that none of the warriors waist-deep in a booby-trapped rice paddy felt particularly uplifted by the so-called "hippies" back in the states. The hippies, no doubt, enjoyed their time doing drugs and having sex and calling veterans "baby killers," but it didn't make for a happy mood over in the jungle.

YOU'RE NOT ALONE

If you're like most Americans, the war in Vietnam makes about as much sense as Meghan Fox's choice of Machine Gun Kelly as a boyfriend. You understand, perhaps, a couple of words like "Tet Offensive" and "napalm," but that's about it. Oh, and you know that we lost.

"Vietnam," most Americans say at a cocktail party, "what a waste."

"Just no way we could win it... "

"Yup, no way... "

"Tet offensive."

"Napalm."

"What a waste."

It's okay, friend, you're not alone. The reason you know so little is because explaining our actions, tactics, and strategy is somewhat like explaining Chaos theory: The one sentence description sounds cool, but before long the mathematics become so complex that you're confused, depressed, and hoping the explainer will hurry up and say Tet offensive.

"Ah, yes—Tet offensive."

I am going to give you a short primer on the war, in hopes it will shed some light on an otherwise mysterious subject. Take note that I have italicized words you may want to use during cocktail conversation.

Domino Theory: This is the theory that one's time is far better spent playing dominoes than screwing around in Southeast Asian politics.

Advisors: These were American fighting men who shot the enemy prior to the arrival of network news teams.

Vietcong (or V. C.): These guys were a never-ending pain-in-the-ass for our military, as they were a ruthless, civilian-resistance organization. Post-war analysis revealed that only two South Vietnamese citizens did not have Vietcong ties: A librarian at Saigon Central Library, and that guy in *"Apocalypse, Now"* who said, "terminate with extreme prejudice."

NVA: This was the North Vietnamese Army. They spent 0.4% of the war shooting at Americans, and 99.6% of the war cowering in Laos and Cambodia, where we could not shoot at them. America's fighting men never lost a battle to the NVA.

Gooks: For some reason, the enemy in Vietnam needed more than the usual one nickname (Example, WWII—Japs, and Krauts). In Vietnam, the enemy soldier earned such monikers as Gook, Dink, Slope, Zipperhead, Zip, and Charlie, which was short for Victor Charlie (V. C.).

Hearts and Minds: The Washington concept for winning the war revolved around being such great father figures that we would "win the hearts and minds of the South Vietnamese people." As a general rule, blowing people up doesn't lead to a teenage crush. The saying among our troops became, "When you've got someone by the balls, their hearts and minds will follow."

Hippies: See cowards.

Agent Orange: A turbo-charged *Roundup*-type product sprayed from airplanes to defoliate the jungles. In caused cancer and other horrific side effects in hundreds of thousands of American soldiers, a fact that our government refused to concede for decades to come.

Search and Destroy: This was the tactic whereby we would send out men to search for someone to shoot, thus enabling the enemy to destroy their legs with landmines.

The Draft: This was the filtering system that drew poor kids and patriots into the fight, and allowed William Jefferson Clinton to "abhor the military" and "maintain his political viability." Dubya, however, bravely joined the National Guard. And in the end, Jane Fonda spent more time in Vietnam than both of them combined.

Ho Chi Minh Trail: This was the path that led from Hanoi to South Vietnam, used to re-supply the Vietcong and the NVA. One would think that such an obvious path would be easy pickings for disrupting supply lines, but one would not know all the ingenious, Washington-dictated rules of engagement.

Grunt: An American who fought in the jungle.

Pogue: An American soldier who spent the war "in the rear with the gear."

REMF: A **R**ear **E**chelon, uh, individual who engaged in sexual relations with women who were already moms.

Jody: The civilian back home who took your job, your girlfriend, and your car.

Hard: A term of respect, meaning tough. (Those gooks are hard.)

Number 10: A term of disrespect, meaning lousy. (This food is Number 10.)

Number 1: A term of respect, meaning the best. (You been to Australia? The chicks there are Number 1!)

Bust Caps: To fire one's weapon in anger.

Body Count: Because major engagements were so rare, the higher-ups needed some way to justify their decisions to send hundreds of thousands of America's boys into a meat grinder. Thus was born the body count, where American fighting men were reduced to counting and reporting the enemy dead like a carnival sideshow game.

Tour: Demonstrating from the start how uncommitted America was to outright winning the war, service in Vietnam revolved around a 12-month tour of duty (13 months for Marines). Just as a combat veteran was learning the ropes and becoming exceptionally effective, oops! Time to go home.

Now, armed with some of the lingo from the war, you... you... well, you probably don't know anymore about it, but you *can* sound informed at a cocktail party. Example:

> *"I'm tellin' you, man, those dinks were hard. The grunts were runnin' search and destroy missions round the clock, bustin caps, soakin' em in Agent Orange... getting resupplied by the pogues...*

the friggin body count was to the moon, and still… still! Those little Zips just wouldn't hand over their hearts and minds."

THE TRUTH OF THE MATTER

To discuss the engagements and tactics of the War in Vietnam is pointless. It offered no beginning and no end, just agonizing search and destroy missions that varied in size and scope. It was a war where our troops simply wandered around until they ran into someone willing to exchange gunfire.

As usual, our fighting men performed brilliantly. From the fighter pilots to the infantry riflemen, all hands stood and delivered. Yes, there were problems, but it was a problematic war in a problematic time, run by a bunch of political clowns who watched the circus safely from the cheap seats. For my money, the men who served in Vietnam were, at their very, very worst, much better than the cowards who called themselves "protestors" and cowered back home, forcing others to serve in their place. I think the fact that the United States military never lost a major battle speaks for itself. The fact that the war was lost speaks for the President and the Congress.

THE REPUBLIC JUMPS THE SHARK

The insanity that was the '60s peaked in 1968. It was a year of such madness that it defies the imagination.

It was during 1968 that Martin Luther King, Jr. was assassinated.

It was during 1968 that Robert F. Kennedy was assassinated.

It was during 1968 that the Democratic National Convention resulted in street riots when a bunch of spoiled, coddled, college students decided their life of luxury wasn't fair enough.

It was in 1968 that Lt. William L. Calley machine-gunned the civilians of the South Vietnamese village of My Lai.

It was in 1968 that the North Vietnamese and Viet Cong launched the massive Tet Offensive, which the American military soundly won, but resulted in value-added interpretation by the media who claimed that the war was unwinnable.

It was in 1968 that a sitting president, Lyndon Johnson, announce he wasn't going to run again.

It was in 1968 that we elected Richard Nixon.

And it was in 1968 that the American military won one of its greatest victories: The place was a hilltop village called Khe Sahn, which the U. S. intended to use as a staging point for attacks on the communist supply lines that ran along the Ho Chi Minh Trail. Defended only by the men of the 26th Marine Regiment, a North Vietnamese force of over 20,000 attacked, and attempted to take the position for 71 days. The Marines fought back viciously, aided by brilliantly placed artillery support and U. S. Air Force B-52 strikes. The Marines never... *never* should have survived. And yet they won.

They *won*.

A year later, the position was abandoned; deemed unnecessary because the morons calling the shots changed their minds.

CHAPTER EIGHTEEN

L IKE IT OR not, that's where I choose to strike the tent... on a bloody, windswept hill, where America's finest fought for nothing, and everything. It was then, at that point in time, that America should have *finished* growing up, and looked back at history the way a forty-year-old person looks back at their life, and says, "Holy crap! I'm lucky I even survived all that stuff." And like a forty-year-old, we should have turned to face the future with... well, a clue.

But we haven't.

We're more like the thirty-year-old lottery winner that decides, "Hey, if coke is fun, crack must be *awesome*!" Our history since 1968 reads like a Guinness Book of Bad Decisions.

Shouldn't we have at least noticed that our nation was—literally—founded on the lesson "don't start a land war in a distant country where the enemy is willing to die for their cause and will utilize guerilla tactics, and the war will ultimately cost lots of money and lives and prove unpopular with the nation's citizens."

Really? Seriously? Invade Afghanistan? Known as "the graveyard of empires" for—literally—thousands of years? And doing so after the obvious lessons of Korea and Vietnam?

Are you freaking kidding me?

So what's the problem?

Is it institutions... like plaintiffs, lawyers, politicians, judges, and bureaucrats?

Is it the fact that we've splintered ourselves apart, each person represented by some special interest group?

Is it the fact that we've all become hyphenated Americans?

Is it the fact that half of us care too much, and the other half doesn't care at all?

The package of reasons and explanations for the disastrous years since 1968 could go on for volumes, and everyone would have their own explanations, based on their political leanings. Suffice it to say that Joe Rogan and Don Lemon would have very different takes on the subject.

But *that* is the beauty of history... both Sean and Don would be wrong, because they'd be too close to the issues to see the history.

History just is.

It's the facts.

The facts can, of course, be *interpreted* by the historian—even *slanted*—but a curious student can still uncover the *facts*, then draw their own conclusions independently. It is impossible to write real history about an era you lived through, unless of course you didn't actually do any *living* during that time. The political leanings of the historical writer reflect off every word, as they begin to use adjectives and descriptions to "help" you understand the facts. Trust me, it's obvious who they voted for.

If this book isn't proof of that, well, God bless you—we're cut from the same cloth.

So why have we failed so utterly to learn from our past? A child only touches a hot stove once, and—voila—lesson learned. Why aren't *we the people* kindred souls with that child and those scorched fingers?

I think it's because—in terms of evolution—we have it too easy. We, as a nation, have come so far, so fast, that our brains cannot adjust. We haven't evolved into it. We're surrounded by decadent luxury, while most of the world is trying to figure out how they are going to avoid starving to death. We're tearing down statues for centuries-old sins, and burning, looting, rioting, and seething with rage at the 50% of America that's "gone crazy." Quite literally, 50% of Americans believe our history to be nothing more than genocide, racism, colonization, misogyny, xenophobia, homophobia, and white privilege.

Gang, we the people are light-years ahead of the rest of the world. Our poorest people have clothing, food, and—9 times out of 10—safe shelter with a television. Our basic middle-class lives like the elite of most nations, complete with car, cable, cell phone, fashionable clothing, vacations, and junk food. Our rich… well, let's not even bother.

Is there anything wrong with this?

No! Our forefathers made it possible—It is our national damn-did-we-get-lucky birthright. It's just that we, the human animal, aren't *ready* for it. For two million years we've been very, very slowly refining our *survival* techniques, and suddenly in the past 100 years we've come to consider electricity to be necessary for survival.

Well, it's not. It's necessary for *luxury*, and sustaining the lifestyle "to which we've become accustomed," but it ain't necessary for survival. Ask the rest of the world.

The fact that we are where we are is the ultimate anomaly! It's the miracle of miracles! The true testament to the brilliance that our Creator endowed us with! We should all be waking up—everyday—and staggering out into the sunlight and shouting, "Thank you, God, Buddha, Allah, Great Spirit, Great Pumpkin, Flying Spaghetti Monster for allowing *me* to be born in America!"

Do we?

Nope, despite the fact that the saber-tooth tiger is dead… crops are grown in the grocery store… the cave has been replaced by a cozy little apartment… fire is created at the push of a button… the horse only needs re-shoeing every 40,000 miles… our clothing comes from hides that someone else acquired, tanned, and sewed for us… the weather is of no real consequence… and world-wide communications can be accomplished on a phone or the Internet… still, we complain.

Why? All the really hard work is done, and we're bored and entitled.

And because we don't have to *really* take care of ourselves, we no longer take responsibility for ourselves. Everything is "beyond our control," it seems. Alcoholism, drug addiction, obesity, gambling, pedophilia—these things are all diseases. If in doubt, we sue the manufacturer. If we choose a life of crime, we blame our parents and society. If we need an opinion, we look to the television to provide it. And if we feel threatened, we retreat to our "safe space."

Here, I believe, is the madness of it: We the people are acting more and more victimized, when in fact we are the least victimized people in the world. In America, it takes exactly *three* generations to go from a Black citizen being arrested for riding in the front of the bus to a Black man being elected President.

Is this possible in any other nation?

No.

Why?

Because they didn't have Thomas Jefferson and a team of the greatest thinkers in history create their nation from scratch. Their nations were created like, well, Jello, where eventually over time things just sort of jelled into place. Then unjelled. Then jelled.

Socialism doesn't work.

Communism doesn't work.

Fascism doesn't work.

Anarchy doesn't work.

Feudalism doesn't work.

The world has been there, tried that... and only one system works: Ours.

The one created in the 1770s, which we are trying so hard to screw up.

There are many, of course, who like to blame our strange state of affairs on specific entities and specific people: Our elected officials, our judges, our lawyers, our media, our schools, our social programs, our bureaucrats, our special interest groups.

But, as P.J. O'Rourke explored so brilliantly in *Parliament of Whores*, aren't "they" actually "us?"

Where do "we" end, and "they" begin?

We elect them.

We pay their salaries.

We watch their TV channels.

We read their magazines.

We use them to sue each other.

We live our lives in accordance with their decisions and their opinions. So what do we do?

Perhaps we study, and restudy, history, and look for an answer there. It worked, after all, for our Founding Fathers, as they used the lessons of history to create our Constitution. Learning from the mistakes of others is a great, painless way to solve most problems, and perhaps we could try using it.

Then again, perhaps America is some sort of bizarre divine experiment, on a collision course with destiny, unable to alter our direction, incapable of learning from past examples, unable to keep it in our brains that fire burns... and the saber-tooth tiger bites.

And if that's the case, let's just hope someone learns from us.

Made in United States
North Haven, CT
11 November 2023

43906116R00157